PROCEDURE WRITING
Principles and Practices
Second Edition

Douglas Wieringa

Christopher Moore

Valerie Barnes

 BATTELLE PRESS

Columbus • Richland

Library in Congress Cataloging-in-Publication Data

Wieringa, Douglas, 1960–
    Procedure writing : principles and practices / by Douglas Wieringa, Christopher Moore,
Valerie Barnes. —2nd ed.
       p.   cm.
   ISBN 1-57477-052-7 (alk. paper)
    1. Technical writing. 2. Technical manuals. I. Moore, Christopher, 1957– .
II. Barnes, Valerie Elizabeth, III. Title.
T11.W54   1998
808′.0666--dc21

98-7875
CIP

Printed in the United States of America

Battelle Press
505 King Avenue
Columbus, Ohio 43201-2693, USA
614-424-6393 or 800-451-3543
Fax: 614-424-3819
E-mail: press@battelle.org
Website: www.battelle.org/bookstore

Preface to the second editon

When we published the first edition of *Procedure Writing,* we were pleased to see that it attracted an audience beyond the world of nuclear power and even beyond the world of procedure writing. This second edition is an attempt to better reach this larger audience. We have included more examples and taken them from a range of procedures. We have also attempted to make our guidance more relevant to nontechnical settings; for example we have added chapters on decision tables and flowcharts, which present decision criteria in a matrix format that readers find familiar and helpful. We've expanded the discussion of the procedure writing process, because you can't write a good procedure without a good process. Also, we've expanded and improved the guidance throughout.

Very few books deal with procedure writing, which is strange, considering the number of people who must write procedures. These people usually are technical experts, not communication experts, who are placed in a position where they have to be communication experts to do their jobs effectively. We wrote this book to help provide them with that expertise.

It is somewhat ironic that many procedure writers search for guidance and don't find it, when there is so much out there that can help them. Writers have struggled to make documents understandable for as long as they have been writing them, and a sizable body of professional knowledge has emerged (Schriver, 1997). The key to finding guidance on procedure writing is knowing where to look, because it is seldom labeled as procedure writing guidance. Principles that apply to documents ranging from advertisements to software manuals to maps to Web sites can be adapted to procedures. We have drawn the principles in the book from disciplines such as technical communication, human factors, cognitive psychology, instructional design, and graphic design.

Although this book covers the fundamentals of procedure writing, we also try to address the issues involved with some sophistication. Procedure writing guidance often takes the form of platitudes and absolutes, e.g., never include an action in a caution; don't use italics because they are hard to read; write at an eighth-grade level. While this approach certainly gives useful guidance, it often glosses over the subtleties and tradeoffs involved in communicating clearly. It oversimplifies, and we try not to do that here. See Section 22.1 for a more detailed discussion of these issues.

In addition to again thanking those who helped with the first edition, we would like to thank those who helped with this edition. Our work with Ameritech, Babcock & Wilcox, Entergy, and Children's Hospital and Medical Center of Seattle taught us a lot; and we've drawn on that knowledge while preparing this edition. Our thanks also go to our reviewers: Pete Ashmore, Patsy Cox, and Anita Taylor. Finally, Bea Weaver's editorial eye helped us practice what we preach, and Susan Vianna helped us get it all onto paper.

Preface to the first edition

This book was originally written for the United States Department of Energy as a guide to procedure writers in Department of Energy facilities. As we were working on it, we began to realize that, with slight modification, the principles we were presenting would be useful to procedure writers in a variety of situations.

Procedures, as we explain in Chapter 1, are instructions. Instructions are used in all sorts of situations:

- Nuclear power plants use procedures to govern most aspects of operation and maintenance.

- Procedures are used in the military, again governing the operation and maintenance of complex equipment.

- Procedures are widely used in aviation, from the cockpit checklists used by pilots to the procedures used by maintainers.

- Computer users often rely on procedures. These procedures can be part of the documentation prepared for the hardware or software or they can be written by hand as instructions from one person to another. Companies that write custom software, such as an internal accounting package, often must also write their own procedures for using that software.

- Procedures are used extensively in the petroleum industry and other hydrocarbon industries.

- The ISO 9000 Quality Standard (or most any total quality management system) requires procedures to standardize methods of doing work.

- Pharmaceutical manufacturers must have standard operating procedures in place for all phases of operations and control.

- Many other types of businesses, ranging from banks to volunteer fire departments, use procedures.

It is our hope that this book will be useful in all of these areas.

This book is an attempt to meld theory and practice. Accordingly, we have drawn information from a variety of sources. Traditional books on writing, such as *The Elements of Style* (Strunk & White, 1979), *Modern American Usage* (Follett, 1966), the *Handbook of Technical Writing* (Brusaw, Alred, & Oliu, 1987), and *Words Into Type* (1974), proved valuable sources.[1] Wherever possible, we have supplemented the tried-and-proven techniques from books such as these with the results of scientific studies. Unfortunately, scientific research into procedures and into writing in general is in its infancy, and studies that present useful information for the procedure writer are not as common as we would like. Although more research is being done, the present lack of scientific research is indicative of the character of writing: "Keep in mind that, despite increasingly good research into its nature, writing is a craft and not a science" (Houp & Pearsall, 1988, p. 146).

This book represents the contributions of many individuals, all of whom played important roles. First, we must thank our project sponsors at the Department of Energy, Bob Waters and Maggie Sturdivant. Without them, this book would never have been written. Our appreciation also goes to our colleagues at EG&G Idaho, Susan Hill and Wendy Reece. Sue and Wendy contributed material to this book, edited drafts, and were always responsive to our questions. They also played an important role in our dealings with the Department of Energy. Finally, many of our colleagues at Battelle provided invaluable assistance. In no particular order, they are Charlene Forslund, who wrote and edited material; Ron Wilson, who performed the thankless task of tracking our many references and wrote some material; Sadie Johnson, who worked the long hours necessary to produce this book; Charleen Sager, whose eagle editing eye kept us all honest; and Ali Tabatabai, Bob Gruel, and David Eike, our project managers.

This book also represents all that we have learned working with procedures for over ten years. We have had the good fortune to participate in several challenging procedures-related projects during this time and must also extend our thanks to those organizations with whom we have worked. We would like to thank, in particular, the U.S. Nuclear Regulatory Commission and Arizona Public Service Corporation's Palo Verde Nuclear Generating Station. We have, in fact, drawn some of the examples in this book from Palo Verde's progressive procedures.

---

[1]In this book, references are cited by the author's name, the year of publication, and, if a quotation is used, the page number.

Contents

PART

ONE

The Basics

CHAPTER

ONE

An Introduction to Procedures

Procedures are instructions, and this book explains how to write instructions so that others can understand them.[2] Procedures can range from simple to complex; they describe anything from booting a personal computer to operating a nuclear power plant during an emergency. Plans, mission statements, proposals, and technical articles are not procedures, although parts of these documents may be considered procedures if they present instructions. No matter how simple or complex a procedure is, certain principles govern the way it should be written. This book presents these principles.

1.1   Procedures and why they are important

There are several benefits to good procedures: procedures reduce human error, document the best way to perform a task, and provide an administrative record of their execution. This section discusses these benefits. It also discusses some of the reasons that workers resist procedures and what you, the procedure writer, can do to write procedures that will be accepted.

The benefits of procedures

The most important function of procedures is to assist workers in performing tasks. Even highly skilled workers can use assistance in performing compli-

---

[2]In this book, we use the term *procedure* to refer to the written instructions for performing a task, not the actions themselves.

cated tasks, particularly if a task is performed infrequently or if the consequences of an error are very high. Humans are fallible; we forget things and make mistakes. Properly written procedures reduce the opportunity for these sorts of errors. By reducing error, procedures can improve quality; protect workers, the public, the environment, and machinery; and increase productivity. Chapter 2 discusses the role procedures can play in reducing human error.

Procedures also help ensure that tasks are performed in an efficient, safe manner. A procedure represents (or should represent) a collective agreement on the best way to perform a given task. A worker following an emergency procedure, for instance, is being guided by the collective knowledge and experience of the entire procedure development team, who took the time necessary to develop and test the procedure in a controlled situation. Without a procedure, the worker must decide what to do individually, perhaps without the assistance of others and under the stress of time pressure and even physical danger. Without the procedure, the worker is more likely to perform the task incorrectly. Procedures also provide managers with control over how tasks are performed. If the task must be performed according to the procedure and management has input into how the procedure is written, then management has control over how the task is performed.

Finally, procedures can serve an important administrative function. Many procedures include check-offs or sign-off blanks that are completed as the procedure is performed. Once the task is completed, the procedure can be archived as a record of the task's performance. If a problem arises later that may be connected to the performance of the procedure, investigators can retrieve the archived procedure to determine if it was executed and who signed off at quality assurance points.

Resistance to procedures

These advantages seem straightforward enough, but often procedures are not used. In fact, people often look for reasons not to read a document, procedures included. All kinds of reasons are given:

- Procedures are inaccurate, and users have figured this out.

- Procedures are out of date, and users have figured that out. The procedures may have been correct when they were first written, but things changed and the procedures did not. Perhaps the procedure writers furnished update pages, but no one bothered to file them.

- Users cannot find the procedure they want. Perhaps the procedures are not distributed to work sites, or perhaps there are so many procedures that users cannot find the one they need among the vast procedure set. One telecommunications company had to undertake a major procedure revision and consolidation effort when they realized that their system had collapsed under the weight of the volumes and volumes and volumes of documentation they had created, much of it unnecessary (Wieringa et al., 1996).

- Users don't need procedures. The tasks are simple, and the procedures exist only because someone somewhere thought they should be written.

- Users need the procedures, but don't use them because they see procedures as an affront to their skill. People don't like being told what to do.

- Users see procedures as a tool of management, and they don't like management.

- Procedures are difficult to understand.

Each of these reasons can be interpreted as a deficiency in procedure quality. Basically, if the procedures aren't good, people won't use them. In a study of maintenance procedures in commercial nuclear power plants, one of the key findings was that

> the procedures that do exist are often of such poor quality that personnel avoid or refuse to use them. In general, maintenance procedures are poorly written and difficult to follow. The inadequacy of existing procedures constitutes the single largest reason cited by maintenance supervisors for their unwillingness to encourage procedure use. (Morgenstern et al., 1985, p. vii)

Procedure quality is determined by the user—the worker who uses the procedure. Users are your customers. The importance of considering the user as customer became evident as we were writing this book. As part of our research, we visited various facilities that used procedures extensively and talked to procedure writers and users. The facility that seemed to have the best procedures was the facility that worked hardest to treat the users as customers. Interaction among procedure writers and procedure users was extensive; writers interviewed users before writing or revising a procedure, called users when they had questions, and had users review drafts of procedures. Without this frequent contact, the writers would not have been aware of the users' needs and would have been unable to tailor the procedures to meet those needs. It is a well-accepted principle that such audience analysis is essential to effective communication (Souther & White, 1984; Schriver, 1997). At another facility, where the procedures were not as good, the person in charge of procedure writing proudly showed us a notebook full of tips on effective writing that she had carefully compiled over the years, but she never talked to procedure users and knew very little about them. That notebook of tips is certainly an aid to good procedure writing, but it is no substitute for contact with procedure users.

Another benefit to interacting with procedure users is that as you write procedures, users will see that they can shape the characteristics of procedures and they will begin to feel some ownership of them. That is a good thing. The procedure isn't just something that tells them what someone else wants them to do, it's a tool that they helped design. Solicit their buy-in by involving them.

By involving procedure users, you can help them realize that they can help improve the procedure. Procedure users are somewhat unique as customers, in that they tend to blame themselves for difficulties they have when using the procedure and do not realize that the procedure can be improved. In one study, users were asked to follow procedures for using VCRs, telephones, answering machines, and stereos. Many had difficulty, and 63% blamed themselves. Only 12% blamed the procedure, despite the fact that there were numerous deficiencies in the procedure, such as poor illustrations, incorrect parts lists, missing information, ambiguous instructions, and incorrect location information (Schriver, 1997). These findings corroborate our informal observations of procedure users—they often assume that procedures are the way they are, and the users are unaware of the many things that can be done to improve procedure quality.

Procedures do not have to live up to their unfortunate stereotype of being impediments to accomplishing tasks. If you write procedures that address the needs of those who will be using them, there is a much greater chance that those procedures will be accepted and used. This book will help you do that, by providing information on improving the procedure writing process (primarily in Chapter 3) and by describing the characteristics of high-quality procedures.

1.2 The importance of a writers' guide

This book presents general guidance on procedure preparation. If your organization writes only a few procedures, then this book will probably be sufficient guidance for you. However, if your organization develops many procedures (such as the several thousand in a nuclear power plant), then you are going to need a writers' guide.

A writers' guide (sometimes called a style guide) specifies the format and content of procedures in a very detailed manner—more detailed than this book. This book typically specifies a principle rather than a specific practice; for example, it says that the equipment cited in procedures should be identified in a consistent, unambiguous, precise manner without specifying what that manner should be. The reason for not specifying exactly how location information should be presented is that there are several ways to present location information that meet the intent of the principle. For the purposes of this book, which can be used in many different settings, it would be too restrictive to state that location information *had* to be presented in one manner.

However, the procedure writer needs to know how to present location information at his facility, because all procedures should present identification information consistently. The writer needs guidance that reads something like this: *Identify all equipment cited in the procedure by common name and equipment number. Present the information in that order, with a comma between the name and number.* This guidance meets the criteria of the principle—it is consistent, unambiguous, and precise.

Such detailed guidance belongs in the writers' guide. The writers' guide should present the style and content rules for procedures at a facility. It should be based on the principles in this document, as well as on facility policies. The writers' guide provides the specific information that the procedure writer needs on a daily basis.

Consider another example: this book says that white space should be used to separate steps and substeps in a manner that conveys their hierarchy. The writers' guide would explain exactly how to do that; it might say, *Insert two blank lines (24 points) before a step and one blank line (12 points) before a substep.*

A writers' guide is a good idea in any setting where *any* documents are written, not just procedures, particularly if different documents are written by different writers. Writers' guides are helpful for maintaining consistency in documents, for ensuring that documents are written correctly, for training new writers, and for describing the steps in the process of writing a document (Allen, 1995, 1996). At a minimum, you should keep a notebook documenting the practices that you follow and disseminate it among your fellow writers.

Having said that, we should add that the appendix to this book contains the specifications for the procedure examples in this book. You can refer to that appendix for detailed information on line spacing, fonts, indentation, and so on. This information can help you start your own writers' guide.

1.3   About this book

Finally, before we get started, some information about this book, the procedures it applies to, and the examples we use.

Organization of this book

This book is divided into five parts:

- Part One, The Basics, introduces this book and procedure writing in general.

- Part Two, Writing Basic Steps, discusses the basics of procedure writing, dealing with only simple steps. This information is organized into a series of principles that the procedure writer should follow.

- Part Three, Format and Organization, discusses the appearance of procedures. This information is also presented in a series of principles.

- Part Four, Writing Complex Steps, discusses lists, conditional statements, and other more complex types of steps. Again, this information is presented in a series of principles.

- Part Five, Conclusion, summarizes the book by discussing some of the problems that the procedure writer will face in light of the principles presented in Parts Two, Three, and Four.

This is the first chapter in Part One. Chapters 2 and 3, also in Part One, discuss the reading process and the writing process, respectively.

A word about procedure complexity

Procedures can be simple or complex, depending on the tasks being documented. This book describes techniques for writing procedures in complex technological settings, such as nuclear power plants. When writing a simpler procedure for, say, changing a spark plug, it would be unnecessary to adhere to all the specific guidance discussed in this book. The cross-referencing system described in Chapter 19, for example, would be overkill for a simple procedure. However, the underlying principle, that cross-references should be explicit and unambiguous, still applies. Similarly, you may not need the action verb list described in Chapter 6, but that does not eliminate the need to always use the simplest verb that conveys the intended meaning. Basically, you should comply with all the principles in this book as you write procedures. The extent of the effort necessary to comply with the principle will vary with the complexity of the procedure.

A word about examples

This book uses examples from a range of different settings, from simple instructions to complex technical procedures. You may not understand the content of some of the examples, but you should still be able to see the principle being demonstrated. These principles are largely independent of technical content; for example, a step should always begin with an action verb followed by an object, whether that step is *Open the door* or *Decant the supernate*. So, rather than use simple examples that our entire audience would certainly be familiar with, such as writing a shopping list or mowing the lawn, we elected to use realistic procedures. It isn't necessary to fully understand the content of the example to understand the communication principle being presented—we don't fully understand the technical nature of some of the examples we use either!

CHAPTER

TWO

The Reading Process

The preceding chapter explained that the purpose of this book is to help you write procedures that are more usable, and discussed usability in a relatively general sense. As you read through the rest of this book, specifically Parts Two, Three, and Four, you will be introduced to many principles that can make procedures more usable. Before delving into these principles, however, it is valuable to know why usability is so important. This chapter reviews those reasons.

A discussion of usability must center on the reading process. Everything that occurs prior to the point where the procedure is read, such as the writers' research and agonizing over word choice, testing, and even photocopying, has one goal—to ensure that, when reading a procedure, the user performs the task correctly. To perform a task correctly, the procedure user must understand what he has read. Thus, an understanding of the reading process is crucial to presenting usable procedures.

2.1 A model of the reading process

This section presents a model, or simplified representation, of the reading process.[3] Once this model is explained, we can show how procedures can help reduce error.

---

[3]This model was suggested by Jan Spyridakis of the University of Washington's Department of Technical Communication and Michael Wenger of IBM (1990). It is presented with apologies to reading researchers, who will realize that we have glossed over many aspects of the reading process, such as the distinction between top-down and bottom-up processing, the role of long- and short-term memory, and so on. For an excellent overview of these issues, see Spyridakis and Wenger (1990).

Reading is hard work. To a certain extent, it is a wonder that we can read—or, more basically, use language—at all. In *The Language Instinct*, Stephen Pinker (1994) describes all that humans must learn to communicate with language—countless words, the rules for combining them into sentences (which we follow very well, but cannot begin to articulate), and the way we assemble those sentences into coherent descriptions, thoughts, and arguments. We figure out how to do this as infants, and do it so quickly that Pinker argues the ability to use language is "hard-wired" into our brains. Pinker maintains that we use language for the same reason that we have two arms and two legs. It's in the DNA blueprint.

Although the theories of what takes place in our minds as we read can vary, all postulate a very complex process. A simplified description of this process includes the following steps:

- Readers must recognize characters (i.e., letters, numbers, and other symbols).

- Readers must recognize the words formed by those characters and assign meanings to words.

- Readers must use their knowledge of English grammar to recognize how these words form sentences.

- Readers must draw upon information in their memories to understand sentences, paragraphs, and entire documents.

All these tasks require cognitive resources. Cognitive resources represent the attention we can devote to a task.

We have only so many resources available as we read. In many situations, this is not a problem, because we are so familiar with the reading process that we have automated many of the basic activities required, such as word recognition. However, when a document becomes difficult to read, these basic activities require more resources, and this increased demand may "crowd out" the resources that we would otherwise have devoted to understanding what we read. For example, if the reader encounters an unfamiliar word or term, he or she momentarily stops, decides what the word or term means, and then continues reading. In this case, additional resources must be devoted to a process (i.e., word recognition) that is typically automatic. These resources must come from someplace, so perhaps comprehension suffers; the sentence must be re-read because, in sorting out the meaning of a word, the reader has lost his train of thought and must re-read the sentence. Figure 1 depicts this situation.

If you have done your own income taxes (and aren't an accountant), you should be able to easily relate to this phenomenon. Many of us have struggled to understand the instructions provided by the Internal Revenue Service (IRS), and this model neatly explains why this is so. IRS instructions use unfamiliar words or use familiar words in unfamiliar ways. We cannot automate the process of recognizing words and must allocate extra resources

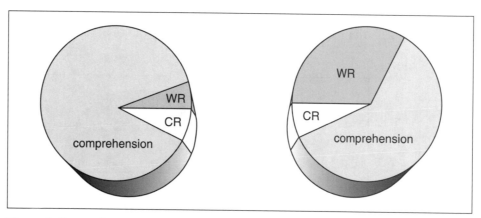

Figure 1. Competing resources. The circle represents the total amount of resources that the reader can devote to reading. On the left, character recognition (CR) and word recognition (WR) require few resources. The diagram on the right depicts the situation when the reader encounters an unfamiliar word. More resources are required for word recognition, so comprehension receives fewer resources and may suffer.

to that process. Similarly, IRS instructions often include conditional information, which can be difficult to understand, especially when expressed in sentence form (see Chapter 16), so understanding what we read also requires extra resources.

Consider the following passage:

> If a charitable contribution deduction is allowed because of a bargain sale of property to a charitable organization, the adjusted basis for the purposes of determining gain from the sale is the amount which has the same ratio to the adjusted basis as the amount realized has to the fair market value. (Internal Revenue Service, 1990, p. 34)

The reader must not only decide what terms such as *bargain sale* and *adjusted basis* mean, but must also decipher the underlying logic of the sentence. Needless to say, these resources detract from the reader's ability to decide what it all means once he or she grasps the terms and their logic.

The demands of the task

This model, as presented thus far, assumes that the reader is concentrating only on the document being read. If he or she is curled up with a good book, that may well be the case—but if the reader is engaged in any other activity, that activity also requires resources. For example, many people have difficulty reading and watching television at the same time or reading and carrying on a conversation at the same time. So, when applying this model to the real world, we must take into account factors beyond the procedure that are vying for the reader's attention.

The procedure reader will always be engaged in at least one other activity—the activity documented in the procedure. Thus, you know that some of the reader's attention will be devoted to the performance of that task and will not be available for reading and understanding the procedure. Figure 2 depicts our model in light of these additional demands.

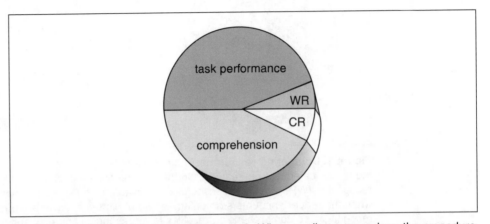

Figure 2. Introducing the demands of a task. When reading a procedure, the procedure user will also be performing a task. The performance of this task requires resources and reduces the resources that can be allocated to the reading task. In this case, character recognition (CR) and word recognition (WR) require the same amount of resources, so comprehension suffers.

Introducing stressors

The resources that can be devoted to the reading task are further affected by stressors. Stressors induce stress. Although we are all familiar with the notion of stress, we probably don't consider stress to have both positive and negative effects on performance; it does. Figure 3 depicts a stress curve, which relates the level of stress to the likelihood of an error (Kantowitz & Sorkin, 1983). Note how performance suffers at low levels of stress as well as at high levels of stress. At a low level of stress, people are bored and tend not to pay attention, whereas at a high level of stress people may be overloaded and also fail to perform optimally.

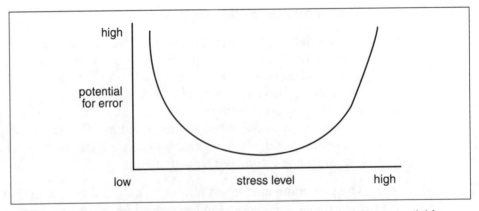

Figure 3. Stress curve. This curve depicts the relationship between the potential for error and stress level. At high levels of stress, errors are more likely. At low levels of stress, errors are also likely because workers are bored.

The effects of stress vary from person to person. Some people fall apart under the slightest stress, while others appear to thrive on stress. Similarly, different types of stress have different effects on people; for instance, a soldier who experiences no fear under combat may be terrified of speaking before a group.

An important point to realize, however, is that we *all* have a threshold of stress above which our performance will deteriorate. The analogy to soldiers, in fact, illustrates this. In one study (Berkin, 1964), soldiers were required to perform various tasks in the face of what appeared to be imminent death. In one task, while under artillery fire, a soldier had to follow a procedure for repairing a malfunctioning radio so that he could call the artillery post and tell them to stop firing. The soldiers, who did not know that the artillery was simulated, performed poorly, although soldiers with combat experience fared better. Assessments of soldiers' performance on the battlefield also bear out the effects of stress; only 25% will fire effectively against the enemy "unless they are compelled by almost overpowering circumstance or unless all junior leaders constantly 'ride herd' on troops with the specific mission of increasing their fire. The 25% estimate stands even for well-trained and campaign-seasoned troops" (Marshall, 1978, p. 50).

Although these are extreme examples, life-threatening incidents are conceivable in situations where procedures are used; examples include emergency procedures in nuclear power plants and, as in the study above, procedures for operating military equipment. Stress can result from other factors as well:

- Workers may be afraid of losing their jobs, or even of doing their jobs poorly.

- A worker may have problems at home.

- A worker may be afraid of looking bad in front of his peers.

- Illness or substance abuse problems may introduce stress.

- Extremes of temperature, noise, or vibration can induce stress (Echeverria et al., 1994).

These factors can introduce stress into the performance of any procedure.

High stress levels reduce the amount of cognitive resources that we can devote to a task—including the reading task. Low stress levels reduce the total amount of cognitive resources that are available; in other words, readers are less likely to pay attention to what they are reading. Figure 4 depicts these effects, as well as other demands on the cognitive resources of the procedure user.

2.2 Applying the model to procedures

Recall Figure 1, where a reader encountered an unfamiliar word, which required excess resources, reducing the resources that were available for comprehension. Now consider the same situation in our "real world" version

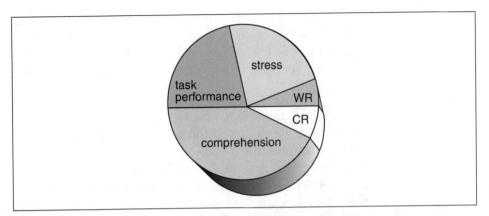

Figure 4. Competing resources—the complete picture. Stress further reduces the resources that users can devote to a task—in this case, comprehending what is being read. If a reader is under extreme stress, he or she must devote resources to dealing with the stress. If a reader is understressed, resources may be devoted to daydreaming or simply may not be available.

of the model in Figure 4, where the user who is performing a procedure under stress encounters a sentence that is difficult to understand. Perhaps he is doing his taxes while tired and ill. His resources become overloaded. He can't understand the procedure, perform the task, and deal with the stress all at the same time. Something's got to go. A variety of scenarios are possible:

- The user may decide that the procedure isn't worth the trouble of trying to understand it and thus will discard it. The demands on his resources are reduced, but now an error is more likely because the user no longer has access to important information in the procedure.

- The user may devote more resources to attempting to understand the procedure and devote fewer resources to the task being performed. Because he is paying less attention to what he is doing, an error in task performance becomes more likely. If the procedure user is working with live circuits or around hot machinery, he may even hurt himself.

- The user may continue in the procedure without understanding the sentence. Again, an error is possible, because he is working without full benefit of the procedure.

Each of these situations is undesirable. As a procedure writer, you cannot do much about the stress the worker is under or the cognitive demands of the task itself, but you can do much to affect the quality of the procedure. By adhering to the guidance in this book, you can make the procedure more usable—and the more usable the procedure is, the fewer cognitive resources it will require. Spyridakis and Wenger (1990, p. 126) sum up the writer's responsibility in this regard:

> Careful writers will lean towards creating documents that, whenever possible, reduce the reader's cognitive load—thus allowing readers to liberate attention for document aspects that cannot be simplified.

As you read through the guidance in this book, remember that there will be other factors competing for the procedure user's cognitive resources. Without considering this fact, you might believe that some of the guidance presented makes a trivial difference in the usability of a procedure. For example, trained users reading the step *Slowly increase flow* (referring to the flow of water through a pipe) will know how slow *slowly* is and are unlikely to make an error. But remember that you are sitting at your desk, under little, if any, stress and probably not doing anything besides reading this book. The object is not to write a procedure that is usable in this situation, but is usable in an extreme situation. If the user is working in a hot, humid, loud turbine building, rushing to complete a valve line-up so that a manufacturing process can begin on time, what then?

Remember that low levels of stress can also be a problem. Assume that you are confronted with a wordy step, presented in paragraph form. Again, perhaps you can plod through the step and understand it; but what about a worker on the graveyard shift, working alone and bored? Chances are higher that he will give the step a cursory read, and then do what he thinks it said. Once more, errors become likely. Unmotivated workers will perform better if procedures are easier to understand. Conversely, highly motivated readers can often deal effectively with text that is difficult to read (Spyridakis & Wenger, 1990).

However, if text is too difficult to read, good readers will adopt the habits of poor readers. Spyridakis and Wenger (1990) recount how, when confronted with demanding and unfamiliar technical text, good readers will (1) recall less information; (2) be more likely to read in a list-wise fashion, ignoring cues as to the importance of ideas; (3) distort the meaning of text in their recalls; and (4) have more difficulty applying the information they have read.

By following the guidelines in this book, you will be taking an important step to guard against these effects in procedures.

CHAPTER

THREE

The Writing Process

In procedure writing, a distinction can be drawn between the product and the process. The product is the procedure itself. Much of this book focuses on the product. It describes what procedures should look like, the proper writing style, and so on. But it is impossible to generate a good product without following a good process. This chapter discusses that process, which begins before the procedure is written, does not end when the procedure is complete, and involves many more people than just the procedure writer.[4]

The Nuclear Regulatory Commission (NRC) found that one cause of the accident at the Three Mile Island nuclear power plant was the poor quality of the emergency operating procedures used by plant operators. As a result, the NRC implemented several requirements for procedures. A few years later, the NRC audited several plants to determine if procedures met the requirements. They found that some procedures did not, and that the reason was that the procedure writing process was deficient (Nuclear Regulatory Commission, 1989).

The procedure writing process consists of seven steps:

- Writers begin by planning. What are they writing? Why are they writing it? What resources will they need?

---

[4]Entire books have been written on effective writing processes; see, for example, *Managing Documentation Projects in an Imperfect World* by Gabriel Lanyi (1994).

- The next step is to investigate. They do preliminary research to collect information and develop ideas about what they will be writing.

- The next step is to organize their thoughts. Outlining is a useful organizational tool.

- Once the outline is completed, the next step is to write a draft of the procedure.

- Once a draft is written, it should be reviewed and revised.

- When the procedure is finished, it should be tested.

- Procedures must be kept up to date. The procedure writer's job is not over once the procedure has been successfully implemented in the field—it is still necessary to maintain the procedure.

It is important to note that these steps are not distinct; they overlap. You may begin one step before the previous step is completed; for instance, you may begin to write before you are finished organizing. This is fine. Some writers cannot completely organize their thoughts until they start writing. Others prefer to have a document fully mapped out before they begin.

3.1 Planning

Procedure writing, like any activity, requires planning. Before a procedure is written, it is essential to know why the procedure is being written, who is going to write it, and how they are going to write it.

Why write the procedure?

It's a simple question but, without a good answer, a good procedure can't be written. What is the main reason the procedure is being written? Consider how different answers to this question can shape the characteristics of the procedure.

- *Manufacturing errors that are directly attributed to human error cost the company $750,000 last year; in the future, all tasks where errors are likely to occur must be performed with a procedure in hand.* This writer, to be successful, will have to carefully craft understandable, technically accurate procedures that (1) describe how to rectify these errors and (2) workers want to use.

- *I'm only writing this procedure because my boss wants me to; no one will use it.* This writer, on the other hand, can simply write something, get his boss to sign off on it, and he's done.

- *Different business units do the same things differently; we need to standardize the way we do business.* This writer will have to do a lot of traveling, talk to many people, and possibly deal with a variety of political problems in his attempts to get everyone to agree on the best way to do things. Otherwise, the procedures are likely to fail.

- *ISO 9000 regulations require procedures.* This writer should be very familiar with the characteristics that ISO 9000 regulators like to see in procedures.

- *Workers need to take procedures home for self-study.* These procedures may need to involve more background information and rationale than procedures that are intended to direct the performance of a task.

- *Staff turnover is high, and we need to quickly educate new workers on our business processes.* This writer should be able to present information in a manner that new workers will be able to understand. (And perhaps someone else should be investigating ways of reducing staff turnover; writing a procedure is not the answer to every problem.)

Once you know why the procedures are being written, take a good, hard look and consider whether procedures are truly the answer to the problem. These are some of the things procedures do well:

- They provide information that users need to perform a task, but that they might not remember when performing that task. By doing so, procedures reduce errors, lower costs, and increase safety.

- They represent the collective knowledge of a group of experts regarding the way a task should be performed. With a procedure, a worker performing the task has access to this knowledge. A related benefit is that processes are standardized throughout an organization.

- They are an "institutional memory" of the way a task should be performed. Information does not reside only in workers' heads, and it does not leave the organization when the workers leave the organization. When workers enter the organization, they can learn by reading the procedure.

- They appease regulators.

- They allow management to have more control over the way tasks are performed.

However, procedures are not the solution to *every* problem. Here are some other things that should be considered in addition to (or instead of) procedures:

- *Engineered solutions.* It is often better to modify the equipment than to tell people to use it better. If you are worried about someone falling off a ledge, it is probably better to build a railing than to write a procedure telling people to watch their step.

- *Training.* As will be discussed in Chapter 7, all procedures require a certain level of user knowledge—the procedure can't tell the user *everything*. Training fills that gap. Further, tasks that do not consist of steps that are performed in a similar order every time are difficult to describe in a procedure. For example, it is difficult to write a diagnostic procedure if you don't know what is wrong with the equipment. You can spend a lot of effort documenting irrelevant eventualities and overlook what is really wrong, Training is essential for these tasks. So, if the task isn't being performed correctly, the problem could lie with training just as easily as with procedures.

- *Personnel selection.* This is related to training—are the right workers doing the job?

- *Supervision.* Procedures cannot make someone perform a task in a specified way. Supervisors sometimes can.

It may be quicker and easier to write (or revise) a procedure than to properly address one of the solutions discussed above. It comes as no surprise that, in some settings, the knee-jerk response to any problem is to revise or write a procedure. The unfortunate result is that procedures become lengthy and poorly focused, and workers don't use them—the original problem still remains.

So, before you begin to write a procedure, or assign the writing of a procedure, ensure that you can articulate the problem you are trying to solve and consider whether a procedure truly will solve that problem.

Who is writing the procedure?

Procedures must be written by qualified writers. Qualifications are determined by two things: technical skills and communication skills. The writer must understand the subject matter and must be able to communicate that information to others.

One question often arises: is it better to train a technical expert to write or to train a writer to be a technical expert? The answer depends on the complexity of the subject. Some subjects are too complex to expect a writer to learn in a reasonable amount of time. If this is the case, then the technical expert must do the writing. Other subjects are simpler and can be learned by the writer.

Another factor is whether management wants to build the technical experts' communication skills (or the writers' technical skills). Cost and availability may also be a factor. It may be cheaper to bring in a contract writer, or the technical experts may simply not have the time to write the procedure.

As writers, the authors of this book would like to think that a good writer can handle any writing task. Unfortunately, writers can wind up over their heads in complex technical subjects. You have to understand something very well to be able to describe it effectively.[5] Something that seems simple at first may grow quite complex once the writer delves into it. Before bringing in a writer to prepare your procedures, ensure that the writer has the necessary techni-

---

[5]Be aware, though, that people who know *too* much about a subject will have difficulty writing about it, as well, because they will have trouble putting themselves in the place of a less knowledgeable reader and figuring out what that person needs to know.

cal qualifications, has access to the resources needed (especially access to knowledgeable people), and is provided with feedback throughout the job.

Similarly, if the technical expert is doing the writing, he should be provided with support. That support may come in several forms. This book is one form—its intent is to describe how to effectively communicate information in procedures. Another is training. A third is the support of an editor or another writer, who can provide feedback and help the author revise the procedure.

There should be one writer per procedure. Attempts to have several writers work on one procedure are likely to lead to inconsistency, redundancy, or missing information. If the procedure is so long that one person cannot write the whole thing, then it should be broken into several procedures.

How is the procedure being written?

Once you have decided why the procedure is being written and who will be writing it, there are many other details that must be planned to ensure that the procedure writing process will be a success.

- Begin with *resources*. Procedure writing takes time, and the writer will need adequate time to do a good job.

- What *software* will be used? Have you taken full advantage of the capabilities of the software to support the writer? The format of procedures can be relatively complex. The best way to easily and consistently apply this formatting is to use style sheets, a word processing feature that allows you to specify a format (e.g., 12-point Times Roman, 13-point line spacing, autonumbered with a hanging indent and 12 points of space before each paragraph), name that format, then apply the format by calling up the name. (The specifications for the style sheet used for the examples in this book are presented in the appendix.)

- Consider the *workflow*, meaning the path the procedure will take through the organization as it is being written. For example, John writes the procedure, Sally reviews it, John reviews Sally's changes, Fred makes Sally's changes online, John reviews Fred's work, Betty reviews the procedure, and so on. Roles and responsibilities should be clear. Those involved should know whether they should be working with a printed version or working online. It should also be clear who owns the procedure—whose responsibility is it to ensure that the procedure is completed and that comments are incorporated?

- Don't overlook *file management*. Will the procedure be kept on a file server or a local hard disk? If it is on a server, who has access to it? If many procedures are being prepared, have file-naming conventions been established so that everyone knows what files are named. Bobpro1.doc may make sense to you, but what about everyone else?

- Is there a *writers' guide*? If not, procedure writers should, at a minimum, keep notes of the stylistic and formatting decisions they make. These efforts will help ensure consistency and simplify future writers' efforts.

- Who *approves* the procedure? In other words, which manager (or managers) confirms that the procedure meets the standards that have been established for it?

3.2 Investigating

Okay, you're ready to begin. When you are writing or revising a procedure, your first step is to obtain the necessary information to write the procedure—you investigate. You perform three activities in this step: reviewing source documentation, interviewing users and subject matter experts, and observing task performance.

Reviewing source documentation

Procedures typically are based on other documents. In technical settings, these may include other procedures, vendor manuals, technical specifications, piping and instrumentation diagrams, training materials, engineering analyses, and other procedures. In other settings they may include memos and management policies. It is important that you gather this material so that you have access to the information you need to write an accurate procedure.

Sometimes, the only document a procedure is based on is the previous version of the procedure. The problem with this shortcut is that there is no guarantee that the old procedure is correct. If you accept what it says without question, you may be perpetuating errors. In going back to the source documents (and adding to it based on your research) you can develop an accurate procedure so that the next writer who works on it *can* take credit for your work and will not have to duplicate it.

When dealing with complex procedures, the key to this process, where a procedure writer can take credit for the previous writer's work, is a *technical basis document*. Technical basis documents present and justify the technical basis for a procedure. A technical basis document does not have to adhere to any specific form; what it must do is explain why the procedure was written as it was written, referring to source documents as necessary. In complex procedures, the technical basis document should include this information for each step. Of course, if a technical basis document already exists for the procedure, you do not have to do this work but can use that document and add to it for your procedure revision.

In some situations, source documentation may not exist. If this is the case, the remaining activities in this step, interviewing and observing, must provide your technical basis. Once you have completed these activities, *leave a written record of what you have learned*. Spare the next writer who works on the procedure the trouble that you have been through.

Interviewing

Not all of the information you need will be contained in technical basis documents. Much of it will be in the minds of procedure users and subject matter experts. To get this information you must talk to these people.

You will typically be interviewing three types of people:

- Talk to procedure users because they are often quite familiar with the technical content of the procedure (including a few tips and hints that never made it into the procedure). Procedure users can also tell you what they want to see in the procedures—and, because they are your customers, this information is important. The discussion of audience analysis in Chapter 7 will return to this point in greater detail.

- Talk to technical experts, such as engineers or vendor personnel, who are not procedure users.

- Finally, talk with managers, who will outline their expectations for the procedure.

Interviews can be structured or unstructured. In an unstructured interview, you simply call up your buddy on the phone and ask some questions. These types of contacts can be very valuable. You should devote some effort to developing a network of people within the facility (or with vendors) that you can call when you have a quick question. However, be aware of the danger of relying too much on such a network—you should talk to people who have the answers to your questions, not who are simply easy to reach or do not mind talking to you.

At other times, you may want to take an approach to interviewing that is more formal. For example, you may be assigned a procedure that you do not know much about, necessitating interviews with people you have never met. In these situations, you probably want to bring a list of prepared questions to the interview; and you should concentrate on taking accurate, complete notes. You may even want to record the interview, so long as your subject will not be disturbed by a tape recorder.

Observing

If you have never seen something done, you will have difficulty writing about it. So if possible, you should perform the task yourself or watch someone perform it. This is a crucial part of the procedure writing process.

Some tasks cannot be easily performed. If you are writing an emergency procedure describing the actions to be taken when a boat takes on water, you probably don't want to go out in a boat, drill a hole in the bottom, then take notes with one hand while bailing with the other. In such cases, you should do the next best thing, which is a form of observation called a procedure walkdown.

During a walkdown, the user "acts out" all of the steps in the procedure in the location where they will be performed. Walkdowns can provide many types of information. The greatest benefit is that you can see what the task entails and thus be able to better describe it in the procedure. Walkdowns can alert you to tasks that will be physically difficult to perform, such as a task that requires users to closely coordinate their activities but is performed in a very loud area. If users cannot hear each other, they may have difficulty coordinating. Walkdowns are also useful for checking the correspondence between equipment labels and the procedure, although it may be too early in the process to worry about that.

Some industries, such as nuclear power and aerospace, use simulators that can model accident scenarios without hazard. If available, a simulator should be used, but it is still important to do a walkdown, because the actual facility may differ from the simulator.

It may be useful to combine a walkdown and an interview with a procedure user. The walkdown can remind the interviewee of things he should tell you and give you an idea of what questions to ask.

3.3 Organizing

Before you begin to write, you should have some idea of what you are going to say and how you plan to say it. You have to get organized. Outlining is a good organizational tool. In the outline, you should determine how the procedure should be broken into sections and what should go into each section (more about this in Chapter 13). Don't become too concerned with the outline format. If numbering is helpful, then number the items in the outline. No, you don't have to use the traditional Roman numeral format that you were probably taught.

You may also find it useful to develop a flowchart as you are organizing a procedure, particularly if the procedure contains several alternative courses of action. Chapter 21 provides guidance on preparing flowcharts. The advantage of a flowchart is that it forces you to systematically consider and account for all alternative courses of action. If there are many possible courses of actions (i.e., many decision points in the flowchart), development of a flowchart can be essential.

3.4 Writing the draft

There is no clear-cut point when you should stop outlining and start writing. Some writers develop complete, meticulous outlines before they begin writing. Others work from a cursory outline. Don't be too concerned with the distinction between the outline and the procedure. Many writers do not distinguish between their outlines and their drafts. Instead, their outline evolves into a finished document. They simply keep fleshing out the outline until it is the document. Whatever approach you take, at some point, your document is going to start looking like a procedure.

This technique has been greatly facilitated by the development of word processors. When writers typed, wrote, or even carved in stone, they were restricted to a basically linear process. For the most part, they had to write words in the order that they would be read. Not so with the word processor—the writer can skip around the document, leaving ideas half finished, with plans to complete them later, leaving notes to himself that will later be erased, shuffling sections around, and so on. With the word processor, you have much more flexibility in the way you write. Consider your writing habits; are you using this flexibility? Word processors offer much more than spell checking and lots of fonts.

Writer's block is one of the biggest obstacles to getting work done. Sometimes, the best technique for overcoming writer's block is to simply sit down and force yourself to write something, anything. You can always revise and change it later. Other times, writer's block is a symptom of too many distractions. Try getting to work early or staying late, and see if working at times when you are free from distraction is helpful.

The *Handbook of Technical Writing* (Brusaw, Alred, & Oliu, 1987, p. 719) provides additional advice on avoiding writer's block:

- Set up your writing area with the equipment and materials (paper, dictionary, source books, and so forth) you will need to keep going once you get started.

- Use whatever writing tools—separately or in combination—are most comfortable for you: pencil, felt-tip pen, typewriter, word processor, or whatever.

- Remind yourself that you are beginning a version of your writing project that no one else will read.

- Remember the writing projects you've finished in the past—you have completed something before, and you will this time.

- Start with the section that seems easiest to you—your reader will not know or care that you first wrote a section in the middle.

- Give yourself a time limit (10 or 15 minutes, for example) in which you will keep your pen or fingers on the typewriter moving, regardless of how good or bad your writing seems to you. The point is to keep moving.

- Don't let anything stop you when you are rolling along easily—if you stop and come back, you may not regain the momentum.

- But stop writing before you're completely exhausted; when you begin again, you may be able to regain your momentum.

- When you finish a section, give yourself a small reward—a short walk, a cup of coffee, a chat with a friend, an easy task, and so on.

With some writers, writer's block is a sign that there is something wrong with what they are trying to say. So, if you find yourself blocked, consider what

you are writing. Do you know what you want to say? Is it logical? Is it necessary to say it? Are you actually being thwarted by an underlying technical
problem?

3.5 Reviewing and revising

Once you have completed a draft, it is time to revise it. Just as there is no
clear-cut line between outlining and writing, there is no such line between
writing and revising. Most writers revise as they write. However, at some
point, you will have completed the procedure and will be ready to read
through it again, enhance it, and correct any errors.

Ideally, you should set the procedure aside for a few days before you revise.
The break will allow you to approach the revision with a clear mind. You will
be able to see problems and discrepancies that were not apparent to you
when you were writing. Although the schedules under which writers work
frequently may not allow this time, you should make every effort possible to
give yourself a break between writing the draft and revising it.

Keep the writers' guide and this book close at hand as you are revising. You
should check for all types of problems, from global (is the procedure accurate?) to specific (are words spelled correctly?). Procedure writing is very
detail-oriented, and this is the stage where you will be checking the details.
Take the time to double-check everything. Don't let things slide with the
expectation that they will be caught by other reviewers. Try to pass off a
procedure that is as accurate as possible.

In addition to the writer's review, it is important to have others review the
procedure, particularly if the writer has worked with technical experts when
developing the procedure. These experts should review the procedure to
ensure that the information they provided has been correctly incorporated.
Other reviews may be helpful as well.

- Users should review the procedure. Remember that they are your
  audience. Only they can tell you whether the procedure will be a useful
  tool for them.

- If an editor is available, the editor should certainly review the procedure. (If a writers' guide exists, it is critical that the editor use it to guide
  his or her review.)

- If an editor is not available, then someone besides the writer should
  proofread the procedure, looking for typos and misspellings. The writer
  is generally quite familiar with the procedure and is not the best person
  to proofread.

- Management should review and approve the procedure.

Always try to limit the number of people reviewing the procedure, however,
because the review process is subject to what's known as the law of dimin-
ishing marginal returns. That's a complicated way of saying that, when

several people review the same document, each additional reviewer tends to contribute a little less than the previous reviewers.

A simplified example can clarify this point. Assume that a procedure has 100 "errors" in it, of varying seriousness. Each reviewer will correct 50 of them and is more likely to correct the serious errors than the minor errors. The procedure is given to four reviewers, each of whom marks 50 errors. The procedure writer then consolidates the reviewers' comments. Once he has incorporated the first reviewer's comments, 50 errors have been corrected. The second reviewer has also made 50 comments, but many of these were also made by the previous reviewer; he has caught, say, only 15 errors that the first reviewer did not. The third reviewer also caught 50 errors, but only 10 that the first two reviewers did not. Out of the fourth reviewer's 50 comments, only 5 were not caught be the first three reviewers. So, each additional reviewer adds less to the document, especially when you consider that the reviewers are more likely to catch the major problems; after some point, as more reviewers are added, everyone is expending a lot of time and effort to catch fewer and fewer minor problems.[6]

Another simplification in this example is the assumption that there are a certain number of errors in a document and, when those errors are corrected, the result will be a perfect procedure. Writing doesn't work that way—there's no such thing as a "perfect" procedure. At best, there is one person's idea of a perfect procedure, which will not be the same as someone else's idea of a perfect procedure. So, when you add more and more reviewers, you really aren't closing in on a perfect procedure, you are bouncing around between a lot of different ideas of what a perfect procedure is. Further, you're expending a lot of time and effort in exchange for minimal or no return.

The point of this discussion is that the procedure does not necessarily improve as more reviewers are added beyond a certain point. The key is to find the appropriate reviewers and solicit their comments without turning the whole process into an exercise in consensus building that is expensive and isn't serving the users' needs. Here are some tips for walking this line:

- Decide what type of input you need and select a limited number of individuals to provide this input.

- Encourage reviewers to refrain from making comments outside their areas of expertise.

- Encourage reviewers to put themselves in the user's place while reviewing the procedure. They should necessarily not revise the procedure so that it is suitable for their own use, because they won't be using it.

---

[6]If there is time, this can be avoided by using a routing slip on a single copy. Carefully choose the order of the reviewers. (Most meticulous or senior person last, junior-level person first.)

- Educate reviewers on the importance of the writers' guide. Writers will need to change their writing habits somewhat to accommodate the writers' guide; reviewers should show similar flexibility.

- As the writer, retain control over the procedure. Someone needs to be in charge; as the writer, it ought to be you.

3.6 Testing

In addition to being reviewed, the procedure should be tested.[7] Someone should use the procedure while the writer watches. For the test to be most useful, the procedure should be performed by someone who has the experience and training that a "typical" user will have. As with observations, it may be difficult to test some procedures. In such cases, the procedure can be tested during a walkdown.

The writer observing the test should let the user perform the task using only the procedure. If the user struggles and stumbles, let him, and figure out what is causing the problem. Once you know what has gone wrong, you can help the user get back on track, if necessary.

The procedure should be revised as necessary after the test and, if substantial changes have been made, reviewed again. The procedure is now ready for use.

3.7 Maintaining

But the writer is not finished working on it. Procedures are living documents—they must be revised as the tasks they describe change. Tasks can change for a variety of reasons: new equipment is installed, new requirements are implemented, other procedures that affect that procedure are changed, or someone figures out a better way to perform a task.

A system should be established for reviewing the procedure on a periodic basis and for collecting feedback on the procedure. It is not necessary to revise a procedure every time a change is suggested. Minor changes can be collected and implemented all at once. If necessary, change pages can be added to the front of the procedure that alert users to changes that have not yet been made to the actual procedure, or changes can be handwritten on the procedure. These are temporary measures, however, and their use should be minimized. Users are unlikely to read and remember all change pages. Handwritten changes can be difficult to read and, because they are not part of the electronic file, can be lost.

The importance of procedure maintenance should not be underrated. If an organization commits to writing high-quality procedures, then it also commits to maintaining them.

---

[7]In some industries, testing is referred to as verification and validation (and people sometimes argue over what is verification and what is validation). We sidestep the issue here (and follow our own guidance from Section 6.2) by using the simpler term *testing*.

PART
TWO

Writing Basic Steps

CHAPTER
FOUR

Introduction: Writing Basic Steps

Beginning with Chapter 5, this book will present a series of principles that guide effective procedure writing. This chapter introduces the collection of principles that pertain to writing basic steps. These principles apply to simple procedures as well as complex procedures.

Steps are the heart of a procedure—they tell users what to do. In fact, the characteristic that most strongly separates procedures from other forms of writing is that information in procedures is presented in steps. In most other forms of writing, information is presented in paragraphs. In procedures, information is typically broken into smaller chunks (Zimmerman & Campbell, 1988). Berry (1981, p. 22) explains why:

> Narrative formats use sentences and paragraphs to separate the steps of a procedure. Sometimes steps are also separated by commas within sentences. Many narrative formats for procedures are ineffective. This format encourages writers to include a lot of unnecessary description and padding. Narrative formats are also more demanding of the user—the narrative steps of a procedure do not stand out clearly.

A comparison of Example 1 and Example 2 demonstrates the superiority of steps over a narrative format for procedures (Wright & Reid, 1973).

Cut the air filters into 1–2 cm² pieces and place the filter pieces into the nickel crucibles. Ash the mixture. Pipette 1 ml of strontium carrier and 1 ml of calcium carrier into the ash. Note that 15 gm of NaOH are required when analyzing 1-5 air filters of smears. Add 5 gm of NaOH pellets for each 1 gm of ash and add 5 gm of NaOH in excess. Be aware that the fusion process will likely result in a splatter that may cause personnel injury, loss of sample, or both unless protective gear is used. Fuse the sample in a nickel-covered nickel crucible.

Example 1. Narrative procedure. Compare this example with the series of steps presented in Example 2.

3.1   Cut the air filters into 1–2 cm² pieces.   ___

3.2   Place the filter pieces into the nickel crucibles.   ___

3.3   Ash the mixture.   ___

3.4   Pipette 1 ml of strontium carrier and 1 ml of calcium   ___
      carrier into the ash.

      Note: *15 gm of NaOH are required when analyzing 1-5 air filters of smears.*

3.5   Add 5 gm of NaOH pellets for each 1 gm of ash and add 5 gm   ___
      of NaOH in excess.

Caution: The fusion process will likely result in a splatter that may cause personnel injury, loss of sample, or both unless protective gear is used.

3.6   Fuse the sample in a nickel-covered nickel crucible.

Example 2. Step-by-step procedure. Here, the information is presented in steps (and a note and a caution). Errors are less likely in this format because the actions are clearly differentiated from each other.

Part Two of this book discusses how basic steps should be written. It concentrates on the content of steps rather then the format. Part Three will discuss format. Part Four will then discuss more complex forms of steps.

Part Two contains four chapters (in addition to this chapter):

- Chapter 5 discusses step syntax—the way steps are actually written. Steps should conform to the rules of English grammar; they should be written as imperatives (i.e., begin with an action verb); and they should be simple, concise, positive statements.

- Chapter 6 discusses vocabulary, word choice, and punctuation in procedures. Simple words are preferable to complex words; consistency is also important.

- Chapter 7 discusses level of detail. Procedures that contain too much detail will be cluttered and difficult to use, while procedures that contain too little detail can contribute to errors.

- Chapter 8 discusses the presentation of numerical information in procedures.

In this chapter...

Write steps as imperatives (5.3).

Essentialize—include only necessary information (5.2).

Follow the rules of English grammar (5.1).

Break a long sentence into short sentences (5.5).

3.1   Select *Customer Info.*
      Customer Info. is on the View menu.

Use standard punctuation (5.6).

3.2   Enter the account number.

Write steps as positive commands (5.4).

3.3   Press F6 (Select Account Info.).

CHAPTER
FIVE

Step Syntax

Syntax is the way in which words are arranged. This chapter discusses the syntax of action steps. It presents six principles.

5.1 Follow the rules of English grammar.

Summary

Procedures that are not written according to the rules of accepted English grammar, through either error or intention, may be misunderstood because they violate the expectations that readers bring to documents. Even if grammatical errors do not lead readers to misunderstand a procedure, they can lessen the procedure's credibility in the eyes of the user.

The word *grammar* has two related meanings, as explained by Brusaw, Alred, and Oliu (1987, p. 273):

> Grammar is a systematic description of the way words work together to form a coherent language; in this sense, it is an explanation of the structure of a language. However, grammar is popularly taken to mean the set of "rules" that governs how a language ought to be spoken or written... .

Here, we consider the second definition of grammar—the rules that govern the correct usage of a language.

The importance of following the rules of grammar

The grammar used in procedures should be very restricted; for example, steps may be written only as imperative sentences (see Section 5.3). However, few (if any) of these restrictions contradict the established rules of English grammar. It is important that procedures adhere to these rules, because readers expect to see documents that adhere to grammatical convention and may be confused by deviations and because ungrammatical writing may be viewed as unprofessional and flawed.

In *Modern American Usage*, Follett (1966, p. 23) portrays grammar as a sort of referee in the game of writing:

> When instinct fails, grammar helps by naming the fault and the remedy.... Anyone is free to dissent, but the rebels are likely to find that the convenience won by anarchy can become terribly inconvenient. Such opportunism has all the disadvantages of changing signals without consultation or the rules of the game without foreseeing all of the consequences.

Simon (1980, pp. 203–204) explains why it is important to adhere to the established conventions of grammar:

> There is, of course, the fundamental matter of courtesy to the other person, but it goes beyond that: why waste time on unscrambling simple meaning when there are more complex questions that should receive our *undivided attention*? [Emphasis added.]

Simon's concern reflects a central theme of this book. The reader of a procedure must, under the best of conditions, divide his or her attention among many tasks. Why add more distractions by deviating from standard grammatical conventions? Adhering to established grammatical conventions helps the reader comprehend and remember information because doing so frees up cognitive resources that might otherwise be needed to work through grammatical puzzles.

Further, correct grammar, like correct spelling, makes our writing more credible. Procedures must sell themselves to their users and, like all documents, they are sometimes judged on characteristics that may seem superficial. For instance, misspelled words are seldom mangled so severely that the reader does not realize which word was intended. So why worry about misspellings? Our audience can figure out what we meant.

We worry because we are making the reader figure out what the word is and because a misspelled word *looks* bad. Too many misspellings are seen as an indication of sloppiness; and if the writer is sloppy about something as basic as spelling, the reader can no longer be certain that the writer was not sloppy with some of the more substantial matters, like checking his facts.

In the same way, the step *Ensure that a safety injection have actuated* may be perfectly understandable, but the user who recognizes the error is likely to think less of the procedure writer and of the procedure itself. (The step should say, *Ensure that a safety injection has actuated*.) The user may wonder whether anyone tested the procedure and what other, more serious mistakes may be lying in wait for him. So, procedure writers should avoid anything that will undermine the procedure, which is exactly what grammatical errors do.

Some *basic* grammatical terminology

We all have taken grammar courses at some point in our lives, perhaps in high school, and most likely disliked the experience and found it of no benefit in later life. And, the fact is, there is no evidence that knowledge of grammar makes us better or worse writers:

> It is quite possible to write adequately without knowing a single thing about grammar (or at least without knowing a single thing that is taught under the heading of "grammar" in the public schools). Furthermore, knowing a whole lot about grammar is not likely to make you an excellent writer. In fact, one survey after another has shown that formal study of grammar in school has no correlation whatsoever with ability to write effectively. So why bother? (Stratton, 1984, p. 377)

We bother because an overview of grammar provides a common ground for discussing procedure writing. Or, as Follett (1966, p. 25) says, "Like the carpenter or plumber, the writer cannot carry on his own trade without technical terms." When the writers' guide says to begin an action step with a verb, a procedure writer should know what a verb is. Hence, this section will define some basic grammatical terms, beginning with some basic parts of speech. (If you are familiar with grammar, you will realize that this section generalizes and simplifies the topic a great deal.)

- A *noun* is a person, place, or thing. In the sentence *John saw the tree*, *John* and *tree* are nouns.

- A *verb* denotes action or state of being. In the sentence *John saw the tree*, *saw* is a verb. It explains the action that John is taking. In the sentence *John is happy*, *is* is a verb, because it describes John's state of being.

- Some sentences use *auxiliary verbs*, also known as helping verbs. Auxiliary verbs indicate mood, voice, and tense. In *The tree was seen by John*, *was* is an auxiliary verb.

- *The*, *a*, and *an* are *articles*. Articles modify nouns by indicating whether they should have a restricted or general meaning. In *John saw the tree*, the article *the* indicates that John saw a specific tree. The sentence *John saw a tree* refers to no tree in particular.

- *Adverbs* modify verbs. (To remember this, think that adverbs add to verbs.) In *John slowly ran*, *slowly* is an adverb. Most adverbs end in *-ly*.

- *Adjectives* modify nouns. In *John saw the big tree*, *big* is an adjective.

These parts of speech are combined into phrases, clauses, and sentences:

- A *phrase* is a group of two or more words that does not contain a subject (defined below) and a verb. *The tree* is a phrase.

- A *clause* is a group of two or more words that contains a subject and a verb phrase.[8] A clause can be a sentence; *John saw the tree* is a clause. Such clauses are called *independent* clauses, because they can stand independently. Other clauses, such as *While John watched the tree*, are not sentences. These are *dependent clauses*, because they depend on the sentence to which they belong for meaning (e.g., *While John watched the tree, Tom cut it down*).

- A *sentence* consists of one or more clauses, at least one of which must be an independent clause.

Sentences consist of subjects, verbs, and objects. Grammatical terminology overlaps here; subjects, verbs, and objects can be phrases or clauses. The terms *subject*, *verb*, and *object* are ways of classifying the phrases and clauses that appear within sentences.

- The *subject* answers the question who or what is performing the action expressed by the verb. In *John saw the tree*, *John* is the subject. Subjects are nouns or phrases acting as nouns. In the *imperative* sentences that make up procedure steps, the subject is the omitted word *you*; for example, in *Open the valve*, the subject is *you*, as in *You open the valve*.

- The *verb* expresses the action in the sentence. A verb (used in this context) can be a verb or a phrase acting as a verb.

- The *object* receives the action of a sentence. Objects are nouns or noun phrases. In *Open the valve*, *the valve* is the object.

Two common errors

A complete discussion of grammatical errors is well beyond the scope of this section. However, a discussion of one common error (subject-verb disagreement) and one intentional practice (omission of articles or auxiliary verbs) that compromise grammar in procedures will serve as an indication of the types of problems that might arise.

Subjects and verbs must agree in number; usually, we make subjects and verbs agree in our writing without really thinking about it. We write *The dogs are back* and *The dog is back* without much difficulty. Subject-verb disagreements typically arise in more complex sentences, where the subject is separated from the verb. For instance, we may write *A census of all fifty states are quite an undertaking*, mistakenly allowing the plural *states*, which is closer to the verb than the subject *census*, to determine the form of the verb. The correct version of the sentence is *A census of all fifty states is quite an undertaking* (i.e., *census... is*).

---

[8]A one-word imperative, such as *Halt!*, is also a clause.

Errors of this type can occur in procedures. Consider Example 3. At first glance, the step appears to be correct. However, it should read *Ensure that one of the following pumps is in service* (i.e., *one... is*). This grammatical error could lead to an error in procedure execution. The danger is that users may base their interpretation of the step on the verb and mistakenly believe that both pumps should be placed in service. With the use of the correct verb, this danger is lessened.

5.7   Ensure that <u>one</u> of the following pumps are in service:
 • Essential Electric-Driven Auxiliary Feed Pump, AFB-P01.   ___
 • Essential Steam-Driven Auxiliary Feed Pump, AFA-P0.   ___

Example 3. Subject-verb disagreement in a procedure. The subject-verb disagreement in this step may be difficult to detect at first glance—the verb should be is. It is a potential source of user error, however, because users may key on the verb are and think that they may place both pumps in service.

Sometimes, procedure writers deliberately violate the rules of grammar in the interest of brevity, omitting words that they feel contribute little to the sentence. The examples that will be considered here are the omission of articles and auxiliary verbs.

Articles (i.e., *a*, *an*, and *the*) indicate whether a noun is intended in a general or a specific sense. As such, they provide important information to readers. Yet, somehow, the notion has evolved in some forms of writing, procedures included, that prose flows better without articles. According to *Words into Type* (1974, p. 372), articles "are often misused and are often omitted without reason." This tendency may be carried to an extreme in procedures. We would never write *I went to store*, yet many procedure writers do not hesitate to write *Ensure that all of following criteria are met*.

Articles provide subtle clues to meaning in prose. The difference between *We were met at the Dublin airport by the officials of the Irish Republic* and *We were met at the Dublin airport by officials of the Irish Republic* is that the first implies that the visitors were met by all officials of the Irish Republic, while the second implies that the visitors were met by some officials of the Irish Republic (Follett, 1966, p. 37). While it is true that, in procedures, we cannot trust the communication of information solely to the subtle clues provided by articles, it is not a wise idea to discard all articles as useless. Readers expect to see articles, and may be confused by their absence. Because articles are such short words, there is simply very little cost to including them in procedures, while the risk of excluding them is that a step may be misunderstood.

A similar case can be made for auxiliary verbs. Why write *Ensure safety injection actuated* when *Ensure safety injection has actuated* is clearer and reads more smoothly, and at only the cost of adding a three-letter word—the auxiliary verb *has*. While in this example the loss of the auxiliary verb has a rather jarring effect, procedure writers often omit auxiliary verbs when a list format breaks up the step, as in Example 4.

> 3.1   Check that:
>   1. The safety function flowcharts have been completed.   ____
>   2. Reactor power decreasing.   ____

Example 4. Omitted auxiliary verb in a list. Although the error is not immediately apparent here, the second item should read, *Reactor power is decreasing*; otherwise, the step says, *Check that reactor power decreasing.*

Auxiliary verbs indicate mood and voice, which are not particularly applicable to procedures, and tense, which is applicable to procedures:

- Mood can be indicative or subjunctive. The indicative mood expresses a fact. The subjunctive mood expresses a possibility. In *If I were a rich man* the auxiliary verb *were* makes the clause subjunctive, indicating that the notion of becoming a rich man is an unlikely possibility.

- Voice can be first, second, or third person. Different auxiliary verbs are used in the following statements: *I am coming*, *You are coming*, and *He is coming.*

- Tense indicates time, either past, present, or future.

The critical issue for articles in procedures is the conveyance of tense. There is a difference between *Check that reactor power is decreasing* and *Check that reactor power has been decreasing*, and the auxiliary verbs convey this information.

5.2 Essentialize.

Summary

Decide what you need to say and say it in as few words as possible, but do not violate established grammatical conventions by writing in a telegraphic style.

Many writers dislike words that end in *-ize*, like *utilize* or *finalize*.[9] We agree, but make an exception for *essentialize*, because it describes a concept that is so important.[10]

When you essentialize, you determine what information is truly necessary to support readers and you include only that information in the procedure, writing as concisely as possible. The issue of deciding what information to include in the procedure will be addressed in more detail in Chapter 7 (Level of Detail). Concise writing will be addressed here.

---

[9]*Use* and *complete* are much preferred.
[10]We were first introduced to the term *essentializing* by Bob Schumacher and colleagues at Ameritech. They borrowed it from Pacific Bell.

Concise writing has long been recognized as good writing. In *The Elements of Style*, Strunk and White (1979, p. 23) write,

> A sentence should contain no unnecessary words, a paragraph no unnecessary sentences for the same reason that a drawing should have no unnecessary lines and a machine no unnecessary parts. This requires not that the writer make all his sentences short, or that he avoid all detail and treat his subjects only in outline, but that *every word tell*.

The Handbook of Technical Writing (Brusaw, Alred, & Oliu, 1987, p. 122) offers similar advice: "Careful writers remove every word, phrase, clause, or sentence they can without sacrificing clarity."

4.3   Be sure to waive any nonrecurring charges that may be
        applied when separate orders need to be issued.   ____

                               ✧ ✧ ✧

4.3   Waive any nonrecurring charges when you need to issue
        separate orders.   ____

Example 5. Concise writing. The version of this step on the top is too wordy. The bottom version is preferable.

Writing should be pruned with care, however. Many shortcuts are naively taken by writers who recognize the need for conciseness but who are not sensitive to the nuances of meaning that adherence to standard grammatical conventions help to ensure. Many of these shortcuts lead to a telegraphic writing style. A telegraphic writing style eliminates words here and there and makes the reader do the work of filling in the gaps. Omission of articles, as discussed in Section 5.1, is one example of telegraphic writing; relying too heavily on acronyms, as will be discussed in Section 6.4, is another. Often the reader can successfully fill in all of the gaps, but the cost in terms of the cognitive resources required to do so will almost always outweigh the advantages of the trivial reduction in length created. Further, there is always the risk that the reader will fill in the gaps incorrectly.

5.3 Write steps as imperative sentences.

Summary

Write action instructions as imperatives in the active voice.

Imperative sentences begin with action verbs: *Open the door*, *Feed the cat*, *Drive the car*. Such sentences clearly state the action to be taken. The implied subject is *You*, meaning the reader. So, those sentences are equivalent in meaning to *You open the door*, *You feed the cat*, and *You drive the car*. Imperative sentences communicate clearly and should be used in procedures for that reason.[11]

Imperative sentences are written in what is known as the active voice. In a sentence written in the active voice—an active sentence, in other words—the verb expresses the action in the sentence and the subject performs the action. *The boy hit the ball* is an active sentence because the action is hitting and the boy is doing the hitting. Imperative sentences are active sentences that begin with an implied *you*.

In a passive sentence, the subject is the recipient of the action. *The ball was hit by the boy* is a passive sentence. The subject of this sentence is *The ball*, but the ball is not doing the hitting—the boy is.

Passive	Imperative
The pressure is set to 700 psia by the operator.	Set the pressure to 700 psia.
The parts should be cleaned by the operator with oil.	Clean the parts with oil.

Procedures differ from other types of writing, where there can be good reason to use the passive voice. Mixing active and passive sentences can introduce sentence variety, which in turn can make a document more pleasurable to read. (Providing sentence variety is not a good goal for procedure writers, who should focus on consistency rather than variety.) Also, in conventional prose, it may occasionally be appropriate to use the passive voice to emphasize the object of a verb rather than the performer of the action. However, as Porter (1991) points out, most of the apparent advantages of the passive voice in technical documents are illusory and the use of the passive voice will, in fact, undermine the tone of a document, force the writer to use long complex sentences, render the writing "immediately forgettable," and bore readers to tears (p. 88). Porter's tongue-in-cheek essay on the advantages of the passive voice, however, barely begins to identify its major weaknesses.

---

[11]An imperative sentence can also begin with a modifier: *Carefully open the door.*

If all other things are equal, the active voice is preferable to the passive voice in procedures because the active voice more closely matches the way people remember and process information. However, all other things are seldom equal and, in fact, the active voice tends to promote a number of recognized good writing practices. Active sentences tend to be shorter than passives (Coleman, 1963; Porter, 1991; Anderson, 1991). Anderson correctly states that the active voice allows "you to speak directly to readers, telling them as briefly as possible what to do" (p. 661).

The active voice also gives procedures more authority (Lannon, 1991) and focuses steps on actors and actions (Anderson, 1991). The subject of an imperative in the active voice is *you*, the performer of the action. The word *you* is omitted because it is so readily understood. The verb showing the action is then placed prominently as the initial word in the sentence. Thus, the imperative sentence *Correct the errors on the printout* focuses on the action the reader is to perform (correcting errors). By contrast, *Errors should be corrected on the printout* treats the object of the action (the errors) as the subject of the sentence and leaves the actor vague—whether you or someone else should correct the errors is not clear. The verb is buried in the middle of the sentence, where it is more likely to be forgotten than if it were placed either at the beginning or the end of the sentence.

Most of the issues discussed above, while important, are somewhat indirect consequences of using the passive voice. When the direct effects of the use of the active and passive voices are considered, the value of the active voice becomes even more evident. Passive sentences clearly place higher cognitive demands upon readers than do active sentences. Slobin (1966) found that subjects took longer to identify whether statements were true or false when the sentences were written in the passive voice rather than the active voice. Herriot (1969) found that subjects also took longer to identify the logical subjects and objects in passive constructions for certain types of sentences when those sentences were cast in the passive voice.

Most importantly, sentences written in the active voice are remembered better than sentences written in the passive voice, and at least some passive sentences are remembered as active sentences (Coleman, 1963; Anderson, 1963). For example, it has been shown that people will recall a previously read passive sentence such as *The mouse was chased by the cat* as an active sentence (*The cat chased the mouse*) and believe that they initially read the sentence in the active form. There are two important implications of this research finding. First, readers will need to devote substantially more attention and cognitive resources to the task of reading passive sentences than they would active sentences. When reading passive sentences, an additional complex task is added to the reading process—the task of recoding the information into active constructions. Second, any intended advantage of using the passive voice is likely to be lost, because readers will translate the text into the active voice and process the information as if it were written in the active voice anyway. Thus, there appear to be many disadvantages to using the passive voice in procedures and few, if any, advantages.

5.4 Write steps as positive commands.

Summary

Write action instructions as positive statements, although concise, nonambiguous negative statements are sometimes appropriate.

Follett (1966, p. 223) warns, "For many reasons, negative statements have to skirt more grammatical pitfalls than do positive statements." Other authorities and many researchers also warn against the use of negative statements. There is substantial evidence to suggest that people do prefer to deal with positive information rather than negative information.

Ensure the valve is not open is a negative statement. *Ensure the valve is closed* is a corresponding positive statement. All else being equal, readers will find it easier to understand the positive statement (Sherman, 1973). Thus, in this particular situation, it is preferable to write *closed* rather than *not open*. A statement containing more than one negation can bring a reader to his knees—*IF the valve is NOT open, THEN do not adjust flow.* These should be avoided at all times (Felker et al., 1981).

Avoiding negative statements

You should avoid negatives, but negative statements are not always harder to understand simply because they are negative. Negative sentences might be more difficult to understand because they tend to be wordier; in the first example above, the negative statement (*Ensure the valve is not open*) is six words long while the positive statement is five words long. Some negative statements also tend to be inherently vague (Sherman, 1973; Harbaugh, 1991). The reader must determine by exclusion what is true; if someone is not happy, then is he sad? Such determinations take effort and introduce the potential for misunderstanding.

5.6   IF the subscriber does **NOT** need a display device,
        THEN go to Step 5.9.   ____

❖ ❖ ❖

5.6   IF the subscriber has a display device,
        THEN go to Step 5.9.   ____

Example 6. Eliminating a negative statement. The top step has been rewritten so that a negative statement is unnecessary. The bottom step is preferable.

Using negative statements when you have to

The authors of this book once prepared a draft of a procedure writers' guide and sent it out for review. When it came back, *every* negative sentence had been rewritten as a positive sentence. Nothing else had been changed. Not only did the reviewer miss several other problems in that particular document, his personal crusade against negative sentences was somewhat misguided. Some sentences were improved by his rewrites, but others were not. In particular, one sentence that began *Do not draw maps to scale...* had been rewritten to begin, *Draw unscaled maps....* The original sentence was perfectly clear; it was certainly clearer than the revision—what's an unscaled map?[12] Sometimes, a negative statement is the clearest.

Negative statements do have a place in procedures, if they are used carefully. Negative statements can be quite emphatic (Burnett, 1990) and a concise, nonambiguous negative statement can communicate quite effectively. Consider *Do not touch the live wires or you may be electrocuted.* Attempt to rewrite the sentence and it loses some of its punch; *Avoid touching live wires...* is not as forceful and *Live wires should not be touched...* is an ambiguous passive.

Note: *The primary scrub column should be filled to a normal level.*

✧ ✧ ✧

Note: *Do not overfill the primary scrub column.*

Example 7. Using negative wording when necessary. These two notes do not say the same thing. If the intention is to tell operators not to overfill the column, then the second note should be used. It would be a mistake to reword the note in a positive fashion, as in the first example, simply to avoid a negative statement.

You should in general avoid using negative statements in your procedures, but do not banish them all without consideration. When you do use a negative statement, ensure that it is concise and unambiguous. You should also be aware of several pitfalls in the use of negatives.

Negating words, such as *not*, should be placed with care; and you should carefully consider what exactly is being negated. The sentence *All of these acids are not found in protein foods* "flirts with the meaning" that no acids are found in any protein foods (Follett, 1966, p. 223). If the author means that some acids may be found in protein foods, a clearer rewrite would be

---

[12]There is another lesson to be drawn here. There are exceptions to every rule; and if you apply rules rigidly and arbitrarily when you write, you may achieve competence but will never achieve excellence. Chapter 22 will discuss this idea further.

Not all of these acids are found in protein foods. All negatives introduce the potential for this kind of misunderstanding.

Negatives may be useful to "suggest the gray area of meaning between the negative and the positive" (Brusaw, Alred, & Oliu, 1987, p. 202). For instance, *not hot* does not mean the same thing as *cold*; something that is lukewarm is neither hot nor cold. Such constructions, however, should be used with care in procedures, which are no place to be introducing subtle shades of meaning. You should also be careful, whenever you use a negative, that any gray area of meaning that might be implied will not introduce confusion. It is worthy of note, though, that in this example the gray area of meaning stems as much from the use of the word *cold* as from the negation. If a specific temperature were used instead, for example, *not above 40°F*, the potential for confusion would be reduced. Even better, of course, would be to say, *40°F or below*, eliminating the negation as well as the vague term.

5.5 Break long sentences into several shorter sentences.

Summary

As a general rule, the sentences in procedure steps should be as short as possible, because short sentences are likely to include fewer actions and be easier to understand. A short sentence containing one long clause may be more difficult to understand than a long sentence containing several short clauses.

In a procedure, short sentences are preferable to long sentences for two reasons. The first is that long sentences in steps may include more than one action and readers may overlook actions if a step contains multiple actions. The second reason is that short sentences can be easier to understand.

Short sentences contain fewer actions

Recall that one reason active sentences are used in procedures is that they begin with the verb, thus highlighting the action. If a step contains several actions, only the first action will be highlighted in this manner; the second or third action may be overlooked.

A step may include more than one action if those actions are closely related.

Short sentences are easier to understand

It has long been recognized that shortening sentences can be an effective way to improve the readability of a document. Chall (1984) writes that, after vocabulary, sentence length has the greatest effect on readability. In fact, readability formulas, which measure how hard a passage is to read, often use

---

6.3   Write down the existing account number, increase the last
        number by one, and add a *0* as the first digit.   ____

                                ✧ ✧ ✧

6.3   Write down the existing account number.   ____

6.4   Increase the last number by one.   ____
        For example, change 62119957 to 6211995**8**

6.5   Add a *0* as the first digit.   ____
        For example, change 62119958 to **0**62119958

Example 8. Breaking up steps. Here, one step is broken into three. There is less chance of an action being overlooked if each is called out in a separate step. An additional benefit is that examples can now be easily incorporated into two of the steps.

the average length of sentences and the average length of words to determine the complexity of the writing.[13]

Short sentences are not a goal in themselves, however—understandable writing is the goal. A consideration of sentence length should therefore be tempered with an understanding of the other factors that affect readability and an understanding that a short sentence is not automatically an understandable sentence.

It is not uncommon to encounter rules in technical communication that specify a maximum (or optimal) sentence length. Huckin (1983) warns against relying too heavily on these rules. He recounts an amusing story of a colleague who had a student whose writing

> was "incontrovertibly soporific." It turned out that the student had once been told by his eighth-grade English teacher that "the average American sentence contained eighteen words," and he thereafter devoted his writing life to producing eighteen-word sentences! Indeed, [Huckin's colleague] counted the words and sentences in one of his papers and found that of the thirty-eight sentences in it, thirty-six were eighteen words long (the two others were seventeen and nineteen words long)! (p. 103)

Huckin is obviously presenting an extreme instance here, but he makes a valid point—sentence-length requirements can be useful, but only as guidelines. Long sentences may be more difficult to understand than short sentences, but this is not necessarily so; and the clarity of a sentence should never be compromised simply to shorten it.

---

[13]See Section 22.1 for more on readability formulas.

The guideline to use short sentences is an oversimplification, and researchers have delved more deeply into the matter. For example, through a series of experiments, Coleman (1963) demonstrated that clause length, rather than sentence length, affects readability. He compared shorter sentences, such as *A detailed knowledge of the lower Mississippi valley would be quite helpful* with longer versions that contained shorter clauses, such as *If you knew the lower Mississippi valley in detail, it would be quite helpful*. He found that sentences such as the second were easier to understand, and attributed the difference to clause length. He writes (pp. 340–341),

> Thus it seems that the advice to prefer short sentences might be better rephrased as a rule to prefer short clauses. If the clauses in a writer's composition are short, he will probably not improve readability much by emphasizing the boundaries between them with periods and capitals.

5.6   Use punctuation that conforms to standard American English usage.

Summary

Punctuation in procedures should conform to standard English usage, because this use of punctuation will conform to users' expectations. Complex or unconventional punctuation should be avoided.

It is not within the scope of this book to include an entire manual of punctuation in technical writing. Many authoritative volumes on this subject are readily available, such as *Words into Type* (1974) and *The Chicago Manual of Style* (1993).

Basically, the guidance here is the same as the guidance regarding grammar. Follow the rules.

An overview of selected punctuation standards and usage, however, may be beneficial. This list is by no means exhaustive, but it does focus on some of the problems that can arise when punctuating procedures.

- *Select a word order that minimizes the need for punctuation.* Break sentences that require extensive punctuation into shorter sentences. Excessive use of punctuation may be an indication that the information is too complex or that the writer is not organized and is perhaps even confused about the subject matter. The procedure writer must appear knowledgeable if a user is to give the written material credibility.

- *Use periods at the end of bulleted items if those items are complete sentences.* If you're one of those people who really get into writing and editing, you've probably realized that bulleted items can be punctuated in many different ways and can become a subject of much contention. This rule isn't perfect, but it is simple; and there is no perfect rule for punctuating bulleted items. So why not use a simple rule?

- *Use the serial comma*, which is the comma that appears before the last item in lists of three or more items. The serial comma appears before the conjunction in the list—*and* or *or*. In the following sentence, the serial comma appears after the word *red*: *Blue, red, and green are my favorite colors*. The sentence could be written correctly without this comma, but lack of this comma can create confusion in other sentences. Consider, *Frank, Bill and Jane completed the manuscript*. Is Frank being told that Bill and Jane completed the manuscript or did the three of them complete the manuscript? With the comma before the *and*, the sentence becomes unambiguous: *Frank, Bill, and Jane completed the manuscript*. All three of them worked on the manuscript.

- *Use a colon (:) to indicate that a list is to follow*. There is an exception to this rule, however: Don't use a colon between a verb or preposition and its direct object(s). In other words, don't say, *Fred went to the store with: Lisa, Tom, and Jane*. Following the logic that a colon must always introduce a list leads to writing sentences such as, *Get: a wrench and a pair of pliers*. Colons should be used to separate an introduction that is a complete sentence from the list; so, it would be correct to write, *You will need two tools: a wrench and a pair of pliers*. A colon should also be used if the list is being formatted with white space, as discussed in Section 10.2.

- *If you are going to use semicolons, use them correctly*. Semicolons seem to be among the most frequently misused marks of punctuation; writers often use semicolons rather than colons. Semicolons are used instead of commas to separate listed items when those items include internal commas and instead of periods to join related sentences. There shouldn't be much reason to use semicolons in procedures—for example, lists should be bulleted or numbered, so there is no need to end each item with a semicolon (or a comma). It is probably better not to use semicolons unless you are certain that you are using them correctly.

- *Don't use an apostrophe to make a word plural*. Dave Barry writes that sign makers use an apostrophe to indicate that the next letter on the sign is an *s*. Apostrophes indicate possession, not plurality. This simple rule is violated all the time. *I have two dog's* is incorrect. Some sources make an exception for abbreviations; however, there is no logic in doing so. If *SG* is the acronym for steam generator, then the plural is *SGs*, not *SG's*. The only exception is when the abbreviation contains internal punctuation (*Words into Type*, 1974)—for example, the plural of *Ph.D.* is *Ph.D.'s*. Here, there is logic to including the apostrophe, because it avoids the awkward construction *Ph.D.s*.

In this chapter...

Use words
consistently
(6.1).

Use short,
simple words
(6.2).

Use abbreviations
carefully (6.4).

Avoid words that
may be
misunderstood
(6.3).

5.6   Ensure that PRV-5 is closed.

5.7   Stop the discharge flow.

5.8   Ensure that PRV-6 is open.
      Turn it to the right-hand position.

CHAPTER
SIX

Vocabulary

Vocabulary refers to word choice. It is important that procedures use words that are easy to understand and convey correct meaning. It is also important that words be used consistently. This chapter presents several principles regarding vocabulary in procedures.

6.1 Use words consistently within and among procedures.

Summary

Words and phrases should be used consistently within and among procedures so that users will not attribute differences in meaning to spurious differences in presentation. A list of action verbs should be developed.

One of the most important differences between technical writing (including procedure writing) and other forms of writing is the importance of consistency. "Once you've started referring to something by a particular name, *continue* referring to it that way," Huckin (1983, p. 101) writes. "Don't vary your terminology simply for the sake of variation."

Farkas and Farkas (1981, p. 6) expand on the need for consistency:

> Every manuscript contains mechanical elements of numerous kinds: abbreviations, hyphenated compounds, numerals, spelled numbers, and so forth. The editor [and writer] must ensure that throughout the manuscript these recurring elements are treated consistently, that is, in a uniform or else logical and

harmonious way. The human mind has an inherent need for order, and if these elements are not treated consistently, the reader may perceive the document to be disorderly and unprofessional and may be distracted by the inconsistencies. Worse still, in some instances, the inconsistent treatment of mechanical elements can be genuinely confusing, because the reader may assume that two treatments of the same thing indicate some distinction in meaning that the reader has failed to understand.

Consistency is particularly important in procedures, which tend to be terse and concise, requiring each word to convey substantial information.

Because action verbs are fundamental to the meaning of a step, special effort should be taken to ensure that they are used consistently. An action verb is (typically) the first word in a simple action step; it specifies the action that is to be taken. In *Open the valve*, *open* is the action verb. A list of action verbs should be developed, and verbs from this list should be used in procedures. Each verb should be clearly defined, and the list should be carefully edited to eliminate redundancy so that, for instance, users do not have to guess at the meaning of such similar verbs as *ensure*, *assure*, and *check*. Further, because users frequently give oral instructions based on procedures, verbs that sound alike but have different meanings should be avoided; for example, *reduce* is preferable to *decrease*, which sounds like *increase;* and *start* is preferable to *commence*, because it is shorter.

If possible, procedure writers should be restricted to using only action verbs from the list. In practice, this may be difficult, however, because the procedure writer cannot foresee all possible actions that the procedure user may take. If this is the case, procedure writers should be instructed to use action verbs from the list whenever possible, but if a specified action verb does not communicate the action they wish the user to take, they should use the shortest, simplest verb that does. The action verb list should be updated to include all new verbs.

Consistency applies to all vocabulary in procedures. Equipment nomenclature should also be presented consistently. A piece of equipment should not be identified by its common name at one place in the procedure and by its assigned number later in the procedure. Cross-referencing terms and conditional terms should also be used consistently.

These consistency requirements apply to phrases as well as words. Certain key phrases will be used repeatedly in procedures. For example, *Continue in this procedure* may be used to indicate that the user may continue in the procedure before the present step is completed; this phrase should not be used interchangeably with *Proceed from this step* or even *Continue on in this procedure.*

If users will be dealing with multiple procedures, especially if the same people will be using different procedures, consistency among procedures can be as important as consistency within a procedure. Consistent presentation also simplifies the work of procedure writers and reviewers. Obviously, if there are discrete sets of procedure users and writers for some classes of procedures, the need for inter-procedure consistency is not as strong.

activate	To set in motion, make active, or make more active: *Activate the air cylinder to raise the element section catch tray.*
actuate	Use **activate.**
add	(1) To combine: A*dd approximately 6 inches of water (approximately 1 liter) to the funnel on the Drum Dryer weigh column.*
	(2) To perform addition: *Add all the Grams U^{235} recorded for each tray.*
adjust	To bring components into a more effective or efficient calibration or state: *Adjust steam pressure to between 5 and 20 psig using <u>any</u> of the following valves:....*
align	To adjust (parts of a mechanism, for example) to produce a proper relationship or orientation: *Align the gasket with the bolt holes.*

Example 9. Example action verb list. Each definition is accompanied by an example. For verbs that should not be used, an alternative is given.

Consistency is ensured through a combination of activities. A detailed writers' guide must set standards for consistency and must be used by procedure writers. Reviewers must be aware of standards for consistency and must take the time and effort to ensure that the procedure is consistent. This is not the most exciting task. Checking for consistency is a meticulous process and can be dull; yet it is important. The fewer people that review for consistency the better. Having a pool of five or ten people who review for consistency is somewhat self-defeating because it increases the possibility of inconsistencies among reviewers.

6.2 Use short, simple words that are common in standard American English.

Summary

Words must be understandable to the intended user. Use the simplest, most common word that accurately conveys the intended meaning and is consistent with other words used in the procedure.

The English language includes many words that are synonymous (i.e., mean the same thing). To choose one of many examples, the words *heroism*, *courage*, and *bravery* mean much the same thing. When choosing among words that mean approximately the same thing, the procedure writer is guided by concerns of accuracy, consistency, and understandability.

Accuracy is critical. Words must accurately convey their intended meaning. The English language is rife with subtle shades of meaning. While the words *inexpensive* and *cheap* can generally be considered synonymous, their connotations are very different. If you buy an inexpensive car, you have gotten a good deal; but if you buy a cheap car, it is likely to break down and give you trouble. Any attempt to universally substitute *inexpensive* for *cheap* (or vice versa) could easily change the meaning of a document. So, when considering issues of consistency and understandability, always ensure that the word *says* what you mean.

That stated, it is important that words be used consistently. Differences in word choice should denote differences in meaning, not a desire to introduce some variety. Consistency was discussed in Section 6.1.

It is also important to use the most understandable word that accurately and consistently conveys the meaning you intend. Complex vocabulary has a strong effect on readability:

> The research in readability has uncovered over one hundred factors related to difficulty—such factors as vocabulary, sentences, ideas, concepts, text organization, content, abstractness, appeal, format, and illustrations. Of these factors, the two found consistently to be the most strongly associated with comprehensibility are vocabulary difficulty and sentence length…. The strongest factor of the two is vocabulary difficulty…. (Chall, 1984, pp. 237–238)

Simple words are easiest to understand. Strunk and White (1979, p. 76) provide sage advice: "Do not be tempted by a twenty-dollar word when there is a ten-center handy, ready and able." *Utilize* is a good example of a twenty-dollar word. Follett (1966, p. 221) singles it out for criticism:

> It should seem as if… no word could be called needless. Exact synonyms are rare, and there is always a feature in the apparent synonym, whether shade of meaning, connotation, length, or rhythm, by which it can make itself useful. Yet some words at some times and others at all times can be shown to be unnecessary. *Utilize* is one of the second class. The occasions when *use* will not do are so rare as to be nonexistent for the workaday writer, and the bad habit of resorting to the longer word becomes incurable.[14]

The Handbook of Technical Communication (Brusaw, Alred, & Oliu, 1987, p. 395) lists other long words and their preferred counterparts: *analyzation* (prefer *analysis*), *certificated* (prefer *certified*), *commercialistic* (prefer *commercial*), *interconnect* (prefer *connect*), *finalize* (prefer *finish*), *orientate* (prefer *orient*), *prioritization* (prefer *priority*), and *visitation* (prefer *visit*).

The requirement to use short words should be applied with some common sense, however. Not all long words are uncommon and not all short words are common: "Multisyllable words like *butterfly*, *everyone*, *however*, and *neighborhood* are… familiar… , while short words like *adz*, *bleb*, *emir*, and *hadj* are not" (Stratton, 1984, p. 435). Further, common words, in this context, are words that procedure users commonly encounter. There is

---

[14] Strunk and White (1979, p. 63), who tend to be much more concise, provide similar, though greatly abbreviated guidance: "Utilize. Prefer use."

nothing wrong with using a long word if you are certain your users will understand it, and no shorter alternatives are available.

Some writers may be concerned that simple, common words cannot effectively communicate complex technical concepts. Yet, simple words can be used effectively with little loss in meaning, as indicated by efforts to develop a simplified English vocabulary set for some technical documents (Gringas, 1987). Although these efforts are intended mainly to facilitate the translation of documents into other languages, a process known as localization, their success indicates that simple words can communicate effectively.

Finally, the illiteracy rates in this country provide an additional reason to use simpler words. It is estimated that approximately 19% of the workforce in the United States cannot read at the eighth-grade level, and 30% of the workforce cannot read at the tenth-grade level (Washington State Office of Financial Management, 1990). Although it is likely that illiteracy rates are lower within the technological or business settings where many procedures are used, as a procedure writer, you must deal with the unfortunate possibility that some of your users may have difficulty reading. The use of simpler, shorter words can make procedures more accessible to these individuals. In the audience analysis (discussed in Chapter 7), you should try to assess the general reading level of procedure users.

6.3 Avoid words that may be misunderstood.

Summary

Procedure writers should avoid words that may be misunderstood, either in written or spoken form. Substitute a clearer word or phrase for the ambiguous word.

It would be impossible to require that words with multiple meanings not be used in procedures. Nearly *every* word in the English language has more than one meaning. These multiple meanings typically are not problematic. It is a normal part of the reading process to attach meanings to words based on context. When we read the sentence, *John will file the memo*, we know that *file* is a verb describing an action and not a noun describing a large metal cabinet, a set of data that can be read by a computer, or a tool for grating metal. We attach different meanings to *file* when we read *John put the memo in the file*, or *Excel can't read my file*, or *The prisoner had a file baked in a cake*.

Problems are likely to arise, however, when the meaning of a word is not evident based on context. As a procedure writer, you must ensure that your instructions will be understood by avoiding ambiguous words. *Open the right valve* is unclear; *Open the right-hand valve* is preferable. *Recover* and *re-cover* (meaning to cover again) would also be confusing; instead of using *re-cover*, you should specifically request that users *cover the opening again*.

Problems may also arise when instructions in a procedure are given orally. Many words sound alike. You should avoid these words also. *Increase* and *decrease*, for example, can be confused with each other; *raise* and *reduce* are preferable.

Some words by their nature are abstract and vague, such as the adverb *slowly* in *He drove slowly*. Houp and Pearsall (1988, p. 147) acknowledge the need for such abstract words, but warn that writers must be cautious: "Abstractions are needed for generalizing, but they cannot replace specific words and necessary details. Words mean different things to different people. The higher you go on the abstraction ladder, the truer this is. Abstract words [can be] interpreted in as many different ways as the writer has readers." Slowly at the Indianapolis 500 is different than slowly in a school zone.

In procedures, vague words are most likely to be adverbs, which modify verbs, or adjectives, which modify nouns. If users are instructed to *Slowly drain the tank*, they must attach a specific rate to the adverb *slowly*. If they read the step *IF the mechanism is rusty, THEN replace it*, what constitutes *rusty* (an adjective)? Whenever possible, adverbs and adjectives should be quantified; say, *Drain the tank at a rate no greater than 10 gallons/minute* or *IF at least 15% of the mechanism's surface area is rusted, THEN replace it*. An illustration of the mechanism showing an acceptable level of rust might also be useful.

Sometimes you are forced to use a vague adverb or adjective. In the example of the rusty mechanism, stipulating 15% may not work because the decision to replace the mechanism hinges on which part is rusted or the nature of the rust. If the issue is simply too complicated to explain, but an experienced maintainer would know whether the mechanism should be replaced, it is acceptable to include the adjective; but during testing you should ensure that it will not be misunderstood.

6.4 Restrict the use of abbreviations and acronyms.

Summary

All abbreviations and acronyms used in procedures should be taken from a restricted list. Users should know the meaning of all abbreviations and acronyms used in procedures without referring to this list.

In the mid 1960s, during the Cold War, the United States military was under pressure to develop new weapons. In response to this pressure, weapons developers began renaming existing weapons to provide the illusion of greater progress. One officer suggested renaming the Nike-Zeus anti-missile system Marathon, because it was taking so long to develop. The name Spartan was chosen instead. Critics were not outsmarted, however—they quickly dubbed Spartan an acronym for *superior performance and range through advanced nomenclature* (Bruce-Briggs, 1988).

It's easy to poke fun at abbreviations and acronyms.[15] Abbreviations are shortened forms of words, such as *fig* for figure, *govt* for government, or *op* for operations. Acronyms are representative words formed from letters (usually initials) of words in a defining phrase. Acronyms may be pronounced as words, such as *NASA* (*na-suh*) for National Aeronautics and Space Administration, or pronounced letter by letter, such as *COD* (*see-oh-dee*) for cash on delivery. In some reference manuals, both of these word-contracting methods are combined under the single heading of abbreviations, because the distinction between acronyms and abbreviations is slight (Towell, 1989). The bottom line is, call them whatever you want (we'll use abbreviations as an umbrella term here for simplicity), but minimize their use.

Used within certain limitations, abbreviations can assist the reader. Often, readers will be more familiar with the abbreviation than the term it represents—quick, what does *laser* stand for?[16] If a word or phrase is commonly understood and used throughout the procedure (e.g., *safety analysis report*), it is appropriate to use its abbreviated form (e.g., *SAR*). This will conserve space on the page while increasing reading speed without jeopardizing comprehension. The shortened visual format of abbreviations, when understood by the reader, can be read faster than the word in full (because fewer letters can be scanned more quickly). In these situations, the use of abbreviations is acceptable and even preferable. However, abbreviations should *not* be used simply for the procedure writer's convenience. Don't include an abbreviation simply to avoid typing the complete word or phrase.

In some documents, it is acceptable to define an abbreviation the first time it appears. This is not acceptable in procedures, however. Procedures are not always performed from start to finish; users may follow a cross-reference to the middle of a procedure and begin the procedure at that point or may only perform one section of a procedure. In these situations, the user may miss the initial definition of the abbreviation. Also, procedure readers have enough demands on them without being expected to learn the meanings of abbreviations as they are encountered. You should use only abbreviations that are familiar to the user and that users will understand without definition (Rogers & Moeller, 1984).

The best way to ensure that abbreviations will be understood is to use only abbreviations from an approved list. This list should be included in the writers' guide. Only in rare cases will it be necessary to deviate from the standardized list (e.g., to copy exact wording from inconsistent nameplates or equipment labels). In these cases, it is more important that the procedural text be representative of the actual equipment markings than that all abbreviations conform in the abbreviation list.

---

[15]A reviewer complained that a document had too many TLAs. What are TLAs? Three-letter acronyms.

[16]*L*ight *a*mplification by *s*imulated *e*mission of *r*adiation.

Several rules govern the abbreviations on this list:

- Users should know the meaning of all abbreviations on the list without referring to the list. User comprehension should be tested before the abbreviation is accepted for use.

- This list should not include abbreviations that have more than one meaning or may be easily confused with other words. Avoid truncating words to create abbreviations that could be confused with other words; for example, don't use *man* for *management*.

- Avoid abbreviations that people do not use when speaking; for example, people say *hardware*, not *HW*, so don't use *HW* as an abbreviation (Miller, 1996).

- Avoid abbreviations that are longer, when spoken, than the terms they replace; for example, there are three syllables in *wide-band switch*, but five in *WBS*. Use *wide-band switch* (Miller, 1996).

- Avoid using abbreviations that end in a period, because users may believe that the period indicates the end of a sentence.

- An abbreviation should represent only one term. For example, *HP* should not stand for both *horsepower* and *health physics*. You should also be careful of abbreviations that can have other meanings when made plural; for example *OPs* (for *operating procedures*) could be confused with *OPS* for *operations*.

- Similarly, do not use more than one abbreviation to represent a single term. For example, the word *manager* could be abbreviated as *mngr* or *mgr*. Using only one of these (say, *mgr*) will reduce the amount of information the reader has to remember, and it will be clear that *mgr* (and only *mgr*) will stand for *manager*. Another example is abbreviating the name of a piece of equipment in two different ways, such as *travel lock* abbreviated as *TRVL LCK* and *TVL LK*; only one of these should be used.[17]

- Simple words are easily recognized and understood, and should therefore be left unaltered. Abbreviating simple words will increase the potential for reader confusion when the only benefit is that an already short word is shortened further.

---

[17]Problems can sometimes arise if abbreviations refer to equipment labels, and those labels are inconsistent; for example, *travel lock* may be labeled *TRVL LCK* in one place and *TVL LK* in another. In this unfortunate situation, if the labeling cannot be corrected, it is more important that the procedure conform to the equipment label, so the procedure writer may be forced into using inconsistent abbreviations.

Remember—the purpose of abbreviating is to increase reading speed and to aid comprehension. Minimize the use of abbreviations, and stick to the list of approved abbreviations when writing procedures.

In this chapter...

Write steps at an
appropriate level
of detail (7.1).

9.3   Open valve H-3 one-quarter turn to add the nitric acid
       solution.

Include
supplemental
detail as
necessary (7.2).

By opening the valve only one-quarter turn, you ensure that
the nitric acid is added slowly; otherwise, the level is
difficult to read accurately.

CHAPTER
SEVEN

Level of Detail

As a procedure writer, one of the most difficult aspects of your job will be to write procedures at the appropriate level of detail—procedures should contain neither too little nor too much information. This chapter discusses this challenge.

7.1 Write procedures at a level of detail that is appropriate for the procedures' intended users.

Summary

Essentialize procedures. Write them at an appropriate level of detail, presenting neither too little nor too much information. The appropriate level of detail will vary according to the type of procedure, the frequency with which the procedure is performed, and the experience level of the users. Procedure writers should solicit feedback from users and interact with training personnel during procedure development. Both these activities are important for ensuring that the level of detail is correct.

Level of detail refers to the match between the information provided in the procedure and the users' knowledge and ability. The procedure should not provide too little information, nor should it be cluttered with excessive detail.

Determining the correct level of detail is a difficult, important task that has a greater effect on procedure comprehensibility than does syntax or sentence structure. Bovair and Kieras (1989, p. 18) discuss a study that evaluated different versions of written instructions where

> the good and bad instructions could not be distinguished by text characteristics likely to affect reading comprehension such as length of text or length of sentences; indeed, some of the best instructions had the most complex syntax and sentence structure. The most important differences between good and bad instructions seemed to be those of content; in particular, poor instructions omitted important details like the orientation of parts in the assembly task, and often included the wrong level of detail.

This section is not going to provide a magic formula for writing procedures at the correct level of detail. Instead, it will explain a process that will lead you to the correct level of detail: learning about procedure users and getting feedback from them, then using that information to make decisions regarding level of detail.

The dangers of too little or too much detail

A procedure can present detail at a variety of levels (Example 10). Few would argue that procedures with inadequate detail can lead to error. If the procedure assumes that the user knows something that the user in fact does not know, users are likely to lose confidence in the procedure and errors are likely to occur. A procedure may tell the user to open a valve, but not explain where the valve is; it may tell the user to complete a form, but not explain which managers must approve it; it may tell users how to overhaul a pump without explaining the tools they will need. The list goes on. The procedure must provide the information that users need.

An unpublished study examining the occurrence of procedure violations in U.S. nuclear power plants points out the consequences that too little detail in procedures can have for safety in nuclear facilities. An inadequate level of detail in procedures was the most frequently cited cause of procedure-related errors in licensee event reports between January of 1984 and July of 1988.[18]

However, it can be just as bad to include too much information in the procedure. Huckin (1983, p. 98) writes,

> Research by information theorists suggests that the use of extended analogies, elaborate examples, and other lengthy explications of important concepts may do more harm than good, if the concepts being explained are already familiar to the reader and can be succinctly related to already-familiar concepts.... Explications that are unnecessarily long raise the proportion of redundant information and risk boring the reader to the point of inattention.

---

[18]Licensee event reports are self-reports of abnormal or unusual occurrences that commercial nuclear power plants file with the Nuclear Regulatory Commission.

7.1   Isolate letdown line.   ——

◇ ◇ ◇

7.1   Isolate letdown line by closing CV1214 and CV1216.   ——

◇ ◇ ◇

7.1   Isolate the letdown line by closing valves CV1214 and
       CV1216. Controls are on panel C18.   ——

◇ ◇ ◇

7.1   Isolate the letdown line by first closing valve CV1214 and
       then by closing valve CV1216.   ——
       Controls are on panel C18. Indicator lights are on panels
       C15 and C16.

◇ ◇ ◇

7.1   Go to panel C18.   ——

7.2   Close valve CV1214 by turning the knob to the right until full
       stop.   ——

7.3   Go to panel C15.   ——

7.4   Check that the lamp indicator for CV1214 is green.   ——

7.5   Go to panel C18.   ——

7.6   Close valve CV1216 by turning the knob to the right until full
       stop.   ——

7.7   Go to panel C16.   ——

7.8   Check that the lamp indicator for CV1216 is green.   ——

Example 10. Various levels of detail. An identical step is presented at varying
levels of detail (Adapted from Zach, 1980).

While procedures are unlikely to include the "extended analogies, elaborate
examples, and other lengthy explications of important concepts" of which
Huckin writes, these findings point out the danger of including excessive
information of any type in the procedure. Because procedure writers may
feel the urge to "play it safe" and include excessive detail, the problem of a
level of detail that is too high is likely.

In the context of emergency operating procedures in commercial reactors,
Fuchs, Engelschall, and Imlay (1981, p. 2–13) address the problem of
excessive detail:

> In several of the procedures evaluated, extraneous explanatory information is
> included…. Sometimes this information is included in steps; at other times it
> takes the form of excessive cautions and notes. Citing this as a deficiency is not
> intended to question the value of such information. Explanatory information
> serves to motivate the operator and, most importantly, help him understand

what is happening. However, such information belongs in training, not in an emergency procedure. In an emergency, the operator needs to know *what to do and how to do it*. If he's faced with an unforeseen situation, it is too late for him to learn how the system works and why certain actions must be taken. Such information should be carried by system explanation manuals to be used in the operator training program.

It is important to realize, however, that the appropriate level of detail in an emergency operating procedure is different from the appropriate level of detail in other types of procedures. Procedures that are seldom performed, are not covered extensively (or at all) in user training, or are not executed under time constraints may have a higher level of detail than emergency operating procedures, which typically present information most concisely.

Further, if too much detail is included in the procedure, the procedure becomes long, becomes difficult to find information in, becomes difficult to revise, and may seem to "talk down" to skilled workers.

Assumed knowledge

Before continuing, it is important to explain that all procedures assume a certain base level of knowledge on the part of users. For instance, an emergency operating procedure requires that operators trip the reactor without explaining how to do so; a maintenance procedure requires that users loosen a bolt without explaining which way to turn it; administrative procedures contain requirements for subordinates to communicate with managers without discussing office protocol.

Users of the procedure in Example 11 must be well versed in laboratory practices and techniques; otherwise, they will be unable to execute the procedure. They must understand terms such as *supernate* and *precipitate*, they must know how to prepare the required solutions, they must know how to operate a centrifuge, and so forth. If the procedure user has these skills, then a procedure written in this manner is not only acceptable, it is preferable, because the user does not have to wade through unnecessary information.

If procedures do not assume some user knowledge, they would be impossible to use; remember that too much detail can make the procedure as confusing as too little. As an exercise, you might try to write a procedure for some common task, say leaving the house in the morning. Include *every* detail you can think of. Is the procedure usable?

Audience analysis

As a procedure writer, you must know what the level of assumed knowledge is for the particular procedure you are writing. The best way to do this is to learn about the procedure's users, or the audience for the procedure. Find

5.1	Add the following to 1 liter of deionized H_2O in a 2-liter beaker:
	• 1 ml strontium, 20 mg/ml, carrier solution ___
	• 1 ml barium, 10 mg/ml, carrier solution ___
	• 5 ml calcium, 2M carrier solution ___
5.2	<u>IF</u> the sample has been acidified, <u>THEN</u> neutralize it with 6N NaOH using a pH meter. ___
5.3	Stir and heat to near boiling on a hot plate. ___
5.4	Add 30 ml 3N Na_2CO_3 with stirring. ___
5.5	Add 1–2 ml 6N NaOH and continue heating for one more minute. ___
5.6	Remove from the hot plate and cool in a water bath. ___
5.7	Decant the supernate and transfer the precipitate to a 250 ml centrifuge bottle. ___
5.8	Centrifuge the solution and discard the supernate. ___

Example 11. Excerpt from a chemistry procedure. This procedure assumes a high level of laboratory expertise on the part of its users.

out what they need to know and how that information needs to be presented so that they can understand and use it. This process is called audience analysis.

The *Handbook of Technical Writing* explains the importance of audience analysis:

> The first rule of *effective* writing is to help the reader. The responsibility that technical writers have to their readers is nicely expressed in the Society of Technical Communication's *Code for Communicators*, which calls for technical writers to hold themselves responsible for how well their audience understands their message and to satisfy the readers' need for information rather than the writer's need for self expression. This code reminds writers to concentrate on writing *for* the needs of specific readers rather than merely *about* certain subjects. (Brusaw, Alred, & Oliu, 1987, p. 550)

To a certain extent, we perform a basic audience analysis without even thinking about it. In *Technical Writing: Process and Product*, Stratton (1984, p. 27) says,

> You will always have some notion of audience and purpose when you write; you will run into trouble only when your notions are too limited or when they fail to line up with those of the people who review and approve your writing. It behooves you, then, as a communicator of technical information to take some specific steps to determine audience, purpose, and other design criteria for each of your communication contexts and to document your analysis.

Basically, you want to stay in touch with the users of the procedures—*don't write in isolation*. As a procedure writer, you are very fortunate because you can meet and talk with the readers of your documents. If they are few, you may be able to talk to *all* the users of your document. Most technical communicators don't have this luxury. They must guess at their audience's characteristics or analyze a small sample of their audience and hope that this analysis will generalize to the audience as a whole. You should take advantage of this opportunity and work at maintaining open lines of communication between yourself and your users. Remember that the procedure user is your customer.

This communication can be formal or informal. During procedure testing, you will receive formal feedback. It is up to you to generate sources of informal feedback. Cultivate relationships with users whose input you value. Bounce ideas off them, especially if you are experiencing writer's block. Pass drafts of your procedures around to your colleagues for review and discuss common problems that you are having.

The feedback that will result from these open lines of communication can be difficult to take; most people dislike having their writing criticized. You should try to separate your ego from your writing and realize that users have a different perspective that will complement and contribute to your writing. No one writes so well that his or her writing cannot be improved by an intelligent, constructive evaluation.

Issues of audience analysis in procedures are concerned primarily with determining the appropriate level of detail. In other types of writing, such as reports, articles, or business letters, technical communicators must also consider issues of style and tone. For example, a writer preparing a memo to the president of a large company must be concerned that the memo is written in a relatively formal style and has a respectful tone (assuming that the president prefers that type of relationship with his or her subordinates). The format and content of procedures are so constrained, however, that these issues largely become moot, and audience analysis reduces primarily to determining the appropriate level of detail—which can still be quite a job.

One warning: it is possible to carry the concept of audience analysis too far, so that each user expects a procedure that is perfectly addressed to his or her particular needs. Obviously, that cannot be done. The best you can do is write for a typical reader, not a specific reader.

Essentializing, again

If you have analyzed your audience, you will have a much better idea of what they need. Now you must include only that information in the procedure. You must essentialize.

The idea of essentializing was first addressed in Section 5.2. When you essentialize, you determine what information is truly necessary to support readers and you include only that information in the procedure, writing as concisely as possible.[19]

Question what you include in the procedure. Much information may be included simply because the writer before you included it in the procedure. Is it really necessary to have a purpose and a scope section—in other words, what does the scope section say that the purpose section hasn't already said? Are you including generic safety requirements (like *Don't touch live wires*) that users are trained to know? Are you including detailed descriptions of how equipment works that users really don't have to be familiar with? Are you including unnecessary steps, like *Ensure the work area is clean when you are finished*?

There is a cost to including such unnecessary detail—it detracts from information that is important. Question everything: how does this piece of information help the user do his job? Then verify your answers through feedback, task observations, and so on.

The relationship between level of detail and training

The passage from Fuchs, Engelschall, and Imlay quoted earlier in this section said that some information should be covered in training rather than included in procedures. In facilities with formal training on procedures, training has a large effect on the user's knowledge level. Consequently, it is important that procedure writers work with trainers (and vice versa).

There are definite advantages to coordinating procedure writing and training. An important advantage is the coordination of level of detail. Training personnel can tell procedure writers that a procedure assumes knowledge that is not covered in the training program or that a procedure unnecessarily includes information that is well covered in training. When such discrepancies arise, they can be addressed either by modifying the procedure or the training curriculum, whichever is more appropriate. Also, if procedure writers and trainers work together, then trainers may be able to use the procedures more effectively during training sessions. Coordination between procedure writing and training is a prerequisite to effective procedures.

---

[19]Essentializing is akin to the minimalist approach to computer documentation: "the minimalist approach entails highly streamlined procedures that provide only information that users will truly need" (Boggan, Farkas, & Welinske, 1996, p. 49; see also van der Meij & Carroll, 1995). Some software documentation is *too* minimalist and fails to provide information that users need.

7.2 Use a format that allows you to present supplemental detail without cluttering the procedure.

Summary

If you present supplemental detail in the procedure, use white space to distinguish it from steps and other information. Two useful techniques are to place details in paragraphs that follow steps or to include a separate column for details.

The previous section discussed level of detail as though one level of detail is suitable for all users. Common sense should tell you that this is not the case. When you do your audience analysis, you will learn the needs of a "typical" user. Unless all users are rigorously trained to the same level, specific users may require more or less detail on different topics. This section will describe ways of writing a procedure so that it includes the detail that may be necessary to some users but not others.[20]

The trick is to format the procedure in a way that allows users to quickly identify detailed information, so that they can skip the detail if they do not need it. This section will describe two ways of doing this: placing details in paragraphs and using a two-column format.

Placing detail in paragraphs

In Example 12, detailed information is presented in paragraphs that follow steps. This information includes specific control manipulations, control locations, and verification steps. Users have the option of reading this information or of skipping to the next step, which is identified by a step number.

Using the actions-details format

Example 13 further distinguishes details by presenting them in a separate column.[21] The advantage of this format over that in Example 12 is that the details are more clearly distinguished from the steps—users who wish to skip details can read the actions column only and bypass the details column entirely. The disadvantage is that this format is more complex to present.

Example 12 and Example 13 use white space to separate details from actions. White space is simply the blank space on the page. In Example 12,

---

[20]However, if there is a large gap between the skill levels of the most and least skilled users, then the techniques described in this section are unlikely to work well. You are confronted with a problem that will be difficult to address effectively with a procedure. Instead, the problem should be rectified through changes in training, work assignments, or the like.

[21]There is another two-column format that presents actions in the left-hand column and contingency actions in the right-hand column. It is used in some nuclear power plant emergency operating procedures. Users must be specially trained on this format, as it can be confusing to the uninitiated.

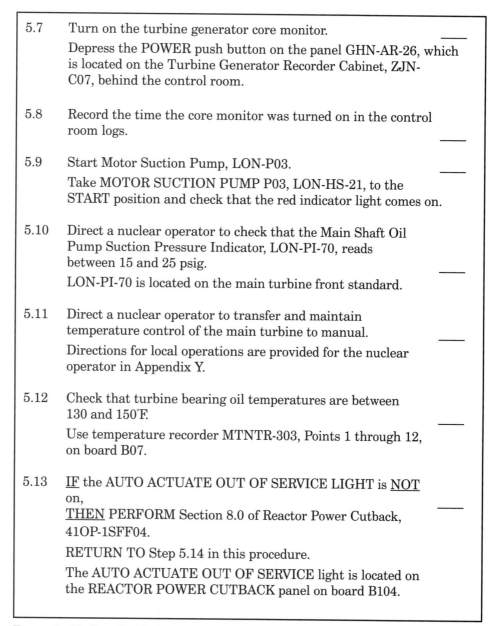

5.7   Turn on the turbine generator core monitor.   ___

Depress the POWER push button on the panel GHN-AR-26, which is located on the Turbine Generator Recorder Cabinet, ZJN-C07, behind the control room.

5.8   Record the time the core monitor was turned on in the control room logs.   ___

5.9   Start Motor Suction Pump, LON-P03.   ___

Take MOTOR SUCTION PUMP P03, LON-HS-21, to the START position and check that the red indicator light comes on.

5.10   Direct a nuclear operator to check that the Main Shaft Oil Pump Suction Pressure Indicator, LON-PI-70, reads between 15 and 25 psig.   ___

LON-PI-70 is located on the main turbine front standard.

5.11   Direct a nuclear operator to transfer and maintain temperature control of the main turbine to manual.   ___

Directions for local operations are provided for the nuclear operator in Appendix Y.

5.12   Check that turbine bearing oil temperatures are between 130 and 150°F.   ___

Use temperature recorder MTNTR-303, Points 1 through 12, on board B07.

5.13   IF the AUTO ACTUATE OUT OF SERVICE LIGHT is NOT on,
THEN PERFORM Section 8.0 of Reactor Power Cutback, 41OP-1SFF04.   ___

RETURN TO Step 5.14 in this procedure.

The AUTO ACTUATE OUT OF SERVICE light is located on the REACTOR POWER CUTBACK panel on board B104.

Example 12. Detailed information presented in paragraphs. Detailed information that may be helpful to some users but unnecessary to others is not presented in the step, but is presented in a separate paragraph that follows the step.

one-half line is skipped before and one line is skipped after the paragraph containing the detailed information, so the paragraph stands out. Section 10.2 will discuss the use of white space in more detail.

The actions-details format is particularly well suited to facilities with a verbatim compliance policy of procedure execution. A verbatim compliance policy requires that procedures be executed exactly as they are written. The advantage of a verbatim compliance policy is that it allows management greater control over work processes. The disadvantages are that the procedure *must*

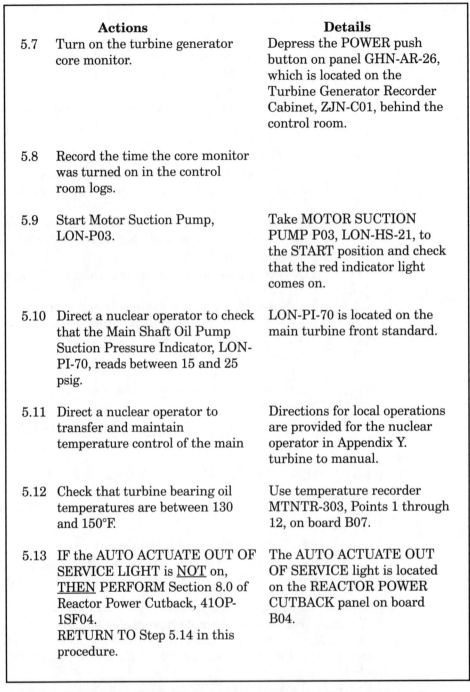

	Actions	**Details**
5.7	Turn on the turbine generator core monitor.	Depress the POWER push button on panel GHN-AR-26, which is located on the Turbine Generator Recorder Cabinet, ZJN-C01, behind the control room.
5.8	Record the time the core monitor was turned on in the control room logs.	
5.9	Start Motor Suction Pump, LON-P03.	Take MOTOR SUCTION PUMP P03, LON-HS-21, to the START position and check that the red indicator light comes on.
5.10	Direct a nuclear operator to check that the Main Shaft Oil Pump Suction Pressure Indicator, LON-PI-70, reads between 15 and 25 psig.	LON-PI-70 is located on the main turbine front standard.
5.11	Direct a nuclear operator to transfer and maintain temperature control of the main	Directions for local operations are provided for the nuclear operator in Appendix Y. turbine to manual.
5.12	Check that turbine bearing oil temperatures are between 130 and 150°F.	Use temperature recorder MTNTR-303, Points 1 through 12, on board B07.
5.13	IF the AUTO ACTUATE OUT OF SERVICE LIGHT is <u>NOT</u> on, <u>THEN</u> PERFORM Section 8.0 of Reactor Power Cutback, 41OP-1SF04. RETURN TO Step 5.14 in this procedure.	The AUTO ACTUATE OUT OF SERVICE light is located on the REACTOR POWER CUTBACK panel on board B04.

Example 13. Actions-details format. In the actions-details format, the left column presents actions while the right column presents detailed information on the performance of those actions. Users who are familiar with the procedure need only look at the actions column; users who need more information can refer to the details column as necessary. The procedure effectively presents two levels of detail.

be correct or the procedure user is put in the bind of being required to follow an inaccurate procedure. Some procedure users may also see a verbatim compliance policy as an affront to their skill and experience. The actions-details format allows a verbatim compliance policy to be implemented in a more flexible fashion. If verbatim compliance can be required only for the actions column, users may follow the details column if they wish, but are free to deviate from it as long as they accomplish the instructions included in the actions column.

In this chapter...

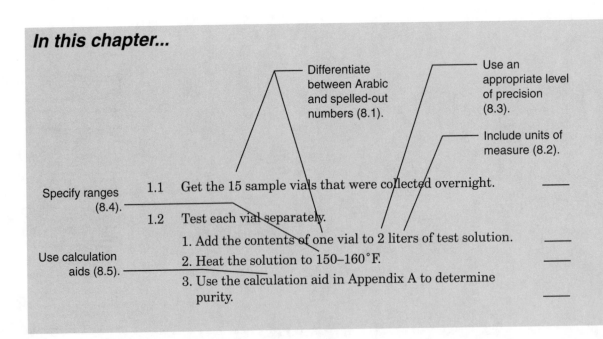

Differentiate between Arabic and spelled-out numbers (8.1).

Use an appropriate level of precision (8.3).

Include units of measure (8.2).

Specify ranges (8.4).

Use calculation aids (8.5).

1.1 Get the 15 sample vials that were collected overnight. ———

1.2 Test each vial separately.

1. Add the contents of one vial to 2 liters of test solution. ———

2. Heat the solution to 150–160°F. ———

3. Use the calculation aid in Appendix A to determine purity. ———

CHAPTER
EIGHT

Numerical Information

Numerical information is any information associated with numbers presented in a procedure. Numerical information can include readings from instrument displays, calculated values, or control settings.

8.1 Differentiate between the use of Arabic and spelled-out numbers in a consistent, useful fashion.

Summary

As a general rule, procedures should use Arabic numbers (e.g., 0, 1, 2, 3) rather than spelled-out numbers or Roman numerals.

Of all the issues facing writers, the presentation of numerical information is one of the simplest yet most troublesome. The important point is to develop a rule that addresses the few basic issues discussed in this section and to apply that rule consistently. The guidance provided in *Words into Type* (1974, p. 125) is sound: "In scientific and technical writing the rule is to use numerals for all physical measures and for most quantities of 11 and over." Some organizations may prefer to use numerals entirely; this guidance is also sound, provided that spelled-out numerals are used in the few instances where the use of numerals could be confusing.

Numbers in procedures will often refer to physical quantities (i.e., are accompanied by a unit of measure) and are most concisely presented in numerals. Hence, *90 dB(A)*, *5 seconds*, *1200 rpm*, *4.16 kv*, and *2%* are all acceptable.

If a number is not accompanied by a unit of measure and is 11 or greater, numerals should again be used. If a number is not accompanied by a unit of measure and is less than 11, it may be spelled out or presented in numerals, depending on the specifications in the writers' guide; in other words, *Start 1 reactor coolant pump* is acceptable, as is *Start one reactor coolant pump*. It is important, however, that a consistent approach be adopted.

Yet, in two instances, a spelled-out number is preferable for preventing confusion. The first of these occurs when a number without a unit of measure is followed directly by a number that is accompanied by a unit of measure, as in *Energize one 4.16 kv bus*. In this case, the first number should be spelled out; if the step read *Energize 1 4.16 kv bus*, users might misread it as a 14.16 kv bus.

The second instance occurs when a number (particularly a single-digit number) is emphasized. Compare the examples in Example 14.

Use <u>1</u> of the following:	Use <u>one</u> of the following:
Use **1** of the following:	Use **one** of the following:
Use *1* of the following:	Use *one* of the following:

Example 14. Emphasis of numerals. Because single-digit numerals are physically so small, the spelled-out version of the number is more effectively emphasized when typographic emphasis techniques are used.

Example 14 shows how typographic emphasis techniques (discussed in Chapter 12) are more effective on spelled-out numbers because they are physically larger (i.e., they require more ink on the page) than their numerical equivalents. Thus, numbers that (1) are emphasized and (2) are not accompanied by a unit of measure should be spelled out.

Finally, don't just give up and both spell out the numeral and use it—*Customer credit may be extended three (3) times before management review is necessary*. Presenting the number twice adds nothing (unless you're writing a check), clutters the writing, and basically announces that the writer doesn't know how to handle numbers well.

8.2　Include units of measure with numerical information whenever appropriate.

Summary

Units of measure should always be used to avoid ambiguity. Units of measure must match the panel or instrument markings exactly.

Units of measure provide important information by specifying exactly what a number represents. For example, *60 miles per hour* (miles/hour) specifies exactly what is being discussed, whereas *60* can be 60 of anything. It is a mistake to assume that the units of measure will be obvious to the user.

Units of measure must match the panel or instrument markings exactly (NRC, 1982). For example, if a temperature gauge is marked in degrees Fahrenheit (°F), then any temperatures related to this gauge must be given in degrees Fahrenheit, as in *175°F*. If the unit of measure is incomplete (*175°*), then there is ambiguity in whether Fahrenheit or Celsius is used. Units of measure for pressure can also be problematic. Sometimes *psi* (pounds per square inch) is not a sufficient unit and a more specific unit of measure, such as psia (psi atmosphere) or *psig* (psi gauge), must be used. Users should not be required to convert seconds into minutes if seconds are the unit of measure used on a chronometer.

8.3 Do not specify numbers at a greater precision than can be read from instrument panel displays.

Summary

In presenting numerical information in procedures, it is important to specify numbers only to the precision available on the instrument panel or display, because users cannot read the panels to a greater precision.

Precision refers to the exactness with which a quantity is expressed. For example, a person might express his height as being about 6 feet, or more precisely, 5 feet 11 inches. This person might be even more precise and say that he is 5 feet 11½ inches tall. Or, with access to very accurate measuring equipment, he may say that he is 5 feet 11.39 inches tall. All these expressions of height represent different levels of precision.

In presenting numerical information in procedures, it is important to specify numbers only to the precision available on the instrument panel or display (or whatever the source of the numbers). For example, if an instrument displays only elapsed minutes, then the procedure should not ask for information about elapsed minutes *and* seconds. If an instrument dial can only be read to the nearest 5 (e.g., 95, 100, 105), then the procedure should not required the user to read 97. By presenting numerical information only to the precision that is available, you help the user read the numbers and not make mistakes or waste time trying to guess at numbers that cannot be easily read.

It is also wise to be conservative in the presentation of numerical information depending on the precision available on the instrumentation. If a technical specification calls for a value to be less than 2.57 units, and the instrumentation can only be read to the nearest 0.1 unit, then it is better to be conservative and use the value *less than 2.5 units*, rather than *2.6 units*. Using *2.6 units* could allow the value to exceed the technical specification.

8.4 Specify ranges rather than error bands.

Summary

Use ranges to specify acceptable limits. Explicit statements of the acceptable limits for particular values are easier to understand, and they reduce the chance of error. Error bands should not be used to express a range of values, because they require a mental calculation by the user. The user can make a mistake in adding or subtracting or can remember the numbers incorrectly.

Sometimes a range of values, rather than a single value, is acceptable for a given parameter. A range specifies the extent or limits of acceptable values. There are several ways to express a group of acceptable values. One way is to specify a range, which gives the limits or outer boundaries of acceptable values. For example, *10–20* is a range. Another way to express acceptable values is by using error bands. Error bands show the acceptable deviation from a given number (e.g., *15±5*).

Error bands require users to make a mental calculation. In the above example, the user must take the acceptable value and subtract 5 (to get 10) and add 5 (to get 20) and then hold that range of values (10–20) in memory while he or she checks the instrumentation to see if it corresponds to the acceptable range. Because error bands require a mental calculation, users are more prone to error. The user can make a mistake in adding or subtracting or can remember the numbers incorrectly. Therefore, error bands should not be used to express a range of values.

Instead, use ranges to specify acceptable limits. Explicitly stating the acceptable limits of the values reduces the opportunity for error. By presenting a range, mental calculations are avoided and the burden on the memory is reduced. The values are written and available to check. Optimal or normal values can still be specified, but include the acceptable range rather than an error band. For example, a normal value of 15 with an acceptable range of 10–20, can be expressed as *15 (range 10–20)* or *10–20 (normal 15)*. However, you should avoid cluttering the procedure with optimal values unless they are necessary.

Example 15 rates the various formats for presenting acceptance values.

8.5 Avoid requiring users to make calculations in procedures; if a calculation is required, use a calculation aid.

Summary

Calculations should be avoided whenever possible. There may be times when a calculation must be made. If so, provide a calculation aid. The use of calculation aids increases accuracy and leaves a record of data entries and computations so that they can be verified later, if necessary.

Good:	3.1	<u>IF</u> the temperature is 75–85°F, <u>THEN</u> open the access door.	____
Bad:	3.1	<u>IF</u> the temperature is 80°F (±5°F), <u>THEN</u> open the access door.	____
Ugly:	3.1	<u>IF</u> the temperature is 80°F (±6.3%), <u>THEN</u> open the access door.	____

Example 15. Presentation of ranges. Ranges (the good example) are preferable to error bands (the bad example). In the ugly example, the user must make a complex calculation, increasing the potential for error and slowing procedure execution.

Calculation aids, also known as data sheets, can be problematic in procedures. According to McCallum and colleagues (1994), data sheets and signoffs that are difficult to use are the fourth most prevalent problem in nuclear power plant maintenance procedures.[22]

Calculations require some kind of numerical computing or manipulating. Calculations create opportunities for error. Calculations also require time. It is therefore recommended that calculations be avoided whenever possible. This guidance applies to simple calculations, such as adding error bands to the single value given (e.g., 2.5±0.1), as well as to long and complex calculations.

However, there may be times when a calculation must be made. If so, providing a calculation aid can minimize the problems discussed above. A calculation aid is anything that assists the user in performing the required calculation. Calculation aids should be clear, logically formatted, and include necessary spaces for all data entries (NRC, 1982). Examples of calculation aids include (1) writing the required formula with blank spaces to insert the appropriate values or (2) using worksheets that describe the needed calculations.

By dictating the calculations to be performed (and their order) and by forcing users to record intermediate steps in a problem solution, a well-designed calculation aid can reduce errors (Larkin & Simon, 1987). Calculation aids spell out the calculation requirements, including units of measure and conversion factors. Aids are used to minimize memory requirements. Users do not have to remember the formula or how to do the calculation.

Calculation aids also provide a way to check the calculation easily. Because all the information is written down and does not need to be remembered, others can verify the accuracy of the calculation. Thus, the use of calculation

---

[22] The biggest problems were, in order, technical inaccuracies, requirements for excessive page turning, and language that was difficult to understand.

aids increases accuracy and leaves a record of data entries and computations so that they can be verified later, if necessary.

Example 16 provides an example of a calculation aid.

5.1   Ensure that the total fissile g content of a waste package placed in any single soil vault is less than 300 g.

    1. Record current vault ^{235}U g content   ___ g

    2. Record shipment ^{235}U g content   ___ g

    3. Record subtotal (sum of Substeps 1 + 2)   ___ g

    4. Record current vault fissile g content other than ^{235}U and multiply by 2

                                  _____ × 2 = ___ g

    5. Record shipment fissile g content other than ^{235}U and multiply by 2

                                  _____ × 2 = ___ g

    6. Record subtotal (sum of Substeps 4 and 5)   ___ g

    7. Record total fissile g content

                        (sum of Substeps 3 + 6) = ___ g

5.2   IF total fissile g content is greater than 300 g, THEN immediately notify the Shift Manager.

Example 16. Example of a calculation aid included in a procedure.
This calculation aid assists users in determining the weight of a shipment.

PART
THREE

Format and Organization

CHAPTER
NINE

Introduction: Format and Organization

Format refers to the way a procedure looks. Many factors affect format, such as type font, indentation, emphasis techniques, and so on. Some documents, such as novels, have a very simple format. They consist of a series of paragraphs, one after another, so each page looks very much like the previous page. Other documents, such as procedures, have a more complex format. In procedures, the format provides useful information to users—indentation differentiates steps from substeps, emphasis techniques indicate the relative importance of items, and so on.

Organization refers to the order in which information is presented and how that information is structured. Organization entails two things: (1) logical relationships in information (e.g., steps are grouped into sections) and (2) the sequence in which items are performed.

Part Three is divided into four chapters (besides this chapter):

- Chapter 10 discusses step format, including type size and font, white space (i.e., the blank space on the page), margins, and step numbering.

- Chapter 11 discusses placekeeping aids.

- Chapter 12 discusses emphasis techniques.

- Chapter 13 discusses procedure organization.

In this chapter...

Use a readable
font (10.1).

Use ragged-right
margins (10.3).

Use white space
according to the
rules of graphic
design (10.2).

Note: *Water is added to the primary dryer column in the next step to prevent crystallization of any concentrated butyl nitrate that may drain into the column during the dryer run.*

3.5 Drain the primary dryer column by performing the following steps:

1. Add approximately 12 inches of water (approximately 1 liter) into the funnel on the primary dryer drain column. _____

2. Note the current time: _____ : _____

3. Wait 10 minutes. _____

4. Open DV-12 to drain the column. _____

5. Close DV-12. _____

CHAPTER
TEN

Step Format

This chapter discusses step format, or the way steps should look.

10.1 Use type that is readable in the worst conditions of expected use.

Summary

Select a type size and font based on their appearance and legibility. Do not use all capitals.

This section discusses type size, type font, and type case in more detail:

- *Type size*, which is still defined based on the conventions used by printers who worked with mechanical printing presses, is the height of the block of lead in which a letter would be cast. This size is typically greater than the height of the letter.

- A *font* is the complete assortment of letters and characters of a single design, such as Times or Helvetica. Typeface is a synonym for font.

- *Case* refers to whether letters are uppercase (i.e., capital), lowercase, or some combination.

Type size

We'll begin this section by cutting to the chase: Use a type size that is large enough to read, based on feedback from users. What follows is a more lengthy discussion that leads to the same conclusion. We present this discussion to give you an idea of the many factors that affect type size, and how assessing these factors is more of an art than a science.

The readability of type is greatly affected by its size; obviously, if type is too small, it cannot be read easily. Three considerations enter into an effective determination of type size:

- A visual angle formula can be used to calculate whether type is of sufficient size to be distinguished by the human eye, given a certain reading distance.

- Type size can be based on the length of a line of type.

- Type size can be determined subjectively.

This section will begin with a discussion of the visual angle formula, which is presented as a sort of a "straw man." Explaining why the visual angle formula falls short makes an important point about trying to characterize type size, or any other aspect of a procedure, in a mathematical formula.

The visual angle formula is a calculation that can be performed to ensure that a letter is sufficiently large for the eye to discern it. Obviously, the farther a letter is from the eye, the larger the letter must be. A convenient method for considering distance and type size together is to specify the visual angle that must be subtended by the letter. Figure 5 depicts the visual angle.

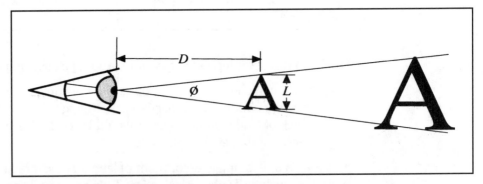

Figure 5. Visual angle. The visual angle (Ø) is the angle subtended at the eye by the letter. Visual angle is used to conveniently take the size of a letter and its viewing distance into account. A single visual angle specifies a size for a letter at all viewing distances.

The following formula expresses the relationship between letter size (L), viewing distance (D), and visual angle (Ø). The visual angle is specified in degrees; L and D must be specified in identical units (e.g., inches).

$$\tan 0.5f = 0.5 \frac{L}{D}$$

Some design standards recommend that the visual angle be 0.172° for letters to be discernible to 90% by the population and 0.401° for letters to be discernible by "virtually 100%" of the population (Smith, 1979, p. 661). By setting Ø equal to these values and solving for L, equations specifying L as a function of D emerge:

$$L_{90\%} = 0.003D$$

$$L_{100\%} = 0.007D$$

Thus, for a viewing distance of 18 inches, the letter size specified by this formula would be 0.054 inches to be discernible by 90% of the population ($L_{90\%}$) and 0.126 inches to be discernible by 100% of the population ($L_{100\%}$). Type size is typically measured in points; there are approximately 72 points in an inch, making the appropriate type sizes four and nine points (i.e., $0.054 \times 72 = 4$, $0.126 \times 72 = 9$). In other words, 90% of the population should be able to discern four-point type at 18 inches and 100% of the population should be able to discern nine-point type at 18 inches.

Four-point type, however, is very small; this fact is an indication of the danger inherent in calculating type size without understanding type size conventions. These conventions were developed when type was cast in lead blocks and set in a printing press. A type font's specified size is the height of this block of lead, which includes the shoulder, the area above and below the letter. The shoulder ensured that there was space between lines of type. As shown in Figure 6, the font size will be greater than the height of an upper-case letter and much greater than the height of a lower-case letter. As a consequence, the results of the visual angle formula cannot be equated directly with a type's specified size.

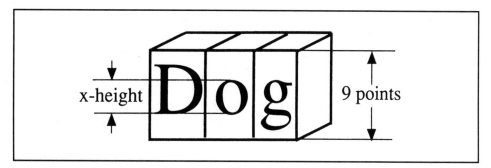

Figure 6. Type size versus actual letter size. A type's size corresponds to the size of the block of lead in which the letters of that type would be cast. The height of a lower-case letter is thus substantially less than the specified size of the type. The x-height is the minimum height of a letter.

The height of the lowercase letter x (and a, c, e, and so on) is known as the x-height. If the visual angle formula is used, it is better to equate the results of that formula with the x-height of the letters in the font than with the font size itself. The visual angle specifies the minimum letter height that the human eye can discern; because the eye must discern these lower-case characters, they should not be smaller than the size specified by the visual angle. Poulton (1972) agrees that type size should be based on the x-height rather than the type size. Brown (1989, p. 75) says that point size "does little to indicate type's actual appearance."

You should, however, remain wary of the visual angle formula even when it is applied to x-heights rather than point sizes. In the first place, it is pretty tough to do, because you will have to measure the x-height yourself. In the second place, a variety of factors besides the x-height affect the apparent size of a typeface, including the width of the character strokes and the width of the letters themselves. Figure 7 shows how typefaces of an identical specified size appear to be different sizes. The issue is further complicated because the readability of type is also affected by the length of a line of type and the spacing between lines of type. All other things being equal, type will be more readable as spacing between lines is increased or as line length is reduced.

This is 12-point Times New Roman.

This is 12-point Arial.

This is 12-point Courier.

This is 12-point Garamond.

Figure 7. Various type fonts of the same size. Even when various fonts are of the same specified size, there can be a difference in their apparent size.

In fact, typesetters and writers seldom use a visual angle calculation when determining a type size.[23] Instead, many prefer line lengths. The shorter the line length, the smaller the type size that can be used. Compare the type size in a dictionary, where line lengths are quite short, to the type size in this book, which has relatively long lines. Turnbull and Baird (1980) recommend that type size be based on a line length of one-and-a-half alphabets (i.e., a sequence of lowercase letters from a to z and then from a to m with no extra spaces), with two or three alphabets as a maximum line length and one

---

[23]The visual angle formula can be very useful when type must be read from a greater-than-normal distance—for example, when determining the type size on a wall sign that is read at a distance of 10 feet. That's about it, though.

alphabet as a minimum. A minimum line length is important because readability will suffer when lines become too short; the frequent transitions from the end of one line to the beginning of the next disrupt the reading process.

So, according to Turnbull and Baird, once the width of a procedure column is known, a type size should be chosen that allows one-and-a-half alphabets to fit on a line. However, this approach may present problems in multi-column procedures, where line length may be artificially shortened; in such a case, it would be a mistake to choose a type size so small that it would enable the procedure designer to squeeze one-and-a-half alphabets on a line in a single column. Like the visual angle rule, this rule is flawed as well.

The upshot of all of this is that determination of optimal type size, like so many other aspects of writing, is more of an art than a science (Hartley & Burnhill, 1977). As a general guideline, 12-point laser-printed text is a good, conservative starting point for text to be read from 18 inches. It is important to be conservative in the choice of type size because procedures may be read under inadequate lighting (e.g., a maintenance procedure performed locally). You should then be prepared to adjust your choice as necessary. It is also important to address any comments that arise during testing regarding type size and readability.

The final, and perhaps most useful, concern for determining type size is a subjective evaluation. According to *Guidelines for Document Designers* (Felker et al., 1981, p. 77), "Choose typesize according to visual size, not point size alone." Can users read the procedure? If so, the type is fine. Be certain to have older users as well as younger users evaluate your choice of a type size because, in general, vision among older workers is poorer (Echeverria et al., 1994). It is also important to evaluate type in the conditions under which it will be used, particularly if light levels are likely to be low. Finally, you should photocopy text in that type a few times (making copies of copies) to determine if legibility is maintained. For hand-held text, these subjective evaluations can be as useful, if not more useful, than the visual angle or line-length calculation.

In addition to varying type size, you can also vary the space between lines. Most people know that type can be single-spaced, double-spaced, or set space-and-a-half. However, these are crude distinctions that are a carryover from the days of typewriters. Typesetters will often add a point or two of space between lines of type rather than increasing type size. The results are often the same—the text is easier to read. This process is known as leading, a term that is also a carryover, from the days when type was set manually (with blocks of lead such as that shown in Figure 6) and strips of lead were placed between the blocks of type. This book uses 11-point type with 2 points of leading, so each line is 13 points high.

Type font

A type's appearance, or font, affects readability. As indicated in the preceding section, the appearance of different fonts varies greatly. And, also as stated in the previous section, the selection of a type font is more of an art than a science. Aesthetic criteria are typically sufficient to ensure that a type font is readable. Obviously, ornate or complex fonts should be avoided. Choose a font that is easy on the eye, and double-check your choice by consulting procedure users.

The biggest distinction in font appearance is between serif and sans serif fonts. This section will focus on that distinction, rather than to attempt to compare the hundreds of type fonts that are available.

Serif fonts include short lines at the ends of some of the lines that form the letter, as shown in Figure 8.

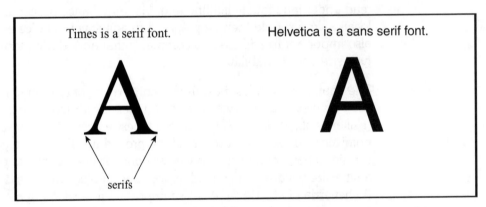

Figure 8. Serif and sans serif fonts. Serifs are short lines at the end of the strokes in letters. *Sans* is French for *without*; hence, sans serif fonts are "without serifs."

The research on serif versus sans serif type is basically inconclusive (Barnes et al., 1989), although much time and effort has been devoted to it.[24] Some authors consider serif typefaces to be easier to read (e.g., Mackh & Rew, 1991), while others find that readers have no preference (e.g., Hartley & Rooum, 1983; Tinker, 1963) and that there is no difference in reading speed (e.g., Gould et al., 1987). Schriver (1997) considered the type of document, and found that users preferred sans serif type faces for instruction manuals. (They preferred serif type for continuous prose, such as in a short story.)

---

[24]Many early studies of typeface have been criticized because they do not apply to real-world reading situations; for example, subjects in an experiment may be recognizing individual letters rather than reading passages of text (Schriver, 1997).

Turnbull and Baird (1980, p. 86) describe a consensus in the field of typography:

> Typographers have long contended that legibility is maximized by the use of standard Roman [i.e., serif] faces. Tests to date have neither confirmed nor refuted this contention, although researchers have been inclined to conclude that it is valid. Typographers believe that familiarity and design factors render legibility to such faces. They point out that we learn to read from books printed in [serif type] and that the majority of what we read thereafter in books, magazines, and other literature is also printed in [serif type]. Further, the more irregular design features of [serif] faces help the reader grasp word forms more rapidly in the reading process than in [sans serif type]. Contrasting strokes give a rhythmic structure to words and serifs assist horizontal eye movement.

However, readers' familiarity with typefaces may be changing. In 1980, the date of Turnbull and Baird's assessment, the personal computer was not yet a fixture in our lives. Now, writers in business settings have access to a broader range of fonts, so perhaps we are seeing more fonts, and thus more sans serif fonts, and are becoming more familiar with them. Schriver (1997, p. 301) writes that her findings suggest that

> the widely held assumption about Americans preferring serif typefaces is a myth. We found no across-the-board preference for serif typefaces. This may be an artifact of the changing face of contemporary typography, which in many publishing areas has been moving towards sans serif.

As with type size, the final assessment of type font must be subjective. Use a font that is readable.

Type case

Type case, on the other hand is not subjective—use mixed case, not all capitals.

Type case refers to whether the type is presented in all capitals, mixed case, or all lowercase. For blocks of text, mixed case is easier to read than all capitals; thus, text in all capitals should be used sparingly in procedures (e.g., cautions should not be presented in all capitals). All capitals will not cause problems, however, for words appearing in isolation or in short phrases, such as emphasis of a single word.

A variety of studies have shown that blocks of text appearing in all capitals are difficult to read. Blocks of text written in mixed case are read approximately 12% faster than text written in all capitals (Tinker & Paterson, 1928; Tinker, 1955; Poulton & Brown, 1968; Hartley & Burnhill, 1977; Turnbull & Baird, 1980; Benson, 1985). According to Tinker (1955, p. 444), "The retarding effect of all-capital print is relatively large. In fact, few typographical variations in printing practice produce differences as large as this."

Figure 9 depicts the reason we have difficulty reading all capitals. When text is presented in mixed case, each word assumes a unique shape, which assists

Figure 9. Blocks of text presented in mixed case are easier to read. This figure shows two paragraphs, one in all capitals and the other in mixed case. The shaded areas beneath each paragraph depict the shapes of the words that comprise the paragraphs. In mixed case, words assume unique shapes, helping readers to recognize them. As a result, mixed case is easier to read than all capitals.

us in recognizing the word; when text is presented in all capitals, each word is a rectangle. Two other factors add to this effect: (1) all capitals occupy more space on the page, requiring our eye to physically cover more area and (2) we are accustomed to reading text in mixed case (Tinker & Paterson, 1928).

In some instances, however, it is beneficial to present text in all capital letters. Words in all capitals are larger than words in mixed case. This increased size allows readers to recognize isolated words in all capitals more quickly than in mixed case (Vartabedian, 1971). The key is that all capitals must be used sparingly (e.g., for conditional terms, cross-referencing terms, or equipment names) or else reading time will suffer, as discussed above.

10.2 Use white space according to the conventions of graphic design.

Summary

Use white space to convey step structure, for emphasis (e.g., of step numbers or placekeeping aids), and for including meaningful line breaks (e.g., in conditional statements).

White space is, as the name implies, the blank space on the page. It is one of the graphic designer's most powerful tools:

> White space frames content, separates ideas, defines sections, gives relief from print, and works with other visual markers to highlight information. It is simple to use and extremely effective. (Mackh & Rew, 1991, p. 210)

Parker (1988, p. 46) lists some of the many uses of white space:

- White space can open up the area surrounding a headline [or a heading]. The readability of a headline [or a heading] is often enhanced more by adding white space around it than by increasing type size.

- The margins of [a] . . . publication are white space. Wide margins push the reader's attention to the center of the page.

- The space between columns of type is white space. The wider the columns, the more space should be between them.

- The space at the ends of the lines of unjustified or ragged-right type is white space.

- Indented sentences have white space.

- White space also refers to the area between lines of type. Tightly packed lines of type darken a publication.

- White space can also be added between paragraphs to open up a publication.

White space is also one of the most misused tools of graphic design. One of the most common errors in page layout is to use inadequate white space. We have all seen documents that appear dense and cluttered; the problem often is that they lack adequate white space or have not used white space effectively.

The following sections discuss two forms of white space—line spacing and indentation.[25]

Line spacing

Line spacing in procedures results primarily when lines are skipped before and after steps or between items in lists. As shown in Example 17, line spacing clearly differentiates steps and items in a list. (Lists will be discussed in Section 15.1.)

Line spacing can also be used to associate items. Note in Example 17 how there is one-half blank line between items in a list (actually 3 points) and one blank line (12 points) between steps. This use of spacing associates the items in the list, because they are closer to each other, while differentiating steps, which are further apart (Hartley, 1985). The same principle is used for the headings in this book: there is more blank space before a heading than after it, so the heading is visually associated with the text that follows in, rather than the text that precedes it.

---

[25]This discussion is simplified, but adequate for procedures. In visually complex publications, such as advertisements, there is much more white space than just line spacing and indentation (see, for example, White, 1982).

3.6	Perform an autostart test of the emergency seal oil pump by performing the following:	
	1. Depress pushbutton SON-P02 TEST HS-13B.	____
	2. Observe that the red light goes on and the green light goes off.	____
	3. Turn GEN SEAL OIL EMER PUMP P02, LON-HS-14 to STOP.	
	4. Observe that the red light goes off and the green light goes on.	____
3.7	Turn on the turbine generator core monitor.	____
3.8	Record the time that the core monitor was turned on in the control room log.	____

Example 17. Use of white space. In this portion of a procedure, white space is used effectively by placing one-third blank line (3 points) between each item in a list and one blank line (12 points) between each step. Indentation, another form of white space, is used to make step numbers and placekeeping aids stand out and to differentiate listed items from steps.

White space, correctly used, shows the relationships among items on the page: things that belong together are closer together than things that do not belong together.

Indentation

Another way to use white space effectively is through indentation:

> One can consider the horizontal spacing of text [i.e., indentation] in much the same way as…[line] spacing. This is to say we can look to see how the [indentation] can be used to separate and group components of the text, and how one can vary the stopping point of…text in accord with its content rather than by using arbitrary rules about line lengths. (Hartley, 1985, p. 31)

In Example 17, notice how the step numbers are indented so that subsequent lines of text align with the beginning of the first line of the step or the listed item. This use of indentation makes the step number stand out. Additional indentation is used to indicate that listed items are subordinate to the steps that contain them. Computer programmers frequently use indentation in this manner to simplify the structure of the code they write. Finally, indentation is used to make the placekeeping aid stand out on the right margin. Compare Example 17 with Example 18, which fails to use indentation in this manner.

3.6   Perform an autostart test of the emergency seal oil pump by performing the following:

1.   Depress pushbutton SON-P02 TEST HS-13B. ___

2.   Observe that the red light goes on and the green light goes off. ___

3.   Turn GEN SEAL OIL EMER PUMP P02, LON-HS-14 to STOP. ___

4.   Observe that the red light goes off and green light goes on. ___

3.7   Turn on the turbine generator core monitor. ___

3.8   Record the time that the core monitor was turned on in the control room log. ___

Example 18. Ineffective use of horizontal white space. Here, horizontal white space is not used effectively. As a result, placekeeping aids and step numbers do not stand out readily and it is difficult to match listed items to steps.

Indentation is also used to make the placekeeping aids stand out. The placekeeping aids (the lines that users check off as they perform a step; see Chapter 12) are on the right margin. Compare the placekeeping aids in Example 17 to those in Example 18. The placekeeping aids in Example 17 are much easier to locate.

Indentation can also be controlled by establishing rules for ending lines of type (Hartley, 1985). For example, line breaks in logic statements (see Chapter 16) can be positioned so that a line break occurs after each clause, as shown in Example 19. There are advantages to this approach that may make the step easier to comprehend (Hartley, 1982). One is that the conditional terms are emphasized by consistently being at the start of a line, as well as by full capitalization and underlining. Another advantage is that the two conditions are clearly differentiated from each other, and from the action, by the line breaks.

8.5   <u>WHEN</u> the main turbine is at rated speed
       <u>AND</u> turbine oil temperature has been stable for 20 minutes,
       <u>THEN</u> return temperature control to automatic.

Example 19. Line breaks in a logic statement. Line breaks are inserted after each clause in a conditional statement. These line breaks can make the step easier to understand.

10.3 Use ragged-right margins.

Summary

Right-justified text is more difficult to read than ragged-right text because of the variation among the spaces between words necessary to justify the right margin. For this reason, ragged-right margins should be used in procedures.

Practically all text is left-justified, meaning that all lines begin the same distance from the left margin. The right margin is a different matter. If text is right-justified, all lines end the same distance from the right margin. The spaces between the words (and sometimes between letters) in a line are varied to adjust the length of that line. If text is ragged right, lines are of unequal length; no attempt is made to adjust line length. The text you are reading now is ragged right. Example 20 shows the different forms of justification.

Fully-justified text can be more difficult to read because, unless it is done just right, gaps can appear between words. These gaps, as well as the varying spaces between words that can result, can be distracting. Hyphenation is often used to break words between lines, thus allowing more control over the spaces between words; but hyphenated words can also be more difficult to read. Trollip and Sales (1986) found that, although there were no differences in comprehension between right-justified and ragged-right text, the right-justified text was read more slowly. Other researchers also recommend ragged-right margins (Benson, 1985; Hartley & Burnhill, 1977; Turnbull & Baird, 1980).

Line length also affects the readability of right-justified text. In a longer line, the space that must be added can be divided among more spaces; in shorter lines, there are fewer word spaces to which this extra space can be added; hence, the spaces become proportionally larger. Because procedures have a short line length, due to the indentation and white space that are used, they should not be right justified.

This text is left-justified and ragged right, which is the alignment preferred in procedures.	This text is right-justified and left-justified (also known as fully justified).
This text is right-justified and ragged left. Avoid this uncommon combination.	This text is centered (making it ragged right and ragged left).

Example 20. Justification. There are four ways that type can be justified.

Ragged-left text, incidentally, should be avoided in all procedures. When we read, it is easier if our eyes return to a common anchor point as we reach the end of a line of text. In left-justified text, this anchor point is always in the same place—a given distance from the left margin. If the text is ragged left, we must hunt for the beginning of a line, as its location will vary. Reading is impeded. The same problem occurs with centered text, although it is permissible to center one- or two-line figure captions.

In this chapter...

Use placekeeping aids (11.1).

5.11 Close MSV-12.

CHAPTER
ELEVEN

Placekeeping

This chapter discusses placekeeping aids, which are boxes or blanks that users check as they perform a step. Placekeeping aids can also be referred to as check-offs or sign-offs.

11.1 Provide placekeeping aids to help users track their progress through the procedure.

Summary

Provide usable placekeeping aids for actions in procedures if they will be of benefit to procedure users. It may also be useful to provide placekeeping aids for conditions in conditional statements.

Placekeeping aids are blank lines or boxes that appear with each step or each action in a step. Users check the placekeeping aid as they perform the step or the action, tracking their progress through the procedure. Place-keeping aids prevent duplication or omission of actions and help users find their place if execution of the procedure is interrupted. Placekeeping aids are important in all types of long procedures, and become critical when proce-dures include cross-references (see Chapter 19), as users are likely to lose their place as they move from one procedure to another. Users can also use tables of contents, tabs, and ribbon markers to help trace their progress through the procedure.

In some procedures, placekeeping aids also serve an administrative function, by providing a record of the procedure's execution. These procedures are archived and may be checked at a later date. For example, maintainers may be required to initial a step instructing them to torque a bolt to specifications. An initial signifies that the bolt was torqued correctly, and may be checked at a later date if a question arises. Critical activities may require independent verification by a second person and a second set of initials.

Placekeeping aids are not suitable for all procedures. Placekeeping aids should not be included in a procedure if the procedure will be reused, because the first person to use the procedure will check them off, rendering them useless (and perhaps confusing) to subsequent users. Placekeeping aids should also be avoided if the procedure user will not be able to use them because his hands are full or otherwise occupied, or if the procedure is short and simple.

Some steps contain more than one action. In these instances, it is a sound practice to provide a placekeeping aid for each action, as shown in Example 21. Depending on facility administrative practices and user expectations, it may or may not be appropriate to include a placekeeping aid for the step as a whole. Example 21 does not include a placekeeping aid for the introductory conditional statement, on the logic that such a placekeeping aid is redundant; once the three placekeeping aids for the actions are checked, the step has been performed. In some cases, however, users prefer to see a placekeeping aid for the entire step; in others, facility administrative requirements may specify that such a placekeeping aid be used.

Placekeeping aids may also be useful for conditions in conditional statements, as shown in Example 22.

Placekeeping aids should be located so that they are surrounded by white space and so that they are easily associated with the items to which they correspond. The best locations are either along the left margin, beside the step number, or the right margin.

5.19   <u>IF</u> no RCPs are running,
      <u>THEN</u> check that the following criteria are met:

- RCS ΔT is less than 10°F.   ____
- RCS T_c is between 552 and 568°F.   ____
- RCS is at least 28°F subcooled based on T_h RTD.   ____

Example 21. Placekeeping aids for multiple actions. The placekeeping aids are the lines along the right margin. This example includes a placekeeping aid for each action, rather than a placekeeping aid for the step as a whole, allowing users to verify the performance of each action.

3.1   IF all of the following conditions exist:

• Pressure in at least one steam generator is decreasing   ____

• RCS pressure is decreasing   ____

• Containment radiation is stable   ____

THEN use this procedure.   ____

Example 22. Use of placekeeping aids for conditions in a conditional statement. Users may mark placekeeping aids if the conditions are met, reducing demands on short-term memory.

In this chapter...

Use emphasis
techniques consistently
and effectively (12.1).

5.5   Ensure:

- PRIMARY CIRCUIT BREAKERS—Switch is **on**   ____
- POWER ON 480 VAC—Green Light is **on**   ____
- RIGHT DOOR CLOSED—Amber light and switch are **on**   ____
- HOIST UP MAXIMUM—Green light is **on**   ____

CHAPTER
TWELVE

Emphasis Techniques

Emphasis techniques are typographical, graphical, spatial, and verbal cues that visually distinguish information within a body of text. Typographical emphasis techniques include:

- **bolding**
- *italicizing*
- <u>underlining</u>
- ALL CAPITALS
- [brackets]
- "quotation marks"

Graphical emphasis techniques include framing (i.e., enclosing in a box), shading, or coloring. Cautions, for example, can be framed.

Spatial emphasis techniques refer to the use of white space to surround the item that is emphasized. Emphasis occurs because the item contrasts with the blank space surrounding it. Section 10.2 discusses the use of white space. Consistent placement of something on the page is also a spatial emphasis technique; for example, the procedure name could appear at the top of each page.

Verbal emphasis techniques include the use of identifying terms, such as *Important*, *NOTE*, or *Caution!*.

12.1 Consistently use emphasis techniques to code and highlight information.

Summary

Emphasis techniques should be used consistently throughout a text to code and highlight specific types of information. Avoid overemphasis.

Emphasis techniques, such as bolding or using white space, are frequently misused in procedures. This section discusses the use of emphasis techniques. It begins by distinguishing between true emphasis and coding, and explains how emphasis techniques should be minimized and used consistently.

Emphasis versus coding

Emphasis techniques, when implemented correctly, actually perform two functions:

- They let the reader know that something is important. This is known as *true emphasis*.

- They let the reader know what something is (e.g., if something is in a box, then it is a caution). This is known as *coding*.

These two functions differ, and often the coding function is more important than the true emphasis function.

True emphasis techniques make something appear important because of the visual difference between the emphasized item and its surroundings. The reader's eye is drawn to the word or section that stands out from its surroundings.

True emphasis techniques make things stand out on the procedure page. Something should stand out for one of two reasons: so readers will see it when scanning the page or so readers will realize that it is important. Headings, for example, should stand out so a reader scanning the procedure can quickly locate a particular section. It may also be useful for control panel markings or equipment labels to stand out when quoted in the procedure, so the user can quickly locate the label when looking back at the procedure to verify that the label corresponds to the label cited in the procedure. True emphasis can also be used to indicate importance, but this should be done with care because, in a terse procedure, every word is important. When emphasis is used to indicate importance, overemphasis, as discussed in the next section, can be a danger, because almost every word in a procedure can be considered important for one reason or another.

But emphasis techniques do more than highlight important information. Emphasis techniques also code, or identify, information. For example, if all warnings are printed in red ink, the reader can identify a warning at the first notice of red printing.

Coding is important. The emphasis of conditional terms, for example, serves as more of a coding function than a true emphasis function. Consider the following conditional statement:[26]

IF you have less than 50 ml of the sample
OR you have less time than 1 hour to complete the test,
THEN GO TO Attachment 2, Measuring SR-89 and SR-90 in Air Samples.

The conditional terms IF, OR, and THEN are capitalized and underlined not simply because they are important to understanding the step. Granted, the step would be difficult to understand if any of these words were missing, but it would also be difficult to understand if almost any other word were missing. The primary reason that these words are emphasized uniquely is to mark (or code) the parts of the conditional statement. When the user sees IF, he knows the condition of a conditional statement follows; when he sees OR, he knows that another condition follows and that either one or both of the conditions must be true; when he sees THEN, he knows that the action that is contingent on the preceding conditions will follow. The conditional terms function as labels for the various parts of the conditional statement. This is a coding function.

Use of emphasis techniques

Whether used for true emphasis or coding, emphasis techniques should be minimized and used consistently. Users should know what the various emphasis techniques mean.

Emphasis is relative; true emphasis techniques work because they contrast with their surroundings. If emphasis techniques are overused, then the "emphasized" information has no subdued surroundings to contrast against. The result is that nothing is emphasized, as illustrated in Example 23.

✳✳✳✳✳✳✳✳✳✳✳✳✳✳✳✳NOTE✳✳✳✳✳✳✳✳✳✳✳✳✳✳✳✳✳

[Eight hours operating fuel *required* **by the NFPA.**]
Fuel consumption for this engine per the
Manufacturer's Specifications is
14 gal/h under NORMAL LOAD CONDITIONS, or
112 gal/8h.
• **Minimum** *allowable fuel level* is 120 gal.

✳✳✳✳✳✳✳✳✳✳✳✳✳✳✳✳✳✳✳✳✳✳✳✳✳✳✳✳✳✳✳✳✳

Example 23. Overuse of emphasis. When everything is emphasized, nothing is emphasized. This (admittedly exaggerated) example demonstrates how overemphasized text can be distracting and unprofessional, if not downright confusing.

---

[26]See Chapter 16 for more information on conditional statements.

Overuse will also detract from coding. For effective coding, the user should be able to distinguish the different techniques used. If too many techniques are used, the user will not be able to keep track of them all. Once this happens, the coding techniques contribute little more than clutter and confusion.

It is also necessary to use emphasis techniques consistently in order to transfer this qualitative information to the reader. If, for example, component names are italicized in the first section of a procedure but not throughout the remainder of the procedure, the reader's speed and understanding may decrease as he or she scans unsuccessfully for a component name in italic print. Important information might be overlooked with this type of inconsistency. Inconsistent coding will lead to confusion, decrease reading speed, and increase the potential for misinterpretations.

Users should be trained to understand the ways in which emphasis techniques are used. Research suggests that typographical emphasis is most effective when the reader knows in advance what the various cues mean (Hartley & Burnhill, 1977; Glynn, Britton, & Tillman, 1985). This information can be provided during organized training for the procedure or within the procedure text. Within the text, for example, an introductory section can be provided that states which emphasis techniques are used and what each one represents, such as, *In this procedure, action verbs are printed in bold lettering, warnings are printed in red, and equipment names are italicized.* A better approach, however, might be to ensure that users are trained on this critical information.

Finally, we would like to suggest that you minimize underlining. Typewriters couldn't easily print italics, so underlining emerged as a substitute. Computers now can italicize, but many people still underline out of habit. Underlining can make text difficult to read and is unattractive. Consider italics instead. In the examples in this book, underlining is used only for conditional terms (such as <u>IF</u>) and in introduction to lists (such as *Perform <u>one</u> of the following:*). Such limited usage is acceptable, but don't underline large blocks of text.

Graphical and verbal emphasis techniques

A complete discussion of graphical emphasis techniques is beyond the scope of this book. A few general caveats are presented here. Background shading should be avoided because it reduces contrast between the type and the background, making the type more difficult to read, particularly if the procedure has been photocopied. If you shade, do so as lightly as possible. Color can be highly effective for emphasis, but it is difficult to produce colored documents, although this is changing with the introduction of color printers and copiers. Color can easily be misused; some color combinations can be illegible or just plain garish. Icons or symbols can also be used effectively as emphasis techniques; for example, a radiation symbol could be used to mark steps where users are working with radioactive material. Such icons will be most effective if users understand their meaning.

Remember, too, that white space can be one of the most effective graphical emphasis techniques. If you surround something with nothing, it stands out.

Verbal emphasis techniques in procedures are generally restricted to headings on cautions and notes. As with other emphasis techniques, verbal emphasis techniques are most useful when their use is minimized; if *every* step is marked *Danger!*, users will quickly come to ignore them.

Coding revisions to procedures: An example

Many procedures are living documents, meaning that they are updated as the need arises. It is important to draw users' attention to any changes in the procedure so they will be aware of changes and will not perform the procedure the old way out of habit. This subsection discusses the criteria that affect the choice of a coding technique for alerting users to revised information and provides an example of the types of factors that a procedure writer should consider when deciding whether a coding or emphasis technique is appropriate and, if so, which technique should be used.

The technique used to identify revised information should not be intrusive, or it may conflict with other emphasis and coding techniques. Bold type, for example, would be a poor choice for this purpose, as a substantially *revised* procedure would have page after page of bold type, which would not only be difficult to read, but would overwhelm any other emphasis and coding techniques that were used. In fact, most forms of typographical coding would probably be unacceptable, given the rather extensive use of typographical techniques for other purposes. Similarly, spatial emphasis techniques are also likely to be of little use, as spatial coding (i.e., white space) is also used rather extensively for other purposes. Verbal techniques are also likely to be intrusive, as the use of words to identify new information would grow tiresome to the reader, particularly if they were incorporated in the step (e.g., *Revised step: Trip the 4.2 kv breakers*).

Graphic emphasis techniques are better suited for identifying revisions. One graphic technique is, in fact, widely used to indicate revised portions of procedures—the change bar. A change bar is a vertical bar that appears near the right or left margin and is aligned with text that has been revised. Being off to the side, the change bar is not intrusive, even if it runs down the entire page, indicating that the entire page has been revised. Yet, it still effectively alerts users to revisions. Example 24 shows a change bar.

4.19	<u>IF</u> no RCPs are running,	
	<u>THEN</u> check that the following criteria are met:	
	1. RCS ΔT is less than 10°F.	
	2. RCS T_c is between 552 and 568°F.	___
	3. RCS is at least 28°F subcooled based on T_h RTD.	___

Example 24. Change bar. The horizontal bar in the left margin indicates that items 1 and 2 have been changed since the last version of the procedure.

In this chapter...

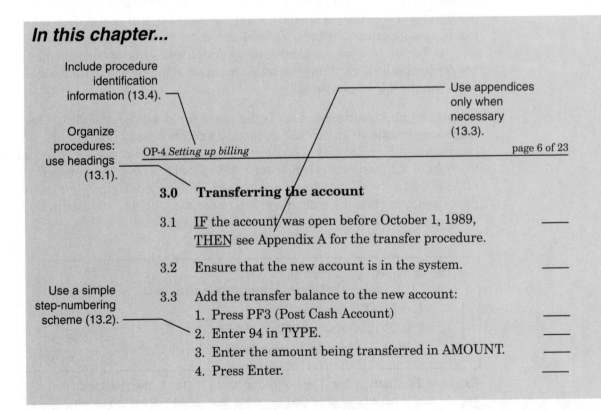

Include procedure identification information (13.4).

Organize procedures: use headings (13.1).

Use appendices only when necessary (13.3).

3.0   Transferring the account

3.1   <u>IF</u> the account was open before October 1, 1989, <u>THEN</u> see Appendix A for the transfer procedure.   —

3.2   Ensure that the new account is in the system.   —

Use a simple step-numbering scheme (13.2).

3.3   Add the transfer balance to the new account:
1. Press PF3 (Post Cash Account)   —
2. Enter 94 in TYPE.   —
3. Enter the amount being transferred in AMOUNT.   —
4. Press Enter.   —

CHAPTER

THIRTEEN

Procedure Organization

The way that material is organized can be as important as the material itself. In his book *The 100*, Michael Hart (1998) presents his ranking of the 100 most influential persons in history. Euclid is number 14, primarily because of the way he organized *Elements*, a geometry text.

> The importance of *Elements* does not lie in any one of the individual theorems it demonstrates. Almost all of the theorems in the book had been known before Euclid, and a good many of the proofs as well. Euclid's great contribution was his arrangement of the material and his overall formulation of the plan of the book. . . . The *Elements* has been used as a textbook for more than two thousand years, and is unquestionably the most successful textbook ever written. . . . It is an outstanding example of a complete deductive structure and as such has fascinated thinkers ever since its creation. (p. 76)

This chapter presents four principles regarding procedure organization. They may not earn you a place in the next edition of Hart's book, but they will improve the quality of the procedures you write.

This discussion focuses on the portion of the procedure that presents the steps because that's what this book focuses on—instructions. Procedures may contain many sections that do not present instructions, such as scope, responsibilities, references, and so on. These sections are not discussed here, because their content can vary greatly. The general rule about such sections? Essentialize. These sections are sometimes included out of tradition rather than need. Keep them short, and don't include them if you don't need them.

13.1 Organize procedures in a hierarchical, logical, consistent manner and reveal that organization to users through the use of headings.

Summary

Procedures should be organized hierarchically; that is, related steps should be grouped into sections. These sections should describe tasks that will be performed and be given names that reflect their content. Headings should be emphasized in a manner that makes them stand out and that provides progressively less emphasis to lower-level headings. Tables of contents should be included in procedures that are more than a few pages long.

Many researchers emphasize the importance of organization. Jonassen (1982, p. 10) says, "The stronger the organization of the text, the more likely it will be assimilated by the reader.... *The importance of organization to text cannot be denied*" [author's italics]. Meyer (1985, p. 70) makes a similar point: "Research shows that a communication is vastly more efficient (it saves effort) and effective (it gets results) if it follows a plan rather than being a miscellaneous sequence of sentences or paragraphs." Although procedures are not presented in paragraphs, Meyer's point remains applicable—the procedure should not be a miscellaneous collection of steps.

In all procedures, the overall organizational scheme will be dictated by the order in which steps are performed. Clearly, the steps that must be performed first should appear first in the procedure. Prerequisites, such as a list of tools that will be needed or a set of conditions that must be met before the procedure is executed, should appear before steps. However, organization is more than the sequence of the steps; it also applies to how steps are grouped into sections. Through the effective use of sections and the effective identification of those sections by headings, much information can be imparted to the procedure user.

The importance of a hierarchical structure

Many researchers believe that a hierarchical structure is best for presenting procedures (Bovair & Kieras, 1989; Fuchs, Engelschall, & Imlay, 1981; Huckin, 1983). Hierarchical procedures are easier to comprehend (Dixon, 1987) and to learn and remember (Holland, Charrow, & Wright, 1988, p. 35): "If procedures are to be learned and remembered, then hierarchical structure appears to be essential."

Hierarchical structures are very common. Businesses, for example, are often organized hierarchically, with a president at the top of the hierarchy, the vice presidents beneath him or her, middle managers beneath the vice presidents, and so on. Figure 10 shows how procedures can also be organized hierarchically.

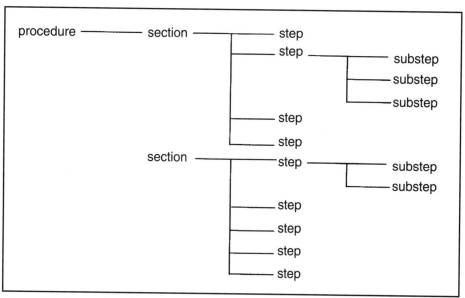

Figure 10. Procedure hierarchy. In a hierarchical procedure, procedures consist of sections, which consist of steps, some of which include substeps.

In procedures, the opposite of a clearly revealed hierarchy is an unstructured list of steps. Example 25 depicts an unstructured list.

5.1	Depress EMER BEARING OIL PUMP TEST SWITCH A, LON HS-52A.	____
5.2	Observe that the red light goes on and the green light goes off.	____
5.3	Take EMER BEARING OIL PUMP P05, LON-HS-8, to STOP.	____
5.4	Observe that the red light goes off and the green light goes on.	____
5.5	Ensure that the emergency seal oil pump is in standby.	____
5.6	Depress pushbutton SON-P02 TEST HS-13B.	____
5.7	Observe that the red light goes on and the green light goes off.	____
5.8	Take GEN SEAL OIL EMER PUMP P02, LON-HS-14 to stop.	____
5.9	Observe that the red light goes off and the green light goes on.	____

Example 25. An unstructured list of procedure steps. No attempt is made to group these steps. Compare with Example 26.

Example 26 revises Example 25 by grouping many of these actions as listed items beneath a descriptive higher-level step.

In the grouped version (Example 26), the relationships among the steps is evident—the procedure is performing three tasks, identified by each of the three steps, and two of those tasks include four subtasks each. This hierarchy is not easily evident to the reader of Example 25.

Although Example 26 depicts a portion of the hierarchy at the step level, the same principles of organization apply when combining steps into section—namely, related steps should be grouped into sections and the name of these sections should reflect the common theme in the steps.

> 5.1   Perform an autostart test of the emergency bearing oil pump by completing the following:
>
>   1. Depress EMER BEARING OIL PUMP TEST SWITCH A, LON HS-52A.   ____
>
>   2. Observe that the red light goes on and the green light goes off.   ____
>
>   3. Take EMER BEARING OIL PUMP P05, LON-HS-8, to STOP.   ____
>
>   4. Observe that the red light goes off and the green light goes on.   ____
>
> 5.2   Ensure that the emergency seal oil pump is in standby.   ____
>
> 5.3   Perform an autostart test of the emergency seal oil pump by performing the following:
>
>   1. Depress pushbutton SON-P02 TEST HS-13B.   ____
>
>   2. Observe that the red light goes on and the green light goes off.   ____
>
>   3. Take GEN SEAL OIL EMER PUMP P02, LON-HS-14 to stop.   ____
>
>   4. Observe the red light goes off and the green light goes on.   ____

Example 26. Grouping used to show the hierarchy of actions. This example revises Example 25 to group steps beneath upper-level steps that summarize the actions that follow (e.g., *Perform an autostart test of the emergency bearing oil pump by performing the following:*).[27]

---

[27]Example 25 and Example 26 deal with steps rather than sections because steps are more concise; it would have required too much space to show an example of a series of steps that were grouped into sections. But the same principle applies.

Task orientation

So how should information be divided into sections? One way to explain that is to consider an example.

You're shopping for a do-it-yourself car repair manual. You don't know much about car repair procedures, but you've decided to give it a try. You find two and compare the tables of contents.

Smilin' Jack's Guide to Auto Repair is organized by the major systems of the car. *Fix it and Save!* is organized by the tasks that you are likely to perform. It is task oriented.

Smilin' Jack's Guide to Auto Repair	*Fix It and Save!*
Brakes 1	Changing the oil and filter 1
Electrical System 10	Setting the valve clearance 4
Engine 17	Setting the timing 9
Exhaust system 45	Checking and adjusting the
Fuel system 48	brakes 14
Suspension 51	Replacing the starter 21

There are advantages to the task orientation in *Fix it and Save!*. The writer of this manual divided it in a manner that more closely matches the way that you will use it. You can find things more easily. For example, if you want to change the oil, you can go straight to the chapter with that title; Smilin' Jack would have you look through the (quite long) chapter on the engine to find the information you wanted. There is also less ambiguity in *Fix It and Save!*. If you need to change the starter, you can refer directly to the chapter of that name; in the other manual, you must first decide whether Smilin' Jack considers the starter as part of the electrical system or the engine. You may need to refer to both sections to get the job done.[28]

Failure to use a task orientation creates extra work for users, because they are often required to follow several different sections at the same time to perform a task. This can be known as the "five-fingers" problem, because

---

[28]This is not to say that there are not advantages to Smilin' Jack's approach. The task orientation of *Fix It and Save!* would probably necessitate some redundancy, because the same system would be covered by several different procedures. An experienced mechanic, who knows the steps of the repair process very well, might prefer Smilin' Jack's leaner approach. This user would only need to refer to the manual for specific bits of information, like the specifications for front wheel alignment, which he or she could easily find in the section on suspension. But if this mechanic isn't following the manual in a step-by-step fashion, then he isn't really using it as a procedure. Task orientation is best for procedures and it does not work as well for documents that are not used as procedures.

they are using five different fingers to mark their place in five different procedures (McCallum et al., 1994).

When you organize procedures, think about the tasks that users will perform. Devote a section to each task. Break that task down into a hierarchy of steps and substeps.[29]

Headings

Headings present the names of sections. As discussed in the following sections, headings help readers comprehend and access text:

- Headings help readers comprehend a procedure by very briefly summarizing the content of a section. For instance, the heading *Starting the Main Turbine* tells the reader that the steps in that section deal with start-up of the main turbine (Hartley & Jonassen, 1985).

- Headings serve as access aids by helping readers locate information in a procedure. If the procedure user is looking for the steps that will start the main turbine, the heading *Starting the Main Turbine* indicates where those steps begin in the procedure. Note that, for headings to effectively aid in access, it is important that they be emphasized so that they stand out on the page (Hartley & Jonassen, 1985).

In a hierarchical document, headings can be referred to by their levels. A first-level heading is at the highest position in the hierarchy. In this book, first-level headings identify Parts One, Two, Three, and so on. Second-level headings are lower in the hierarchy; in this document, second-level headings identify chapters. This pattern continues through the lowest level of the hierarchy.

Headings should provide specific, useful information to readers (Hartley & Jonassen, 1985). For this reason, vague headings like *Action Steps* should be avoided. Instead, headings should describe the content of the section; for example, a series of headings such as *Turning Gear Operation*, *Turbine Warming Operations*, and *Turbine Start-Up* provides more information than the single heading *Action Steps*.

Headings facilitate comprehension

Headings can help readers comprehend information by providing a context for that information. Consider the following passage, which is presented without a heading (Anderson et al., 1977, p. 373):

> Rocky slowly got up from the mat, planning his escape. He hesitated a moment and thought. Things were not going well. What bothered him most was being held, especially since the charge against him had been weak. He considered his present situation. The lock that held him was strong but he thought he could break it. He knew, however, that his timing would have to be perfect. Rocky was

---

[29]Section 19.1 provides a further discussion of task orientation.

aware that it was because of much of his earlier roughness that he was being penalized so severely—much too severely from his point of view. The situation was becoming frustrating; the pressure had been grinding on him for too long. He was being ridden unmercifully. Rocky was getting angry now. He felt he was ready to make his move. He knew that his success or failure would depend on what he did in the next few seconds.

What is this passage about? Suppose that it had been preceded by the title, *The Wrestling Match*. Read it again with that title in mind. Now suppose that it was preceded by a different title—*Escape from Alcatraz*. Read the passage again. This example demonstrates the power of headings in shaping the way that readers will perceive writing.[30]

Evidence suggests that headings do help readers understand what they read. Huckin (1983, p. 97) is convinced of the support in the research for the notion that headings aid in comprehension, stating that "many psychological studies have demonstrated the powerful effect of headings and subheadings on comprehension." Spyridakis and Standal (1987) found that headings did aid in comprehension, producing the greatest effects when a passage was neither too easy nor too difficult for its readers. Further, the notion that headings aid comprehension is somewhat buttressed by studies that have found that headings that have no relation to or are contrary to the text adversely affect comprehension (Hartley & Jonassen, 1985). On the other hand, Spyridakis (1989b) found that headings had no effect on immediate recall. She expected this, "based on much of the literature that has failed to find immediate effects for headings" (p. 410).

The research regarding the ability of headings to facilitate comprehension does not clearly point in one direction, and perhaps never will. However, these results should by no means discourage writers from using headings. Spyridakis and Standal (1987, p. 294) sum up the issue nicely: "Because there is ample reason to believe that signals [i.e., headings] help and no reason to believe that they hinder, it seems reasonable to suggest that a reader may be best served through the inclusion of [headings]."

Headings facilitate access

On the other hand, there is little question that headings help readers locate parts of a document. Mackh and Rew (1991, p. 211) explain how headings facilitate access: "Headings flag information for readers, helping them to scan and locate sections quickly. They act as mini-overviews, indicating what information is contained within document sections and subsections."

---

[30]It could be argued that this passage is not a realistic example. Research by Anderson et al. (1977) on headings, from which this passage is drawn, does set up a straw man, in the form of a deliberately ambiguous passage. Hartley and Jonassen (1985, pp. 240–241) discuss one of Anderson's earlier experiments in this regard: "The effectiveness of headings needs to be affirmed with natural, less ambiguous prose.... Few studies have examined this question posed in this particular form." We include the example here simply to make a point.

A consistent organizational scheme will also facilitate access. If the first few sections of every procedure are (for instance) *Introduction*, *Precautions and Limitations*, and *Prerequisite Instructions*, users will be able to locate these sections more easily. The writers' guide should specify these generic procedure sections or should provide criteria that procedure writers can use when dividing a procedure into sections.

Headings can also facilitate access during cross-referencing. It is often best to refer users to an entire section rather than a series of steps, because a section is a logical unit of information. Most cross-references should be to complete sections.

Format for headings

Brusaw, Alred, and Oliu (1987, p. 293) say that "there is no correct format" for headings. Experimental findings bear this out. Hartley (1985) found that position and form of headings made no significant difference in the headings' effectiveness. Hartley and Trueman (1983) found that position of headings made no difference. Thus, much is left to the writers' discretion regarding the format and position of headings. What is important is that (1) headings are emphasized so that they stand out and (2) upper-level headings are emphasized more heavily than lower-level headings.

A variety of techniques emphasize headings. Headings may be surrounded by white space, bolded, italicized, underlined, fully capitalized, initially capitalized, or set in a larger font. Generally, no one of these techniques is any better or any worse than any other.[31] However, these emphasis techniques should be used in combinations that convey the hierarchy of the headings; in other words, in a document with four levels of headings, first-level headings should have the most emphasis, second-level headings should have less emphasis, third-level headings even less, and fourth-level headings should have the least emphasis. The table below shows one way of placing progressively less emphasis on each level of heading.

	Centered	All capitals	Bold	2 blank lines before, 1 after
First level	✔	✔	✔	✔
Second level		✔	✔	✔
Third level			✔	✔
Fourth level				✔

It is often tempting to include more levels of headings than will be useful to readers; writers often feel the need to include fifth- or even sixth-level headings in documents. Many researchers warn against this. Brusaw, Alred, and

---

[31]Because headings are (or should be) short, they can be presented in all capitals. The loss in legibility is slight, because the heading does not constitute a block of text, and is offset by the benefit coding effect of all capitals.

Oliu (1987, p. 289) write, "In extremely technical material as many as five levels of [headings] may be appropriate, but as a general rule it is rarely necessary (and usually confusing) to use more than three." The problem is that readers cannot keep track of a detailed hierarchy of headings, so the headings wind up conveying some global, complex scheme that is evident only to the writer.

Tables of contents

Headings are typically listed in a table of contents. While it is a good idea to include a table of contents in any procedure that is more than a few pages long, writers should be aware that, according to one source, users refer to tables of contents and indexes only 25 percent of the time (Sticht, 1985), so it is not a good idea to rely on them. Procedures should include other means of helping readers locate information; these include properly emphasized headings, which will stand out as readers scan the pages of the procedure, and tabs to indicate section breaks for long procedures.

Several concerns govern the design of a table of contents (Wright, 1985). Readers should be able to easily link the table of contents' entries with corresponding page numbers. A horizontal line of periods is often used between the entry and the page number for this reason. A table of contents should reflect the hierarchical organization of a document; in other words, first-level headings in the table of contents should be emphasized more heavily than lower-level headings. It may not be necessary to include all heading levels in the table of contents. Think about what readers will actually want to look up.

13.2 Use step numbering and structure that provide useful information to users and is not overly complex.

Summary

Step numbers should be formatted so that they indicate that a step is to follow, they should uniquely identify steps, and they should provide information regarding the location of the step in the hierarchy of the procedure, unless this information is provided in another manner. Hierarchical step numbering should not be overused.

Steps are numbered for three reasons: (1) a step number indicates an item in a procedure is a step; (2) step numbers identify individual steps, which facilitates cross-referencing; and (3) step numbers can indicate how sections, steps, and substeps are related. When numbering steps, or other information in procedures, it is important to keep these purposes in mind so that the step numbering scheme is useful and is not too complex for the procedure. Example 27 depicts effective step numbering.

7.0   Night Shift Operation

7.1   Transfer the solution by performing the following steps:
1. Open drain valve D-34.   ____
2. Open:
   - Inlet valve I-45   ____
   - Outlet valve O-2   ____
   - Outlet valve O-3   ____
3. Start the transfer pump.   ____
4. <u>WHEN</u> the solution is approximately 1 foot below the
   maximum level mark on the column,
   <u>THEN</u> stop the transfer pump.   ____

Example 27. Effective step numbering. This example demonstrates one method of effectively numbering steps. Steps have a two-part number to identify the section they are in (Section 7) and the number of the step (Step 1). Substeps are simply designated with numbers. Bullets are used to distinguish listed items. Compare with the more complex numbering scheme used in Example 28.

Procedure users should readily recognize the steps in a procedure as steps. A step number is one cue that a step, and thus an action, is to follow. Unique identification of steps allows users to differentiate the essential directions from supporting information. Other information in the procedure, such as the references at the beginning of the procedure, should not be numbered in the same manner as a step, or the information may be confused with a step. If these items are numbered, step numbers could be surrounded by square brackets, for example, to differentiate them from other numbered items.

Step numbers also help users find specific steps. Identification of specific steps is particularly important in cross-referencing. Users must be told in an unambiguous manner which step they are going to. One means of accomplishing this is to use a hierarchical step numbering scheme. In such a scheme, the third step in Section 5 is Step 5.3, the first step in Section 12 is Step 12.1, and so on. Under this scheme, each step in the procedure will have a unique number, so a cross-reference to, say, Step 17.1 will unambiguously denote a specific location in the procedure.

Hierarchical step numbering also provides useful information to users regarding the relationship of the step to the overall procedure; when a user sees Step 4.3, he knows that it is in Section 4. This knowledge can provide information on the context under which the step is being executed. Research indicates that hierarchical step numbering can provide useful information to procedure users (Benson, 1985). The NRC (1982) recommends that step numbers be used hierarchically.

Hierarchical step numbering is not the only means of providing this information; for example, a section title repeated at the top of the page will also provide this information, perhaps more clearly than a step number, because users do not have to associate the first part of the hierarchical number with a section title. In other words, it is easier to attach a useful meaning to *5.0 Post-maintenance testing (continued)* at the top of the page than to remember that the *5* in Step 5.23 corresponds to the post-maintenance testing section.

It is quite possible to carry the notion of hierarchical step numbering too far. Example 28 shows an excerpt from a computer procedure where hierarchical step numbering has been overused. Consider Items 5.1.1.2.1 and 5.1.1.2.2 in Example 28. What purpose is accomplished in numbering them? The number is not an indication that actions follow, because headings, steps, and listed items are numbered according to an identical format. The numbers would not be an aid to cross-referencing, as there would be no justifiable reason to cross-reference to so brief and fragmentary a piece of information as *a delay in delivery to data entry.* Finally, the numbers do not convey any useful hierarchical information, as it is obvious from indentation and context that Items 5.1.1.2.1 and 5.1.1.2.2 are subsumed under Item 5.1.1.2. Further, the hierarchical information presented is not useful to the user, who should not be expected to remember that items 5.1.1.2.1 and 5.1.1.2.2 are subsumed under item 5.1.1.2, which is in turn subsumed under *Discrepancies in Turnaround Time*, which is subsumed under *Run Date and Date Keyed*, which is subsumed under *Interpreting Discrepancies.* The hierarchy is too complex; it goes five levels deep in half a page.

5.0   Interpreting Discrepancies

    5.1   Run Date and Date Keyed

        5.1.1   Discrepancies in Turnaround Time

            5.1.1.1   If the run date is equal to or just slightly greater than the date the client information sheet went to data entry, then the system is functioning properly.

            5.1.1.2   If the run date is several days greater than the date the client information sheet went to data entry, at least one of the following conditions exists:

                5.1.1.2.1   a delay in delivery to data entry

                5.1.1.2.2   a problem at the data entry level

---

Example 28. Overuse of the hierarchical numbering scheme. The hierarchical numbering scheme as used here serves no useful purpose at the lower levels of the hierarchy. No benefit is realized by numbering Items 5.1.1.2.1 and 5.1.1.2.2 (adapted from Horn & Kelly, 1981, p. 18).

13.3 Use appendices and attachments to present information that would otherwise be difficult to integrate into the procedure.

Summary

Appendices and attachments can be used to present information that cannot be easily incorporated into the procedure, such as contingency actions, actions performed by someone other than the procedure reader, and periodic steps. Because transitions to appendices and attachments are disruptive to readers, the use of appendices and attachments should be minimized.

There is no universal distinction between the terms *attachment* and *appendix*. Because any distinction can be vague and of little use to users, it is not recommended that you distinguish between appendices and attachments unless necessary. In the remainder of this section, we will use only the term *appendix*.

The following types of information may be included in an appendix:

- Appendices can include lengthy sequences of contingency actions that are not normally performed when the procedure is executed. In an appendix, these actions are out of the way but available should they be needed. They would be accessed via a conditional cross-reference (see Chapter 19). Frequently performed actions should not be included in appendices, however, unless they meet other criteria expressed in this section.

- Appendices can include actions that are performed by someone other than the person who is using the procedure, allowing the person who will be using the appendix to remove it from the procedure.

- Appendices can include steps that are performed repeatedly, allowing the user to refer to the appendix periodically.

- Appendices can include data sheets and other lengthy forms that would be difficult to incorporate in the procedure.

- Appendices can present supplementary and background information that may be useful to procedure users.

- Figures can be included in appendices; however, figures should be placed in appendices with care, as users are much more likely to refer to graphics that are on the same page as the portion of the procedure that refers to them (or on the facing page).

These are all useful functions for appendices; however, the danger in using appendices is that it is often easier to shove something into an appendix than to figure out where it really belongs within the organization of the procedure. One study (McCallum, et al., 1994) found this to be a high-priority potential problem in nuclear power plant maintenance procedures, second only to technical inaccuracies. Figures, for example, are commonly included in appendices. Originally, this may have been because they were difficult to incorporate into the procedure at the appropriate point. Computer technology has changed this, however, making it much easier to include a picture as part of the electronic file and include it at the appropriate point in the procedure. Similarly, it is often easier to include a series of steps in an appendix than it is to revise a procedure to include those steps where they really belong. These are practices that benefit the procedure writer and hurt the procedure user.

Transitions to appendices are disruptive for the procedure user, who must abandon his location in the procedure, locate the appendix, read the appendix, and (if necessary) perform tasks as directed, and then return to his place in the procedure. This process is complicated by the fact that transitions to appendices are often implicit rather than explicit; in other words, rather than including an explicit cross-reference to the appendix, the procedure writer simply expects that the user will know to look in the appendix. Again, this simplifies the writer's job and complicates the user's job.

Excessive use of appendices is a danger sign. Consider moving information from the appendices to the procedure, converting appendices to separate procedures, and so on. If it remains essential to use a great number of appendices, then provide help for the user in locating information in the appendices, in the form of explicit cross-references, indexes, and so on.

13.4 Include adequate identification information in procedures.

Summary

The cover page should include the procedure name and number, the procedure objective, and any necessary administrative information. The header or footer that appears on every page should include the procedure name and number, the page number, and any necessary administrative information.

When a user picks up a procedure, he should know exactly what procedure it is, what the procedure applies to, and whether it is the current procedure. By including this information in the procedure, you are taking an important step towards ensuring that it is usable. This information appears on the cover page, the page header, or both.

Cover page

The cover page is the first page of every procedure. The cover page identifies the procedure and should contain the following information:

- The *procedure number* is also important. If procedure users typically identify procedures by number rather than title, then the number is more important than the title and should be more prominent.

- An *objective* can also be useful. The objective is a short description of the procedure that supplements the title. It describes what the execution of the procedure will accomplish.

- The *procedure number* is also important. If procedure users typically identify procedures by number rather than title, then the number is more important than the title and should be more prominent.

- The cover page should *identify the facility or business*. In large facilities, it may also be useful to identify the department or branch to which the procedure pertains.

- Finally, the cover page should include *administrative information*, such as review and approval signatures, the revision number, and the effective date of the procedure.

Page header and footer

The page header appears at the top of every page; the footer appears at the bottom of each page. The header or footer includes the identification information that must appear on every page:

- The *procedure title* and *number* should be repeated in the header or footer so that users can identify the procedure without referring to the cover page.

- In long procedures, it may be useful to repeat the *section title* in the header or footer.

- The *page number* must appear on every page. The page number should also include the total number of pages (e.g., *Page 7 of 32*) so that users are aware of the total number of pages in the procedure. This can be useful information, as the last page of a stapled procedure is sometimes separated from the procedure.

- Finally, the header should include adequate *administrative information*, such as the revision number or the effective date, so that users are certain they are working with the most current version of the procedure.

PART
FOUR

Writing Complex Steps

CHAPTER

FOURTEEN

Introduction: Writing Complex Steps

Part Two of this book discussed basic steps. While this discussion covered the fundamentals of step writing, it did not address the more complex types of steps that you frequently must write. Part Four turns to a discussion of these steps.

- Chapter 15 discusses lists, which are frequently used to present a series of items (typically actions or conditions) in a step.

- Chapter 16 discusses conditional statements (which are also known as logic statements). Steps written as conditional statements contain actions that are taken only if a condition is met (e.g., *IF the ambient temperature is less that 45°F, THEN turn on the heater*).

- Chapter 17 discusses logic tables, which can be used to present complex conditional information.

- Chapter 18 discusses warnings (which signal danger to workers), cautions (which signal danger to machinery), and notes (which provide supplemental information).

- Chapter 19 discusses cross-references, which direct transitions in procedures (i.e., send users to another step).

- Chapter 20 discusses the special types of steps, including steps that are performed out of sequence, steps that verify that a given condition is met, steps that present equally acceptable alternatives, steps that assist users in diagnosing a situation, and steps that must be performed immediately in an emergency.

- Chapter 21 discusses flowcharts.

In this chapter...

Use lists to organize and group information (15.1).

6.8 <u>IF</u> the voucher is <u>NOT</u> turned in by the deadline
<u>AND</u> the traveler still asks to be paid before he departs,
<u>THEN</u>:

1. Obtain verification from the traveler's manager that the trip is essential. ___

2. Obtain approval from your manager for special payment. ___

3. Ask accounting to cut a special check. ___

4. Inform travel processing of the actions you have taken. ___

CHAPTER
FIFTEEN

Lists

A list is a sequence of items. This chapter presents one principle regarding lists.

15.1 Use lists to group and organize information.

Summary

Present a sequence of three or more items (e.g., actions or conditions) in a list format. Introduce the list with an overview. Provide a placekeeping aid for each item in the list.

Lists "condense information into related groups that help readers to understand, organize, and remember information" (Mackh & Rew, 1991). Lists can present actions, conditions, criteria, equipment, and other types of information. Lists are pervasive; everyone uses them. William Horton (1991, p. 135) writes,

> Whether probing the limits of machine intelligence or making a shopping list, we rely on the simple organizing principle of the list. The list is fundamental to our language, even our experience of life…. Who has not relied on laundry lists, shopping lists, wish lists, to-do lists?

This section will discuss the format for lists and the use of overviews to introduce lists.

The format for lists

Lists can be embedded into a step or emphasized with white space. Compare Example 29 and Example 30. Example 31 presents another example of a list.

The formatted list in Example 30 is preferable when the list contains three or more items. According to Hartley (1985, p. 51), "Research suggests that readers prefer text which has lists or numbered sequences spaced out and separated, rather than run on in continuous text." Each item in the list is emphasized by being surrounded by white space so that readers can easily and efficiently scan through the list (Benson, 1985). Each item has its own placekeeping aid, reducing the chance that an item will be overlooked. When a sequence of three or more items must be presented in a procedure, that sequence should be presented in a list.

If a list contains only two items, then the use of white space to emphasize and differentiate the items is optional. If a list consists of actions that require placekeeping aids, then the list format should be considered for lists of even two items.

Overviews

It is important to provide a smooth transition into a list so that the user can deal effectively with the information presented (Mackh & Rew, 1991). This transition is created by the overview that introduces the list. In Example 30,

| 5.6 | Ensure that <u>all</u> of the following tests have been completed: SP-EG-105 series, SP-EG-100 series, and SP-EG-1 series. ____ |

Example 29. Embedded list. Compare this list with the list in Example 30.

5.6	Ensure that <u>all</u> of the following tests have been completed:
	• SP-EG-105 series ____
	• SP-EG-100 series ____
	• SP-EG-1 series ____

Example 30. White space used to format a list. In this list, each listed item stands out more clearly and has its own placekeeping aid.

6.34	Ensure that lights and switches are configured as follows:
	• Primary Circuit Breaker—switch is **on** ____
	• POWER ON 480 VAC—green light is **on** ____
	• POWER ON 120 VAC—green light and switch are **on** ____
	• Right door closed—amber light is **on** ____

Example 31. Another example of a list. Here, a list is used to present an equipment configuration.

the overview is *Ensure that <u>all</u> of the following tests have been completed:*. The overview "sets the stage" for the list, alerting users to the type of information that is to follow.

Overviews are analogous to the topic sentences in a paragraph. A topic sentence is the first sentence of a paragraph; it should introduce the idea that will be developed in the paragraph. An overview does much the same thing, introducing the items in the list. Thus, much of the research on topic sentences can be applied to lists. The general conclusion in the research is that effective topic sentences are useful to readers. Lorch and Lorch (1985) found that topic sentences aid in recall. Kieras (1978) found that topic sentences (followed by "connected, coherent sentences" [p. 13]) minimized memory load. Spyridakis (1989a, 1989b; Spyridakis & Standal, 1987) also found that topic sentences were beneficial. These findings indicate that effective overviews will aid in the comprehension and recall of listed items as well.

The overview should summarize the actions the user will be performing as the steps in the list are executed. Compare Example 32 and Example 33 below. In Example 32, the overview is simply the first item in the list. Example 33 uses a correct overview.

6.12   Remove the end plate from the column:
1. Drain the liquid into an approved container.   ____
2. Rope off the area.   ____
3. Post contamination warnings.   ____
4. Tell health physics that you have sealed off the area. ____

Example 32. Incorrect overview. Here, the "overview" is simply the first item in the list. Compare with Example 33.

6.12   Clear the plugged column by performing the following actions:
1. Remove the end plate from the column.   ____
2. Drain the liquid into an approved container.   ____
3. Rope off the area.   ____
4. Post contamination warnings.   ____
5. Tell health physics that you have sealed off the area. ____

Example 33. Correct overview. This overview correctly summarizes the list.

The overview should clearly indicate how many items in the list apply or should be performed. One possible approach for indicating this information is shown in Example 30, where the word <u>all</u> indicates that all tests must be performed. Similarly, the words <u>any</u> and <u>one</u> could be used to indicate that any test may be performed or that only one test should be performed. These words are underlined for emphasis, but they are not capitalized so that they do not detract from the emphasis of conditional terms. The overview should also end with a colon, so that it is apparent that the overview is related to the list that follows.

In this chapter...

Use conditional
terms accurately,
appropriately, and
consistently (16.2).

Use conditional statements
to present simple
conditional information
(16.1).

Use <u>AND</u> and <u>OR</u> to
join conditions, but
avoid complex logic
statements (16.3).

5.1   <u>IF</u> monthly revenue is below $50,000
      <u>AND</u> labor cost exceed 45% of total cost for that month,
      <u>THEN</u> complete Form 12-4B, Labor Cost Variance.

CHAPTER
SIXTEEN

Conditional Statements

Many steps unconditionally direct users to perform an action or a set of actions. In some instances, however, procedure writers must place restrictions on particular steps and direct users to perform an action only if specific conditions are met—if your work is done and your boss is gone, then go home early. These steps can be among the most difficult to understand in procedures. To prevent confusion, the step must clearly specify the conditions to be met and must identify the relationship between that condition and the action to be taken.

This chapter will explain how to present conditional statements using the rules of Boolean logic. Steps written in this manner can also be called logic statements. Conditional statements can unambiguously express actions that are contingent on conditions. Chapter 17 will present an alternative means of presenting complex conditional statements—logic tables. Logic tables may be less confusing to users who are not used to conditional statements. Chapter 21 will discuss a third alternative for presenting this information— flowcharts. Flowcharts present complex decision criteria more clearly than conditional statements.

16.1 Use conditional statements to present simple conditional information in procedures.

Summary

Conditional statements should be used to present simple conditional information in procedures. These statements describe a condition first and then describe the action to be taken if that condition is met. These statements use the conditional terms IF or WHEN to present the condition, THEN to present the action, and NOT to negate conditions. Conditional terms should be consistently emphasized throughout procedures.

Steps that consist of conditions and actions tend to be long and complex. In addition, different writers may convey the same conditional information in different ways. For example, a simple conditional statement can be written several ways, as shown in Example 34.

5.1   If the pretrip alarm for LO SG PRESS CH PRE-TRIP actuates, direct the secondary operator to lower the automatic steam generator-low set point.

❖ ❖ ❖

5.1   Direct the secondary operator to lower the automatic steam generator-low set point if the pretrip alarm for LO SG PRESS CH PRE-TRIP actuates.

❖ ❖ ❖

5.1   Direct the secondary operator to lower the automatic steam generator-low set point, but only if the pretrip alarm for LO SG PRESS CH PRE-TRIP actuates.

❖ ❖ ❖

5.1   Do not direct the secondary operator to lower the automatic steam generator-low set point unless the pretrip alarm for LO SG PRESS CH PRE-TRIP actuates.

❖ ❖ ❖

5.1   The secondary operator shall be directed to lower the automatic steam generator-low set point if the pretrip alarm for LO SG PRESS CH PRE-TRIP actuates.

Example 34. Different ways of writing the same step. Without the consistent use of conditional statements described in this chapter, a step could be written several different ways. This step instructs nuclear power plant operators to make an adjustment if an alarm sounds.

In order to decrease the complexity of conditional statements and make them more consistent, conditional statements should be written according to the rules of formal logic. Conditional terms are the specific words that indicate conditions and the subsequent actions to take when certain conditions exist. The conditional terms commonly used in procedures are <u>IF</u>, <u>WHEN</u>, <u>THEN</u>, <u>AND</u>, <u>OR</u>, and <u>NOT</u>. These terms derive from Boolean logic. George Boole (1815–1864) was an English mathematician and logician who devised this system of formal logic. There are many books devoted to discussions of formal logic, such as *Formal Logic: Its Scope and Limits* by Jeffrey (1967), for those who are interested in learning more.

If these conditional statements were rewritten according to the rules of formal logic, the various statements in Example 34 would all look something like this:

> <u>IF</u> the pretrip alarm for LO SG PRESS CH PRE-TRIP actuates,
> <u>THEN</u> direct the secondary operator to lower the automatic steam generator-low setpoint.

Writing conditional statements according to the rules of logic increases their consistency; there is only one way to construct the syntax of a given conditional statement according to these rules. Also, using a formal, structured approach to writing conditional statements decreases the likelihood that the statement will be misunderstood. The reader can apply the same rules when interpreting the step as the writer used when writing the step. Thus, it becomes easier for users to understand conditional information that is presented in conditional statements.

The most important rule to remember about conditional statements is that the condition always goes *before* the action. If the action comes first, the user is likely to perform the action regardless of whether the condition has been met. Here the action precedes the condition:

> Direct the secondary operator to lower the automatic steam generator-low set point
> <u>IF</u> the pretrip alarm for LO SG PRESS CH PRE-TRIP actuates.

If a user were to encounter this procedure step, he or she could read the first part of the step and direct the secondary operator to lower the automatic steam generator set point without realizing that the steam generator set point should only be lowered when a specific condition exists; that is, only if the pretrip alarm for LO SG PRESS CH PRE-TRIP actuates. Because carrying out an action at an inappropriate time may have serious consequences, *always* write the condition before the action in a conditional statement so that the user encounters the condition first.

> <u>IF</u> the pretrip alarm for LO SG PRESS CH PRE-TRIP actuates,
> <u>THEN</u> direct the secondary operator to lower the automatic steam generator-low setpoint.

Conditional terms should always be emphasized in procedures. As discussed in Section 12.1, emphasis on conditional terms actually serves more of a coding function. An approach common in the nuclear power industry is to use capitalization and underlining to emphasize conditional terms. Therefore, throughout this chapter (and this book) you will notice that the terms <u>IF</u>, <u>WHEN</u>, <u>THEN</u>, <u>AND</u>, <u>OR</u>, <u>IF NOT</u>, and <u>NOT</u> are capitalized and underlined to clearly indicate that a step is a conditional statement. Other emphasis techniques, such as those discussed in Chapter 12, could be used to emphasize these terms, but capitalization and underlining were chosen here as an example of one effective technique.

Regardless of which emphasis technique is chosen to make conditional terms stand out, the emphasis technique for conditional terms should be used *only* for conditional terms, not for other words in a procedure as well. For example, if conditional terms are capitalized and underlined and occasionally other non-conditional term words are also capitalized and underlined, the conditional terms are longer uniquely identified by the coding technique of capitalizing and underlining. A user could no longer look at a capitalized, underlined word in the procedure and identify it as quickly as a conditional term.

The use of white space can also add emphasis in conditional statements. By always having the conditional terms <u>IF</u>, <u>WHEN</u>, and <u>THEN</u> start new lines, the white space created by the line break adds emphasis and helps the user distinguish between the conditions and the actions in the conditional statement (Barfield, 1986; Hartley, 1982; Stevens, 1981). More information on the use of white space is presented in Section 10.2.

Emphasizing conditional terms clearly divides the conditional statement into conditions and actions. Example 35 demonstrates this effect. At a glance, the user can not only recognize a conditional statement, but can also quickly distinguish the various parts of the conditional statement. The user can clearly see the condition (*<u>IF</u> the status light is green,*) and the action (*<u>THEN</u> push the override button*) by virtue of the line break between the condition and the action. Dividing conditional statements into conditions and actions so that the user can readily identify the discrete parts of the statement becomes even more critical as conditional statements become more complex.

3.5   If the status light is green, then push the override button.   ____

◇ ◇ ◇

3.5   <u>IF</u> the status light is green,
<u>THEN</u> push the override button.   ____

Example 35. Use of emphasis in conditional statements. Capitalization, underlining, and line breaks make conditional terms, conditions, and action stand out.

Check conditional statements to ensure that the statements are clear and logically correct. In other words, the conditional statement must cover *every* eventuality for a particular condition and action. As you write a procedure, walk through the logic of all conditional statements (or a series of conditional statements), step by step. Ensure that conditional statements make sense and clearly direct users to take appropriate actions. For example, if a step tells users what to do if a temperature is above 70°F, another step should tell them what to do if temperature is below 70°F. A third step may be necessary as well, to tell operators what to do is temperature is equal to 70°F. (As Chapter 17 will discuss, this information can also be presented in a logic table.) A good way to test a sequence of logic statements is to try to present them in a flowchart, which will force you to consider all alternatives. Chapter 21 discusses flowcharts in more detail.

16.2 Use conditional terms accurately, appropriately, and consistently.

Summary

Each conditional term in a procedure has a specific meaning and a specific use. The conditional term <u>IF</u> signifies a condition that may or may not happen. <u>WHEN</u> signifies a condition that is very likely to occur. All steps containing <u>IF</u> and <u>WHEN</u> should also include the conditional term <u>THEN</u>. <u>THEN</u> signifies the action that should be taken if a condition is met. <u>THEN</u> should not be used to combine actions or items. The conditional term <u>NOT</u> is used to clearly distinguish a negated condition. Whenever possible, however, writers should phrase conditional information positively. Do not use <u>NOT</u> if another word can convey information more clearly. Finally, use the phrase <u>IF</u> <u>NOT</u> to express action to take if a condition is not met.

This section individually discusses the conditional terms used in procedures.

Using <u>IF</u>

Use <u>IF</u> to introduce conditions that may exist. In the condition <u>*IF*</u> *the bearing is worn*, bearing wear is a possible but not an expected situation.

<u>IF</u> should only be used at the beginning of conditional statements, otherwise the action will come before the condition; <u>IF</u> should not be hidden inside action steps. Example 36 illustrates why <u>IF</u> should not be hidden inside action steps.

> 9.6   Establish cooling water to secondary systems <u>IF</u> any
>   non-vital 4.16 kv buses are energized.   ____
>
>   ✧ ✧ ✧
>
> 9.6   <u>IF</u> any non-vital 4.16 kv buses are energized,
>   <u>THEN</u> establish cooling water to secondary systems.   ____

Example 36. Hidden Condition. The first step illustrates an <u>IF</u> hidden within an action step. The user is likely to perform the action first and then read the statement, only to discover that perhaps the action should not have been performed. The second step illustrates the correct use of <u>IF</u>.

Using <u>WHEN</u>

Use <u>WHEN</u> to introduce conditions that are expected to occur.

> 3.3   <u>WHEN</u> at least 3 class inverters are energized,
>   <u>THEN</u> reset <u>all</u> of the following:
>   • SIAS   ____
>   • CSAS   ____
>   • RAS   ____

Example 37. Conditional statement using <u>WHEN</u>. At least three class inverters are expected to be energized at some point during the procedure. When that happens, the user knows it is then time to reset the SIAS, CSAS, and RAS.

<u>WHEN</u> can actually have two related meanings. One meaning is that the user must stop and wait until the condition is met before continuing on with the action. The other meaning is that the user can expect the condition to occur, but the user does not have to wait for the condition to occur before continuing on with the procedure. It is important to give the user guidance about how to interpret <u>WHEN</u> in a procedure by including the phrase *Continue in this procedure* (or a similar phrase) in steps where the user can go on in the procedure while waiting for the condition to be met (see Example 38).

> 6.5   <u>WHEN</u> the STA arrives in the control room,
>   <u>THEN</u> direct him to monitor safety function status
>   and trending of plant parameters.   ____
>
>   Continue in this procedure.

Example 38. Instructions to continue. Here, users continue in the procedure if the STA (Shift Technical Advisor) has not arrived in the control room. They take the action when he arrives.

Note that the instructions to *Continue in this procedure* are separated from the conditional statement by one blank line. This white space emphasizes the instruction and helps ensure that the user will not overlook it.

You must use *Continue in this procedure* carefully because you are requiring the user to remember this step as he or she continues on to subsequent steps. When the phrase *Continue in this procedure* is appended to the conditional statement, the step becomes a *concurrent* step. Although they are essential at times, concurrent steps should be used sparingly because they require users to remember information. You should remind the user to perform the concurrent step on subsequent pages of the procedure. This reminder should appear in a consistent location (e.g., on the facing page) and should be emphasized so that it stands out. Section 20.1 discusses concurrent steps in greater detail.

As with IF, WHEN should only be used at the beginning of a conditional statement; WHEN should not be hidden inside action steps.

Using THEN

All steps containing IF and WHEN should also include THEN. This convention promotes consistency and uniquely distinguishes conditional statements from other kinds of steps. This convention also assures you that *every* conditional statement has an associated action and that the action is consistently identified.

> IF the level for any steam generator is less than 0% wr,
> THEN restore the level.

THEN should not be used to combine non-conditional items or to make run-on sentences. An incorrect use of THEN is *Place the mechanism into the bin, THEN close the lid*. In this case, there is no conditional information in the sentence, just two actions connected by THEN. Use of THEN in this situation is likely to be confusing.

Remember that the action introduced by THEN should begin on a new line.

Using NOT

The conditional term NOT is used to distinguish a negated condition.

> IF the diesel generator is NOT running,
> THEN direct the primary operator to manually start the diesel generator.

NOT is emphasized with capitalization and underlining to make sure that users do not misunderstand and read the condition as a positive statement. As a general rule of thumb, use NOT in place of a negating prefix such as *in-* or *un-* to negate a condition. For example, rather than say, *IF the demineralized water system is inadequate,* you should say, *IF the demineralized water system is NOT adequate*. The rationale for using NOT in this situation is that it clearly indicates that the condition is negated; *inadequate*, on the other hand, could be misread as *adequate*.

However, you should minimize the use of <u>NOT</u> because readers must often read and reread a negative statement to understand its meaning. Positively phrased sentences are usually easier to understand and less prone to misinterpretation (Wason, 1959, 1961). Therefore, whenever possible, phrase conditions positively. When one word that does not begin with *in-* or *un-* can denote the negative state (such as saying *<u>IF</u> the valve is closed* instead of saying *<u>IF</u> the valve is <u>NOT</u> open*) you should use the one word instead of <u>NOT</u> to negate the condition. Section 5.4 discusses the presentation of negative information in more detail.

Using <u>IF</u> <u>NOT</u>

So far this section has discussed how to write simple conditional statements that direct a user to take an action when a condition is met. When you must write a conditional statement that directs a user to take action when a condition is *not* met, you should use the conditional term <u>IF</u> <u>NOT</u>. The term <u>IF</u> <u>NOT</u> allows you to express two actions that depend on the same condition: one action is performed if the condition *is* met and the other is performed if the condition *is not* met (see Example 39).

3.32   <u>IF</u> the condenser is available,
          <u>THEN</u> use the SBCS to reduce RCS temperature and
          steam generator pressure.   ____

          <u>IF NOT</u>, <u>THEN</u> use the ADVs to reduce RCS temperature
          and steam generator pressure.   ____

Example 39. Use of <u>IF NOT</u>. <u>IF NOT</u> introduces a contingent action for reducing coolant temperature and pressure in a nuclear power plant that is taken if the preferred piece of equipment (the condenser) is not available.

Although <u>IF</u> <u>NOT</u> is useful for writing some conditional statements, it should be used only for simple statements that contain one condition and one action. Using <u>IF</u> <u>NOT</u> after multiple conditions or multiple actions may cause a user to misinterpret the conditional statement and make an error. For example, the term <u>IF</u> <u>NOT</u> should not have been used in Example 40.

10.7   <u>IF</u> the power for the trick head system is off,
          <u>THEN</u> perform the following:

          1. Plug in the 120 V ac power.   ____
          2. Record the date and time at which power was applied   ____
             <u>IF NOT</u>, <u>THEN</u> energize the main busses.

Example 40. Incorrect use of <u>IF NOT</u>. <u>IF NOT</u> should not be used in conditional statements containing multiple actions.

Given this conditional statement, the user might ask, "IF NOT what?" It is not immediately clear that the IF NOT in this step applies to the trickle head system being off. Literally, the step is saying, *IF the trickle head system is NOT off,* but you can see how a user might become confused and make an error in executing this step. The term IF NOT should not have been used here because two listed actions separate the IF NOT action from the condition and require the user to not only remember the original condition but also to interpret the double negative *not off*. A clearer way to convey this information would be to dispense with IF NOT altogether and write two steps, as shown in Example 41.

10.7   IF the power for the trick head system is off,
       THEN perform the following:
       1. Plug in the 120 V ac power.
       2. Record the date and time at which power was applied   ____

10.8   IF the power for the trickle head system is on,
       THEN energize the main busses.   ____

Example 41. Avoiding IF NOT in complex steps. Here, Example 40 is corrected by breaking it into two steps.

Remember that IF NOT is best used only for simple conditional statements. If multiple actions separate the IF NOT action from the original condition, or if the IF NOT action requires the user to interpret a double negative based on the original condition, users may easily become confused and make an error in executing the step.

16.3 Use the conditional terms AND or OR separately to combine conditions when necessary, but avoid complex sequences of conditional terms.

Summary

AND and OR combine two conditions. AND indicates that all conditions must be met before action is taken. Usually the conditional term OR is inclusive in procedures and is used to combine conditions for statements in which one or more than one condition must be met before an associated action can be carried out. Writers should maintain the distinction between AND and *and* as well as the distinction between OR and *or*. Finally, to keep conditional statements from becoming too long and complex, avoid using AND and OR in the same conditional statement.

This section discusses the difference between the conditional terms AND and OR. The section also discusses when each of these terms is appropriate to use in conditional statements.

Using <u>AND</u>

If you want to combine conditions in a conditional statement to indicate that *all* of the conditions must be met before the associated action can be carried out, use the term <u>AND</u>. When you use <u>AND</u> in this way you are telling the user to ensure that all of the conditions are met before performing the action.

> <u>IF</u> both 4.16 kv vital buses are de-energized
> <u>AND</u> the 525 kv grid is de-energized,
> <u>THEN</u> direct an operator to perform Attachment 2 of this procedure, Battery Load Control.

In the example above, two conditions must be checked: the status of the 4.16 kv vital buses and the status of the 525 kv grid. *Both* conditions must be met before the action can be carried out. Each condition begins on a new line (Felker et al., 1981).

It can be useful to distinguish between the conditional term <u>AND</u> and the conjunction *and*. <u>AND</u> is used to join two conditions when each condition is a complete clause. (A clause, as discussed in Section 5.1, contains a subject and a verb phrase.) In all other instances, *and* is a conjunction. Example 42 demonstrates the correct use of <u>AND</u>.

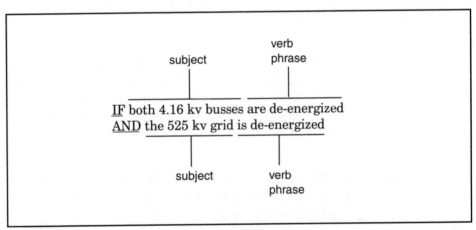

Example 42. Use of <u>AND</u> to join complete clauses. The two conditions joined by <u>AND</u> are complete clauses, meaning that each contains a subject and a verb phrase.

Now consider the following example, which fails to use <u>AND</u> according to this rule:

> <u>IF</u> a safety injection has actuated
> <u>AND</u> pressurizer pressure is greater than 300 psia
> <u>AND</u> stable,
> <u>THEN</u> stop <u>all</u> operating HPSI and CS pumps.

Here, the third "condition" is not a complete clause—it is simply the word *stable*. Hence, it should be introduced by the conjunction *and*:

> IF a safety injection has actuated
> AND pressurizer pressure is greater than 300 psia and stable,
> THEN stop all operating HPSI and CS pumps.

Example 43 shows how the second condition is now a complete clause.

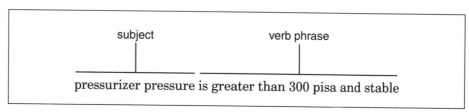

Example 43. Use of *and* in a compound object. This condition is one complete clause. Confusion may arise because the clause includes *and*, but *and* does not join two complete clauses.

There are two advantages to distinguishing between AND and *and*. The first is that if *and* is always capitalized and underlined, then the procedure will quickly become cluttered with ANDs (and ORs, if they are treated the same way). Fully capitalizing and underlining AND will detract from effective true emphasis (due to overuse) and from effective coding, because AND no longer consistently signals the beginning of a condition.

The second advantage to distinguishing between AND and *and* is that failure to do so fragments information that should be grouped. Consider this example again:

> IF a safety injection has actuated
> AND pressurizer pressure is greater than 300 psia
> AND stable,
> THEN stop all operating HPSI and CS pumps.

Use of AND separates *pressurizer pressure is greater than 300 psia* from *stable*, when these words belong together. In other words, the example above makes it look like the user is checking three things, when in fact he is checking only two: (1) the status of safety injection and (2) pressurizer pressure. When the procedure writer distinguishes between AND and *and*, the step clearly conveys this information.

Finally, whenever you have three or more conditions, use a list format rather than multiple ANDs. A user can more clearly identify a list as a group of related items (NRC, 1982). Lists are discussed further in Section 16.1.

Using <u>OR</u>

The conditional term <u>OR</u> is used in conditional statements when only one condition must be met before the associated action can be carried out:

As with <u>AND</u> and *and*, there is a distinction between the conditional term <u>OR</u> and the conjunction *or*. <u>OR</u> is used only in conditional statements according to the rules of logic. Because <u>OR</u> is a conditional term, it should always be emphasized. The conjunction *or* should not be emphasized.

8.9	<u>IF</u> Reactor Power Cutback System Trouble, window 4A11A, is lit <u>OR</u> the AUTO ACTUATE OUT OF SERVICE light is <u>NOT</u> lit, <u>THEN</u> GO TO Reactor Power Cutback, 41OP-1SF04.

Example 44. Combining conditions with <u>OR</u>. In this case, two conditions must be checked: the status of the Reactor Power Cutback System Trouble, window 4A11A, and the AUTO ACTUATE OUT OF SERVICE light. If either condition is met, the action should be carried out. If they are not met, the user uses another procedure.

Also, keep in mind the difference between an inclusive and an exclusive <u>OR</u>. An inclusive <u>OR</u> means that an action can be carried out when one or more than one condition is met. If there are two conditions combined with an inclusive <u>OR</u>, it does not matter whether one or both of the conditions are met. As long as at least one condition is met, the action can be carried out. On the other hand, an exclusive <u>OR</u> means that either one condition or the other, but not both, must be met. An exclusive <u>OR</u> excludes the possibility that more than one condition can be met before an action is carried out. The following table illustrates that distinction.

First condition	Second condition	Inclusive <u>OR</u>	Exclusive <u>OR</u>
true	true	take action	do not take action
true	false	take action	take action
false	true	take action	take action
false	false	do not take action	do not take action

Ordinarily, we can distinguish between inclusive <u>OR</u> and exclusive <u>OR</u> by the context in which the word *or* is used. For example, when a waiter asks, "Would you like something to drink or an appetizer?" you know that you could have a drink or an appetizer or both. The inclusive <u>OR</u> is being used in this case. But when the waiter asks, "Would you like a baked potato or rice?" then you know an exclusive <u>OR</u> is being used. In this case the waiter is saying that you may have a potato, or rice, but not both. However, procedure users should not rely on context to interpret <u>OR</u>, especially in the operation of complex technological systems. Because there is seldom reason to use the exclusive <u>OR</u> to join two conditions, we recommend that you only use inclusive <u>OR</u> in procedure conditional statements. In other words, a conditional statement using <u>OR</u> in a procedure should always mean that one or more than one condition must be met in order for the associated action to be carried out. Consistent use of <u>OR</u> will eliminate confusion and reliance on context.

Finally, whenever you have three or more contingencies, use a list format rather than multiple <u>OR</u>s. A user can more clearly identify a list as a group of related items (NRC, 1982). Lists are discussed further in Section 15.1.

Combining <u>AND</u> and <u>OR</u>

Conditional statements can be difficult to interpret if they are long and complex. In order to keep conditional statements short and simple, break a long, complicated step into more than one logic statement if necessary, or use a logic table (Chapter 17) or a flowchart (Chapter 21). A series of short, unambiguous conditional statements is better than one long, complex, difficult-to-understand conditional statement.

In particular, avoid using <u>AND</u> and <u>OR</u> in the same conditional statement. When <u>AND</u> and <u>OR</u> appear together in the same statement, the user may interpret the statement in two different ways. The conditional statement below illustrates this point. The context is that you are driving to the store and must decide whether to put the top of your convertible down.

> <u>IF</u> it is a beautiful day,
> <u>AND</u> you want to impress your neighbors,
> <u>OR</u> the car needs airing,
> <u>THEN</u> put the car top down.

Borrowing a technique from algebra, we can use parentheses to indicate the two ways to read this statement:

> <u>IF</u> (it is a beautiful day <u>AND</u> you want to impress your neighbors),
> <u>OR</u> the car needs airing,
> <u>THEN</u> put the car top down.

> <u>IF</u> it is a beautiful day
> <u>AND</u> (you want to impress your neighbors <u>OR</u> the car needs airing)
> <u>THEN</u> put the car top down.

This complex conditional statement is ambiguous. The user might wonder, "Should I put the top down on a cloudy day?" Using the first interpretation, the answer would be yes, if the car needs airing, put the top down regardless of the weather. However, using the second interpretation, the answer is no because it must be a beautiful day in order to put the car top down. In the preceding example, the consequences of choosing the wrong interpretation may not be very serious—at worst the user might get wet if the cloudy weather turns to rain. However, in many industrial or business settings a misinterpretation could have very serious consequences.

To avoid writing ambiguous or confusing conditional statements, break complex conditional statements into several simple conditional statements. Assuming the second interpretation is correct, the previous example might be broken into the following simple conditional statements, as shown in Example 45.

3.1   <u>IF</u> it is a beautiful day
        <u>AND</u> you want to impress your neighbors
        <u>THEN</u> put the car top down and GO TO Step 3.3.   ____

3.2   <u>IF</u> it is a beautiful day
        <u>AND</u> your car needs airing,
        <u>THEN</u> put the car top down.   ____

3.3   Drive to the store.   ____

Example 45. Presenting conditional information in multiple steps. It may take more than one step to describe actions that are based on complex conditions. The reference to *GO TO Step 3.3* is necessary because if it is a beautiful day and you are driving your car, there is no need to perform Step 3.2—you already have the top down.

These two simple statements clearly tell the user what actions to take. In addition, by seeing the long, complex conditional statement broken into two simpler statements, the user realizes that he or she need not read the second conditional statement if the conditions of the first statement are met. Example 46 illustrates that both statements lead to the same end point, but the user need only take one of the conditional statement paths to get to that end point.

The inclusion of the instructions to *GO TO Step* 3.3 points out an important fact—you must walk through the logic of the procedure, trying *all* permutations of conditions, to determine that your steps make sense. This can be a complex and subtle process but it is very important.

Example 46 also shows how these two steps can be presented in a flowchart. There is another way to present this information, as shown in Example 47—in a logic table. The next chapter will discuss logic tables.

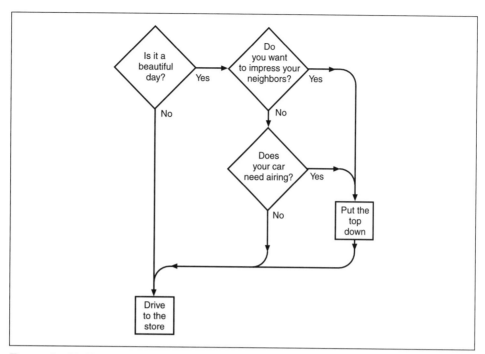

Example 46. Presenting conditional information in a flowchart. This flowchart illustrates that two separate conditional statements can lead to the same end point. The user need only follow one of the conditional statements to the end point.

3.1   Perform the appropriate action from the table below.

Is it a beautiful day	Does the car need airing?	Want to impress your neighbors?	THEN . . .
yes	yes	yes	put the top down
yes	yes	no	put the top down
yes	no	yes	put the top down
yes	no	no	do <u>NOT</u> put the top down
no	yes	yes	do <u>NOT</u> put the top down
no	yes	no	do <u>NOT</u> put the top down
no	no	yes	do <u>NOT</u> put the top down
no	no	no	do <u>NOT</u> put the top down

3.1   Drive to the store.

Example 47. Presenting conditional information in a logic table. Logic tables, which are discussed in the next chapter, are another way to present conditional information.

In this chapter...

Consider using logic tables
to present complex
conditional information
(17.1).

Simplify the
format of logic
tables (17.2).

12.9 Perform the appropriate action from the table below:

IF coolant level is...	THEN...
less than 10 inches wr	open PV-21
between 10 and 18 inches wr, inclusive	open PV-22
greater than 18 inches wr	open PV-23

CHAPTER
SEVENTEEN

Logic Tables

Conditional statements, as discussed in the previous chapter, can unambiguously present decision criteria. However, to the uninitiated, they can appear foreign. One solution that may be more appropriate for audiences that may be confused by conditional statement syntax is logic tables. Tables are familiar to nearly everyone.

> For over 5,500 years people have used tables to organize complex information into neat rows and columns. The basic grid structure of the table permeates technological civilizations which march by rank and file and lay out their cities in a grid of blocks. No wonder, then, that tables are a natural way to organize many separate pieces of information…. (Horton, 1991, p. 140)

17.1 Consider using logic tables to present complex conditional information.

Summary

Logic tables may be easier for some users to understand than a sequence of conditional statements. Logic tables allow users to quickly scan information and locate relevant information. A logic table can duplicate conditional statement syntax, or present a matrix of alternatives.

There are two types of logic tables: logic tables that use conditional statement syntax and logic tables that present a matrix of alternatives. Because of the many ways that logic tables can be designed, the distinction between these two types of tables is not always clear.

Logic tables that use conditional statement syntax

One type of logic table duplicates the syntax of a conditional statement in table form, as shown in Example 48.

<u>IF</u> the insurance is...	<u>THEN</u> GO TO the following procedure...
commercial insurance	Follow-up with commercial insurance (FU-1)
self-pay	Follow-up with parents (FU-2)

Example 48. Logic table using conditional statement syntax. This logic table is a restatement of the two conditional statements in Example 49.

3.1	<u>IF</u> the patient has commercial insurance, <u>THEN</u> GO TO Follow-up with commercial insurance (FU-1). ____
3.2	<u>IF</u> the patient is self-pay, <u>THEN</u> GO TO Follow-up with parents (FU-2). ____

Example 49. Equivalent conditional statements. These two steps present the same information as the table in Example 48.

The advantage of the logic table in Example 48 is that it presents the same information as the two steps in Example 49, but is simpler. Users can quickly scan the alternatives in the left column of the logic table. They cannot scan the steps as quickly, and the relationship between Steps 3.1 and 3.2 is not immediately evident.

Logic tables can be made more complex by adding additional columns, as shown in Example 50.

4.1   Sort the return mail: ____

IF you receive...	THEN GO TO...	because...
a copy of the front of the envelope	Step 4.2	the post office has corrected the address and forwarded the mail to the recipient
an undelivered envelope	Step 5.1	the post office was unable to correct the address and the recipient has not received the mail

Example 50. Complex logic table. In addition to presenting the action that should be taken, this logic table also provides supplemental information.

When creating a logic table of this type, there should be a column for each condition and a column for each action. Generally, you should use the logic terms discussed in Chapter 16 to differentiate the conditions from the actions. However, sometimes headings can be more clearly presented without using logic terms; compare Example 51 and Example 52.

3.3   Enter the account type: ____

For...	enter...
an inpatient account	IP
an outpatient account	OP
a unitized account	U

Example 51. Logic table that does not use logic terms. This logic table states information more concisely than the table in Example 52.

3.3   Enter the account type: ____

IF the account is...	THEN enter ...
an inpatient account	IP
an outpatient account	OP
a unitized account	U

Example 52. Forced use of logic terms. Compared to Example 51, the headings in this table are wordier. The table in Example 51 is preferred, although this is acceptable.

Logic tables that present a matrix of alternatives

For complex combinations of conditions, sometimes the only practical way to design a logic table is to include a column for each condition, and then include enough rows in the table to cover all combinations of conditions. The logic table in Example 47 (page 143) is designed in this manner. This format can lead to difficulties, however, because it requires users to pick the correct combination of *Yeses* and *Noes*.

17.2 Simplify the format of logic tables.

Summary

Simplify the design of logic tables. Avoid unnecessary grids and shading.

Earlier in this book, we included a quote from Strunk and White (1979, p. 23):

> A sentence should contain no unnecessary words, a paragraph no unnecessary sentences for the same reason that a drawing should have no unnecessary lines and a machine no unnecessary parts. This requires not that the writer make all his sentences short, or that he avoid all detail and treat his subjects only in outline, but that *every* word tell.

This is a plea to write concisely. Edward Tufte, in his book *The Visual Display of Quantitative Information* (1983), makes a similar plea to design graphics, such as tables, concisely. Tufte discusses non-data ink, which is ink on the page that does not present information. Non-data ink is clutter, or visual noise. It not only fails to impart information, but can obscure information by needlessly complicating a graphic image. In Tufte's world of minimalist graphics, heavy gridlines, three-dimensional effects, and useless embellishments[32] are examples of non-data ink.

Consider the two tables in Example 53. The upper table includes a grid and borders; the lower table does not. What information do the borders and grid add? The border indicates the boundaries of the table, and the grid clearly separates one cell in the table from another. Yet, the lower table is designed in a way to accomplish the same things, without using a border or grid. The table is in a different font than the text—Arial. Use of this font essentially establishes the boundaries of the table: anything that is in the Arial font is in the table, anything that is in the Century Schoolbook font is not in the table. The cells of the table are separated with white space, so users can easily tell what information is in what cell. Further, the rows are left-aligned, which helps the eye distinguish the columns. The only grid is a horizontal line that separates the table headings (which are further distinguished by being bold) from the body of the table.

---

[32]See any graph on the front page of the newspaper *USA Today* for examples of three-dimensional effects and useless embellishments.

3.3   Align valves as shown in the table below.

	MSV-1	MSV-2	MSV-3
For system startup...	Open	Open	Closed
For system operation...	Closed	Closed	Open
For system shutdown...	Closed	Closed	50% Closed

✧ ✧ ✧

3.3   Align valves as shown in the table below.

	MSV-1	**MSV-2**	**MSV-3**
For system startup...	Open	Open	Closed
For system operation...	Closed	Closed	Open
For system shutdown...	Closed	Closed	50% Closed

Example 53. Table design. The table on the bottom, which is visually simpler, is preferable to the more complex table on top.

The bottom table in Example 53 is superior. It presents the same information in simpler, cleaner manner.

In this chapter...

Warnings and cautions must identify a single hazard and the consequences of that hazard (18.3).

Do not include actions in warnings or cautions (18.2).

Include warnings and cautions in procedures (18.1).

Place warnings and cautions before the steps to which they apply (18.5).

Present warnings and cautions in a unique format (18.4).

WARNING: Do not remove the access panel. Fluids inside are very hot and under high pressure.

Caution: The pressurizer pump will be damaged if allowed to run while there is a leak in the pressurizer system, because the flow will drop and the pump will not be adequately cooled.

6.1 Look through the sight glass in the access panel for evidence of a leak.

Use notes to present supplemental information (18.6).

Note: *Pressure oscillation of ± 20 psi for up to 10 minutes after increasing pump speed is normal.*

6.2 <u>IF</u> there is no evidence of a leak,
<u>THEN</u> increase pressurizer pump speed to 95%.

CHAPTER

EIGHTEEN

Warnings, Cautions, and Notes

Warnings alert users to potential hazards that may result in death or injury to workers or the public. Cautions alert users to potential hazards that may damage machinery or equipment. Notes call attention to important supplemental information that may enhance a user's understanding and performance of the procedure.

18.1 Include warnings and cautions in procedures.

Summary

Inadequate or missing warnings and cautions may result in injury or even death. Warnings and cautions are important because users understand operations without understanding the hazards associated with those operations. Also, we typically do not perceive or estimate risk accurately. Warnings and cautions should not be overused, however.

Warnings and cautions are the most critical type of supporting information in procedures. Because procedure users may deal directly with hazardous equipment, work in hazardous situations, take actions that affect the safety of others, or take actions that may have adverse business consequences, they must be informed of any dangers involved in these activities. This information is provided in warnings and cautions. Inadequate warnings and cautions may result in injury or death. It is your responsibility as a procedure writer to include proper warnings and cautions in procedures.

The importance of warnings and cautions

Don't assume that procedure users will know to avoid dangerous situations. Although users may have enough knowledge to operate a system, their knowledge may not include adequate awareness of the hazards involved in system operation. Further, empirical research has demonstrated that people typically do not estimate or perceive risk accurately. When individuals are asked to make judgments about risk-related events, they typically underestimate the risk for events in which they lack actual personal experience and overestimate the risk for events that receive much media attention (Slovic, Fischhoff, & Lichtenstein, 1982). Also, when making judgments about risk, individuals often use rules of thumb (heuristics) that result in their excluding important available information about risk (Payne, 1976). Even when people are very familiar with a task, they can underestimate the risk associated with the task. In fact, people are likely to minimize the risk of carrying out a very familiar task. It is, therefore, inappropriate and possibly dangerous to rely on the user to know or to figure out the potential risks in operating a system. Proper warnings and cautions must be included in procedures.

You as the procedure writer cannot include proper warnings and cautions in a procedure without a complete understanding of the potential hazards inherent in the tasks, systems, and processes covered by the procedure. Therefore, you (or another appropriate person) must perform an exhaustive investigation to identify all of the potential hazards for each procedure step. Input for this investigation should come from procedure users, technical specialists, subject matter experts (including operations), and all available documentation (including drawings, descriptions, technical specifications, safety documents, administrative documents, accident reports, and so on).

Minimizing warnings and cautions

An automobile owners manual (for a car that will go unnamed) includes the following warnings, among many others:

- "Do not leave the vehicle unattended with the key in the ignition lock. Always lock all doors and take the key."

- "Do not leave children unattended in the vehicle, especially with access to vehicle keys. Unsupervised use of the keys can result in starting of the engine or use of vehicle systems such as the power windows, etc. which could result in serious personal injury."

- "Do not leave children inside the vehicle unsupervised. If the locking knobs of all doors are depressed, the vehicle will be locked. In an emergency, it would be impossible to open the doors from the outside without the key."

- "Do not stick anything on the windows or windshield that may interfere with the driver's vision."

Although these are certainly important concerns, one could argue that this manual is simply telling people things that they already knew—if you lock all the doors, you can't get back in the car without the key.

These examples are taken from the first few pages of the manual. After encountering these warnings, a reader might decide that the warnings really aren't telling him anything he doesn't already know and he may begin to skip the warnings. People do that—they adopt reading strategies that they believe will allow them to extract the most important information from a document in the least time. They do not read things that they do believe are unimportant. In doing so, they may skip warnings such as the following, which also appear in the manual:

- "Accident statistics have shown that children are generally safer in the rear seat area than in the front seating position."

- "Never touch the radiator fan, it is temperature controlled and may switch on suddenly."[33]

If a procedure includes too many unimportant or irrelevant warnings or cautions, users may ignore the important or relevant warnings or cautions. Carefully consider each warning or caution. Omit those that are not necessary. This may call for some hard decisions, but you should always consider the cost of the warning or caution (that it clutters the procedure and may de-emphasize important information) as well as the benefit.

18.2 Ensure that actions do not appear in warnings and cautions.

Summary

Including actions in warnings and cautions may confuse users. Actions in warnings and cautions may also increase the likelihood that a user will overlook an action. Finally, to ensure that you do not "hide" an action in a warning or caution, use the active voice, negative imperative mood for warnings and cautions.

One of the most difficult aspects of writing effective warnings and cautions is writing them so that they do not include actions that belong in steps instead. The main reason we do not include actions in warnings or cautions is so that actions are not overlooked. Further, steps offer a better format for presenting actions. Steps include placekeeping aids and step numbers to help users track their place in the procedure.

---

[33]The run-on sentence is theirs.

Why actions do not belong in cautions

The example below shows an incorrect caution that includes an action.

Caution: <u>WHEN</u> dc voltage has increased to at least 100 V dc, <u>THEN</u> close the input breaker. Closing the input breaker sooner may cause a power surge on the inverter.

Users reading the caution in the above example might not recognize the information as an action. When users see a caution they expect to see supplementary information, not instructional information. Therefore, actions presented in warnings and cautions may confuse users and may increase the possibility of users making errors (Fuchs, Engelschall, & Imlay, 1981).

The action should be presented in a step. If the user must be alerted to a potential hazard associated with performing that step, the information on the potential hazard should be written as an active voice, negative imperative statement *above* the step. Example 54 shows the corrected caution and step.

Caution: Do not close the input breaker until dc voltage has increased to at least 100 V dc; otherwise a power surge on the inverter may occur.

4.3   <u>WHEN</u> dc voltage has increased to at least 100 V dc,
        <u>THEN</u> close the input breaker.   ____

Example 54. Integration of a caution and a step. Here, the action is presented in a step while the cautionary information related to the step is presented in the caution before the step.

Although the caution in the example above is written as an imperative, it is not an action. It instructs the user *not* to do something; in other words, it instructs the user to leave things the way they are—to leave the breaker open. Hence, it is a negative imperative. The step below the caution provides explicit instructions on when to close the input breaker during the procedure. The caution was not the place to tell the user about the action. Thus, a step was added to tell the user when to close the input breaker.

Although Section 5.4 stated that negative statements are often more difficult to understand, warnings and cautions often justify the use of negative statements. Be careful, however, to avoid using double negatives, such as *Do not leave the valve unlocked*, and other convoluted negative constructions in warnings and cautions. The alternative phrasing, *Lock the valve*, is much easier to understand. Further, being able to rewrite the negative statement *Do not leave the valve unlocked* as the positive statement *Lock the valve* indicates that it may be an action belonging in a step format rather than in a caution.

Using the passive voice

Often, writers try using the passive voice to "hide" an action in a warning or caution. For example, a writer may try to eliminate any hint of an action by writing:

WARNING: Bus bars and circuit boards inside the battery charger access doors may be energized, presenting an electrocution hazard.

The warning above is written in the passive voice, as evidenced by the verb phrase *may be energized*. In this particular warning, the object is omitted—the bus bars and circuit boards may be energized, but by *what?* As you may remember from Section 5.3, objects are often omitted from passive sentences if the object is unimportant. Here, the bus bars and circuit boards are energized by the cables that run to them; because this information is not important, the procedure writer omitted it.

But, because the object is omitted from this sentence, the user reading the procedure is left to fill in the missing information. A user could assume that the object was *you* (i.e., himself or herself) and could interpret the caution as an instruction to energize the bus bars and circuit boards—*You may energize the bus bars and circuit boards.*

The example below addresses the potential for this type of error by explicitly wording the warning as an instruction not to touch the bus bars or circuit boards.

WARNING: Do not touch the bus bars and circuit boards inside the battery charger access doors because they may be energized, presenting an electrocution hazard.

Again, we have returned to the negative imperative as the best form for presenting this type of information in a warning or caution.[34] The previous example points out the dangers of using the passive voice in a warning (or anywhere). Although there will be instances when the passive voice is the best way of presenting information, there are other situations where it can get you into trouble. Thus, you should avoid the temptation to use the passive voice to hide an action in a warning or caution because you may introduce the potential for user error and confusion.

Further, if a writer casts an action as a passive sentence in a caution, the action may still be there, it is just more difficult to see because it's implied.

---

[34]The passive clause still exists, but the caution has been clarified by the addition of the imperative instruction.

So, in addition to still presenting an action, the caution is confusing. By using the passive voice, the writer has not solved anything. He has just made the caution more difficult to understand. Look at the following two cautions.

Caution: Temperature must be maintained above 185°F or the solution will gel.

Caution: Maintain temperature above 185°F or the solution will gel.

The writer of the first caution used the passive voice and in doing so mistook a passively phrased action for cautionary information. In reality, this caution does not warn the user of any potential hazard. Instead it directs the user to take action. Rewriting the caution in the active voice, as shown in the second example, allows the writer to clearly see that the caution is really an action step and therefore should be presented in a step.

18.3 Warnings and cautions must identify a single hazard, the consequences of the hazard, and any critical time constraints.

Summary

Complete warnings and cautions identify the hazard, the consequences of the hazard, and time constraints associated with the hazard. Ensure that each warning, caution, and note deals with only one topic.

The best way to avoid something is to know exactly what you are trying to avoid. Unless sufficient information is provided in a warning or caution, the procedure user may not understand and appreciate the risk related to a hazard. At a minimum, each warning and caution must identify the hazard and the consequences of the hazard. Time considerations may also be critical for some hazards. In such cases, the warnings or cautions for those hazards must state important time considerations (Ballard & Rode-Perkins, 1987). Harris and Wiklund (1989) suggest that more threatening warnings and cautions are perceived more effectively. Therefore, do not minimize a potential hazard when writing warnings and cautions. If, for example, death from electrocution is a potential consequence, the warning should explicitly state that the user may die if the warning is not followed. The following warning exemplifies a complete warning.

WARNING: Charging or discharging batteries generates hydrogen gas. Do not smoke, use open flames, or create arcs or sparks in the vicinity of batteries because an explosion may occur.

Notice how information is arranged in the above warning. The warning identifies the hazard first: *Charging or discharging batteries generates hydrogen gas.* The warning further describes the hazard by listing dangerous activities. Note that this description is an imperative instruction telling the user what not to do: *Do not smoke, use open flames, or create arcs or sparks in the vicinity of batteries because an explosion may occur.* This description is an example of the active voice, negative imperative mood. The warning concludes by specifying the hazard—an explosion.

Also, make sure that the action steps below warnings and cautions are clear and concise. Avoid wordiness in the steps that may make the intent of the warning or caution more difficult to recognize or understand.

Finally, each warning and caution must address only one topic. Presenting only one topic in a warning or caution helps the user understand the intent of the warning or caution better and assists the user in recalling or checking the cautionary information presented in a step. The example below illustrates how confusing warnings and cautions become if more than one topic is addressed.

WARNING: Battery electrolyte contains sulfuric acid and will cause burning if it comes in contact with skin or eyes. Do not wear loose clothing near moving equipment.

Given this warning, the user would not quickly understand which potential hazard was more immediate or what steps to take to avoid the hazard. He may even become confused trying to determine the relationship between the two hazards. This warning should be rewritten into two separate warnings: one addressing the hazard of battery electrolytes coming in contact with the skin or eyes and the other addressing the hazard of wearing loose clothing near moving equipment.

18.4 Present warnings and cautions in a unique format.

Summary

Warnings and cautions should be formatted to draw attention to their critical nature. Clearly differentiating warnings and cautions from the rest of the procedure reduces the effort required to determine the purpose of the warning or caution. Also, consider the user's expectations when deciding whether to consistently call potential hazards involving personnel or equipment only cautions or only warnings. Ask yourself whether the user would expect you to distinguish between the two types of hazards.

This section discusses the use of a unique format for warnings and cautions. The section also discusses why a writer must adhere to user expectations when deciding whether to use the terms warning or caution for information on hazards.

Use a unique format

Warnings and cautions in a procedure must be uniquely emphasized to draw attention to their critical nature (Ballard & Rode-Perkins, 1987). (Section 12.1 discusses emphasis techniques.) Some evidence (McCarthy et al., 1984) suggests that people do not pay much attention to warnings. For example, people generally do not read warning labels on products or pay attention to a flight attendant's preflight briefing in commercial air travel. One way to draw the user's attention to warnings and cautions is to present them in a unique format. Using a unique emphasis technique to clearly differentiate warnings and cautions from other parts of the procedure will help users recognize the critical nature of warnings and cautions. If users know what kind of information to expect when they see a specific format, they can more easily and quickly process the information presented.

Simple ways to emphasize warnings and cautions include using a different font, centering, bolding, or underlining the word *warning* or *caution*. Such emphasis will help users to quickly and easily recognize that cautionary information is being presented. Another formatting technique that can emphasize warnings and cautions is to use white space to separate the warning or caution from the flow of action steps in the procedure. Section 10.2 presents more information about the use of white space as an emphasis technique. Boxing around a warning or caution can also be used as a means of separation.

The distinction between warnings and cautions

So far this discussion has made a distinction between warnings, which describe hazards to people, and cautions, which discuss hazards to equipment. However, some facilities may choose not to differentiate between warnings and cautions. In some procedures only the term *caution* or the term *warning* may be used to alert users to both personnel and equipment hazards.

Always present information about hazards in accordance with the users' expectations. At some facilities users expect procedures to differentiate between hazards to people (i.e., warnings) and hazards to equipment (i.e., cautions). Users at other facilities, however, may expect the term *warning* to cover all hazards, while the term *caution* is never used (perhaps because their procedures do not deal with physically hazardous situations). Be sure to keep the users' expectations in mind when you are deciding how to present information on hazards. Whatever choice is made, it should be applied consistently across *all* procedures.

18.5 Place warnings and cautions on the same page as and immediately before the step to which they apply.

Summary

Place warnings and cautions immediately before the step to which they refer to increase the probability that the user will read the warning or caution. Also, to help the user find and recall a warning or caution more easily, place warnings and cautions on the same page as the related step. Repeat warnings or cautions for all applicable steps of the procedure.

Warnings and cautions must be placed immediately prior to the step to which they refer (Fuchs, Engelschall, & Imlay, 1981; Wogalter, Godfrey, & Fontenelle, 1987). Placing the warning or caution before the associated step will reduce the likelihood that an error will occur because a user is performing a step while unaware of a related hazard. Procedure users must be aware of cautionary information and potential hazards before they perform an action that may put someone or something in danger. Warnings and cautions should also be on the same page as the step so that the user has all the information needed to execute that step safely. If the warning or caution is on one page and the action is on the next page, the user may recall the cautionary information incorrectly or even forget it.

Warnings and cautions should also be presented every time they apply to a step. For example, if a particular caution regarding engine temperature is applicable to both Step 6.5 and Step 6.25, then the caution should be placed before each step. Warnings and cautions should be repeated as many times as needed throughout a procedure, but they should not be overused, or procedure users may begin to ignore them.

18.6 Use notes to present supplemental information.

Summary

Much of the information that has been stated previously about warnings and cautions is applicable to notes as well. Notes provide supplemental information in procedures that is different from the information in warnings and cautions. Therefore, notes should look different from warnings and cautions.

Notes are used to provide supplemental information in procedures and are qualitatively different from warnings and cautions. Notes provide additional information that, while useful, is not essential to performing a procedural task safely. Whereas warnings and cautions provide critical information that must be adhered to in order to prevent injury or equipment damage, the information in notes is not as critical.

Notes can be used in several situations:

- Notes can emphasize important information (for example, by reminding users that the company has made a legal commitment to perform a sequence of steps in a particular way).

- Notes can inform users of an expected situation in the facility. For example, a note could inform users that power to a piece of equipment will be interrupted when a circuit breaker is removed. If the expected situation may be dangerous, use a warning or caution to convey the information instead.

- Notes can provide location information regarding equipment.

- Notes can group steps if section headings are not adequate for this purpose. For example, if a group of steps presents pre-start criteria for a pump, you could indicate this fact in a note preceding the first step in the group.

The example below illustrates how a note can be formatted in a procedure. Notice how the note is emphasized by italics, and that this emphasis technique is visually different from that used for warnings or cautions.

Note: *Overriding an AFAS when the steam generator level is less than 0% wr may cause a loss of heat removal.*

Much of the information presented in the previous sections regarding warnings and cautions applies to notes as well. Notes must be clear, concise, and unambiguous. However, a note is not as critical to user performance as a warning or caution. Therefore, the unique format of notes should distinguish the notes from warnings and cautions and need not contain as much emphasis as the format for warnings or cautions.

As with warnings and cautions, a note should be placed just prior to and on the same page as the step to which it applies. Placing notes before an associated action allows the users to see the supplemental information before they perform the associated action.

Finally, actions should not be included in notes. Actions belong in steps. Just as with warnings and cautions, do not hide actions in notes by using the passive voice. Users can easily overlook actions if they are not presented as steps.

In this chapter...

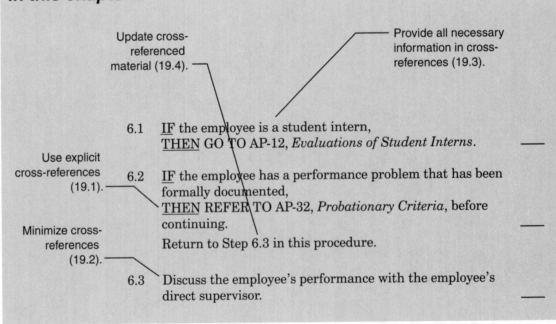

Update cross-referenced material (19.4).

Provide all necessary information in cross-references (19.3).

Use explicit cross-references (19.1).

Minimize cross-references (19.2).

6.1 <u>IF</u> the employee is a student intern,
<u>THEN</u> GO TO AP-12, *Evaluations of Student Interns*.

6.2 <u>IF</u> the employee has a performance problem that has been formally documented,
<u>THEN</u> REFER TO AP-32, *Probationary Criteria*, before continuing.

Return to Step 6.3 in this procedure.

6.3 Discuss the employee's performance with the employee's direct supervisor.

CHAPTER
NINETEEN

Cross-References

Most procedures should be written in a step-by-step format. The user reads a step, performs it, and then repeats the process for the next step. However, not all tasks can be described in a sequential (linear) flow of steps; sometimes it is necessary or advantageous to use cross-references to direct the user to depart from the normal linear flow of information. Cross-references instruct users to go to a specific step in a procedure; an example of a cross-reference is *IF header temperature is above 230°C, THEN GO TO Step 3.4 in this procedure.*

Several types of cross-references can be distinguished. It is useful to draw distinctions between (1) explicit and implicit cross-references, (2) references and branches, (3) conditional and unconditional cross-references, and (4) internal and external cross-references.

- *Explicit* cross-references specifically direct the user to refer to another procedure or another part of the same procedure. *Implicit* cross-references are not stated in the procedure; users are expected to know that a cross-reference is necessary.

- *References* direct the user to temporarily abandon his or her place in the current (i.e., base) procedure, perform the cross-referenced steps, and then return to the base procedure, typically beginning with the step following the cross-reference instruction. *Branches* direct the procedure user to permanently abandon the current procedure (or place in the current procedure) and to go to another place in the procedure set for instructions.

- An *unconditional* cross-reference is always performed. A *conditional* cross-reference is only performed when certain specified conditions are met. Conditional cross-references are specified in conditional statements.

- *Internal* cross-references send the user to a step that lies within the procedure containing the cross-referencing statement. *External* cross-references send the user to a step that lies within another procedure.

The table below provides examples of these different types of cross-references. No examples of implicit cross-references are provided because, by definition, they are not explicitly stated in the text and thus have no format.

As will be discussed in Section 19.2, cross-references should be minimized; if possible, cross-references should be eliminated altogether. Cross-references are a necessary evil in complex procedures, that may not be necessary in simpler procedures. If your procedures are sufficiently simple that you can avoid using cross-references or can restrict use of cross-references to one type (e.g., internal conditional references to additional information), then do so.

Type of cross-reference	Basic format of step
Internal unconditional reference	REFER TO Step [number] in this procedure. RETURN TO Step [number] in this procedure.
External unconditional reference	REFER TO Step [number] in [procedure name and number]. RETURN TO Step [number] in this procedure.
Internal conditional reference	IF condition X exists, THEN REFER TO Step [number] in this procedure. RETURN TO Step [number] in this procedure.
External conditional reference	IF condition X exists, THEN REFER TO Step [number] in [procedure name and number]. RETURN TO Step [number] in this procedure.
Internal unconditional branch	GO TO Step [number] in this procedure.
External unconditional branch	GO TO Step [number] in [procedure name and number].
Internal conditional branch	IF condition X exists, THEN GO TO Step [number] in this procedure.
External conditional branch	IF condition X exists, THEN GO TO Step [number] in [procedure name and number].

19.1 Use explicit cross-references whenever possible.

Summary

Do not expect users to know that a cross-reference is necessary. Whenever possible, include cross-references explicitly in procedures.

Cross-references are actions and, like all actions, they should be specified clearly and unambiguously. Few procedure writers would write a step like *Open the valve* without specifying which valve; yet, procedure users are sometimes instructed to perform a task without being told that additional guidance on performing that task exists in another procedure. In both of these cases, the procedure places unreasonable demands on its users by not alerting them to useful information.

Implicit cross-references can become especially problematic when users are required to perform a task that is described in several different procedures. They may be expected to know that they perform Section 4.5 of this procedure, Section 4.11 of another procedure, all of a third procedure, and scattered steps from a fourth procedure. To avoid this problem, cross-references should be explicit whenever possible—the procedure should specifically say, *REFER TO Section 4.0 of this procedure* or *IF the valve body is corroded, THEN REFER TO Appendix A of this procedure.*

Implicit cross-references are often fostered when procedures are based on systems rather than tasks.[35] For example, at an industrial facility there may not be a procedure for handling a loss of electrical power. Instead, when power fails, workers must know that they have to perform a section of the emergency diesel procedure, another section of a procedure for shutting equipment down, yet another section of an administrative procedure for notifying management, and yet *another* section of a fire protection procedure for maintaining fire safety. The procedures are organized around systems—the various pieces of equipment, mostly—rather than the overall task—handling a loss of electrical power. Because these procedures are written without consideration of the overall task that is being performed, they do not include the explicit cross-references that would be necessary to direct the performance of the subtasks; all cross-references are implicit. This situation reduces the usefulness of procedures, because of the usability problems involved with using many procedures at once and the likelihood that users will overlook a procedure that applies and perform some actions from memory, perhaps incorrectly.

One obvious way to address such a problem is to include explicit cross-references that direct the performance of the many different procedures necessary to perform the overall task. These cross-references could be included in the various procedures or in a separate procedure that directs the performance of the task. While this may be an improvement, it does not

---

[35]Task orientation is also discussed in Section 13.1.

scattered through several procedures. Instead of making the implicit cross-references explicit, the best solution is to develop procedures that address tasks that are actually performed. Thus, in this example, the solution would be to develop a task-oriented procedure (or a set of task-oriented procedures) that addresses reactor start-up (and only reactor start-up) and consolidates all the information that was formerly scattered among procedures.

This solution can create document control problems, however. If procedures address tasks rather than systems, it is likely that some information will be repeated in several procedures. For instance, information regarding equipment shutdown may now have to be incorporated in several different task-oriented procedures, where it was formerly only in one system-oriented procedure. While this duplication will make the user's job easier, it can complicate the procedure writer's, as any revision must now be made in several procedures rather than simply one.

Fortunately, automation can simplify this (and many other) aspects of procedure management. Some technical publishing systems, which are sophisticated word processing systems for complex technical documents, allow the development of document databases. A document database can allow a procedure to be assembled from a database of steps. These steps appear only once in the database. If one step is changed, *every* procedure in which that step appears is automatically changed. See James (1985) for an introduction to this concept. You may also wish to contact various software vendors to learn more about the actual capabilities of various technical publishing systems.

However, if you use explicit cross-references, they must be correct. An attempt to include explicit cross-references for all possible tasks that can be performed with a large procedure set could be a nightmare for writers, and that nightmare will only get worse when the writing is done, because now the resulting web of cross-references must be kept current. A change in one procedure could ripple throughout the entire set. Consequently, implicit cross-referencing is sometimes a necessary evil in the real world of procedure writing. Just do the best you can to minimize it, especially for tasks that are commonly performed. See Section 19.4 for a further discussion of maintaining cross-references.

19.2 Minimize cross-references.

Summary

Minimize cross-references; however, cross-references may be necessary to ensure technical accuracy and to simplify complex conditional information. Cross-references should be used only when absolutely necessary if the procedures are to be executed under stressful situations and time constraints, conditions that can be expected to increase the errors made when cross-references are performed. The amount of lay-down space for procedures must be considered, lest the user end up with one procedure on the table, one in his or her lap, and one tucked under an arm. Also, if a task is performed locally, it is obviously not advantageous to require users to lug an armful of procedures to the work site.

This section begins by discussing the problems that are likely to arise when cross-references are used, then discusses one aim of cross-references—to simplify the logic in the procedure. The following sections discuss the use of conditional and unconditional cross-references.

Problems with cross-references

Cross-references are common in commercial nuclear power plant procedures (Barnes & Radford, 1987; NRC, 1982) and other industries where procedures are used to operate and maintain especially complex equipment. Problems with cross-references are also common. For example, a General Accounting Office Report states that to diagnose and repair one aircraft radar malfunction a technician had to refer to 41 different places in eight documents (Duffy, 1985). Even if in such a case the documents were organized to provide an easy-to-follow path through the 41 different places where the necessary information resided (which is quite doubtful), such excessive cross-referencing would be more difficult than using a single procedure.

Procedure users can have difficulty coordinating procedure steps when cross-references require them to execute multiple series of steps concurrently. However, even cross-references that do not require the concurrent execution of steps can lead to problems associated with the sequencing of actions. When users are forced to bounce around through a procedure or, especially, through a set of procedures, technical errors can occur—for example, users may skip a step. Cross-references can also disrupt the flow of information from the procedure to the user. In addition to these problems, cross-references can create placekeeping problems for users and they can create substantial problems for writers in document revision and control (see Section 19.4).

Barnes and Radford (1987, pp. 29–30) describe how nuclear power plant operators feel about cross-references in operating procedures:

> Operators reported that plant procedures are designed so that operators are frequently required to follow two or more procedures simultaneously. In attempting to use multiple procedures, the operators reported (1) problems in determining how to coordinate steps in the different procedures, (2) difficulties in placekeeping in the procedures, and (3) problems with physically handling more than one procedure manual at a time. The operators stated that these problems had, at times, left them lost among procedures and confused, and that the press of events sometimes required them to abandon efforts to use the procedures and to conduct their tasks on the basis of training and experience alone.

Using cross-references to guide movement through the procedure

The best solution to many of these potential problems is to minimize the use of cross-references. In general, it is better to repeat steps and make procedures longer than to force users to hunt out cross-referenced material; but obviously there are limits. The price of purging unnecessary cross-references is longer procedures, because instructions must be repeated rather than cross-referenced. Thus, the length of potentially cross-referenced passages is one factor that should be evaluated when considering the use of cross-references. Short passages should generally be included in the base procedure, while it may be advantageous to cross-reference longer passages.

While minimizing cross-references is an obvious way to avoid the problems they cause, occasions do exist when cross-references are the lesser evil. Pragmatic issues must certainly be considered when evaluating the degree of cross-referencing appropriate in a procedure set. For example, one must question whether the procedure will be performed by an individual or by a team. A team should be able to handle several procedures concurrently more successfully than an individual.

The problems associated with cross-references can increase as cross-referenced steps are nested within other cross-referenced steps. Thus, it appears advisable to repeat even lengthy portions of procedures rather than cross-reference them, if doing so eliminates multiple levels of cross-referencing.

If it is necessary to include cross-references in a procedure, provide the simplest path possible through the logic under the most likely set of conditions. Construct steps so that (1) it will be easy to follow the logic of the steps, (2) the steps will make sense to the user, and (3) wasted motions will be minimized.

Decisions about when to use cross-references cannot be made in a vacuum at the writer's desk. The writer will need to consider information about the task, feedback from users, and the results of testing to determine when the benefits of cross-references outweigh their costs. This fact is especially true in the case of conditional cross-references. Decisions about when to use and how to construct conditional cross-references can be very complex. In particular, in some procedures it is impossible to avoid internal conditional branches. However, in such cases, the writer still retains considerable control over how the cross-references will be structured. Although the writer may not minimize the cross-references in the *written* procedure, he or she can minimize how often the cross-references will need to be performed when a procedure is executed and control the complexity of the path through the procedure. Thus, the writer focuses on minimizing cross-references and the complex cross-referencing structures in the *procedure's execution* rather than in the written document itself.

Unconditional cross-references

As a general rule, internal unconditional references and branches should be avoided. If the procedure user must always make a transition, then it is generally best to simply include the target steps in the procedure—why make the user make the transition *every* time? However, external unconditional references are sometimes necessary. Some tasks for which procedures are necessary require that many tasks be conducted in tandem. In some cases, the procedure writer will be in a position to determine a good way of integrating the tasks and all of the tasks can be presented in a single series of steps. In other cases, however, the procedure users may be in a better position than the procedure writers to determine how to best integrate the tasks. In this case, external unconditional cross-references lead the user to necessary instructions while giving the user some latitude in how the different sets of instructions will be coordinated.

Unconditional cross-references must sometimes accompany conditional cross-references. Assume that, based on a particular condition, users perform either Section 5.0 or 6.0 (in other words, there is a conditional cross-reference that says, *IF X, THEN GO TO Step 5.1. IF NOT, THEN GO TO Step 6.1*). In either situation, they then go on to perform Section 7.0. The last step in Section 5.0 should then be an unconditional cross-reference to Step 7.1 (i.e., *GO TO Step 7.1*) so that users do not perform Section 6.0 after performing Section 5.0.

Conditional cross-references

Conditional references and branches, either internal or external, can often be useful. Long series of actions may be contingent on complex combinations of conditions. Every path created through the possible combinations of conditions may have unique associated actions. In such cases, explicit cross-references may well be essential to direct the user through the complex path of logic. For example, in Example 55 cross-referencing has been inappropriately avoided at the expense of creating an extremely long and complex step.

4.1   IF the torus temperature is less than 110°F,
      AND any ERV is open
      AND any MSIV is open,
      OR
      IF the torus temperature is less than 110°F
      AND the drywell pressure is less than 3.5 psig
      AND any MSIV is open,
      THEN bypass the low-low water level MSIV isolation interlocks.

4.2   Stop all operating RCPs.

Example 55. Complex step. This difficult-to-understand step can be simplified by the use of cross-referencing, as shown in Example 56.

This step can be simplified by breaking it into two steps and using internal conditional branches to direct the user's movement through those steps and subsequent related steps. One example of how this could be done is shown in Example 56.

4.1 <u>IF</u> the torus temperature is greater than or equal to 110°F
   <u>THEN</u> GO TO Step 4.4 in this procedure.

4.2 <u>IF</u> all MSIVs are closed,
   <u>THEN</u> GO TO Step 4.4 in this procedure.

4.3 <u>IF</u> any ERV is open
   <u>OR</u> the drywell pressure is less than 3.5 psig
   <u>THEN</u> bypass the low-low water level MSIV isolation interlocks.

4.4 Stop all operating RCPs.

Example 56. Use of cross-referencing to simplify a step. Here, Example 55 is simplified by breaking one step into three and using cross-referencing. The logic here is equivalent and easier to follow. Note how conditions have been stated positively rather than using <u>NOT</u>; for instance, this improved example uses *greater than or equal to 110°F* instead of *<u>NOT</u> less than 110°F* and *MSIVs are closed* instead of *MSIVs are <u>NOT</u> open.*

Restructuring the long complex step into multiple steps, with explicit conditional branches to direct movement through the steps, simplifies the original long, complex step in a number of ways. First, all problems of potential ambiguity associated with the use of <u>AND</u> and <u>OR</u> within a single conditional statement can be eliminated (see Section 16.3). Also, note how the improved construction in Example 56 moves the common necessary conditions (torus temperature less than 110°F and any MSIV being open) to the beginning of the step series. If these conditions are not met, the user is directed to skip past the rest of the (now) irrelevant conditional information. This second feature of conditional branches is perhaps their greatest value; they allow for the user to skip past additional conditional information that has been determined to be irrelevant, saving time and simplifying procedure execution (Brooke & Duncan, 1981).

Conditional internal branches should be used when they simplify the presentation of complex conditional information, as in the example above. However, considerable care should be taken to ensure that the cross-references provide the simplest and clearest path possible through the complex information. For example, common necessary conditions can be presented early in the series, as in the previous example. Also, cross-references to short procedure segments are generally preferred to repeating the steps when users must conditionally perform a sequence of steps and when conditions under which they will perform the cross-referenced steps are unlikely. On the other hand, if users will likely need to perform a series of conditional steps, it is probably better to include them in the procedure and require users to skip around the steps when the conditions do not apply. That is to say, when deciding whether to repeat steps or cross-reference the steps, design the procedure so that it is easiest to use most of the time.

An additional caveat should be mentioned here, however. The complexity of the logic should not be evaluated in a vacuum, but in light of what is known about the operational setting in which the procedure will be used. For example, the simplest possible logic sequence may not be better than a slightly more complex sequence if the complex sequence provides a better match with the user's understanding of the situation. Also, the configuration of the operational setting should be considered. You might, for example, want to have an operator check gauges on one side of the control room first and then move to the other side to check additional gauges, rather than having him or her go back and forth across the control room, even if doing so makes for a slightly more complex series of conditional steps.

Often procedures that contain many cross-references can be presented more clearly in flowcharts. Thus, when faced with a procedure that seems to demand the use of many cross-references, consider using a flowchart if that option is available. Chapter 21 discusses flowcharts.

19.3 Write cross-references that provide all necessary information in a usable, consistent format.

Summary

Key words should be used to indicate each type of cross-reference. These key words should be emphasized (i.e., coded). The structure of conditional cross-references should be coded through use of white space. Cross-referenced steps should be fully identified. All cross-references should identify the specific steps to which the user should go (or refer).

The format of cross-references can have a pronounced effect on their usability. Cross-references should provide complete and clear information on where the cross-referenced information is located and, for conditional cross-references, on the conditions under which the cross-reference should be performed. As much detail as possible should be provided about the location of the cross-referenced steps. For example, the instructions to perform a cross-reference should identify the referenced step with information such as the name and number of the procedure containing the step, the number of the step itself, and, if possible, the page number where the step is located. Presumably, revision numbers and dates are not necessary to ensure that the user accesses the most recent revision of the cross-referenced procedure (other document control measures should ensure that users receive current revisions of procedures). However, the inclusion of revision numbers and dates does serve an essential purpose in document control, as discussed in Section 19.4.

In addition to this location information, the step must provide any conditional information that dictates whether the referenced material should be cross-referenced and also provide instructions about how the cross-reference is to be performed. For example, if users are to navigate through the procedure correctly, they must know whether they are performing a reference (which will require that they mark or note the location to which they must return) or a branch. Information that dictates the conditions under which a cross-reference is to be performed must be presented up front—before the cross-referencing instructions—and it must be as clear and explicit as possible. If it is presented after the reference (e.g., *GO TO Step 6.3 but only if…*), the user may erroneously perform a conditional cross-reference before reading that it should only be performed under certain conditions.

The clarity of both the conditional information and the cross-referencing instructions can be enhanced by designing and adhering to specific formats. Rules should be followed for presenting conditional information to ensure consistent and clear presentation. For example, conditional terms should be used and the rules of formal logic should be followed when presenting conditional references and branches (see Chapter 16). Formatting can also code each type of cross-reference to signal information to the procedure user about the cross-reference. Coding can be achieved with verbal, typographical, and spatial cues; as discussed below (see also Section 12.1).

Verbal cues consist of key words that alert the reader as to the type of cross-reference encountered. For example, references could always be indicated with the words *REFER TO… while continuing in this procedure.* Branches could be indicated with the phrase GO TO. If branches are used to indicate that the base procedure should be permanently or temporarily abandoned, key words should provide this information as well (e.g., *Abandon this procedure permanently and GO TO…* or *Abandon this procedure temporarily and GO TO…*).

Typographical cues consist of conventions such as the use of italics, bold type, and different fonts. Spatial cues use both the relative position of elements and the white space created by the positioning to create signals. Spatial cues can be created by using line breaks and indentation to set apart specific pieces of information. These verbal, typographical, and spatial cues are most effective when users are trained to understand their meaning, when cues are used sparingly, and when cues are not overly complex (Duchastel, 1982).

In the following example, a variety of cues are provided for the procedure user. The step format shown uses only techniques that can be accomplished with a standard typewriter or word processor; elaborate desktop publishing technology is not required to present cross-referencing steps clearly.

> 4.17   <u>IF</u> the computer fails to retrieve the data,
> <u>THEN</u> REFER TO procedure 201b, "Manual Data Recovery,"
> Steps 5 through 9 inclusively, beginning on page 3, while
> continuing in this procedure. Observe the note that precedes
> Step 5.

Example 57. Formatting a cross-reference. In the example, typographical cues (capitalization and underlining) signal the organization of the <u>IF</u>... <u>THEN</u> conditional statement that provides the conditional information in this step. The organization of this conditional statement is clarified by the way in which it is positioned on the page. The <u>THEN</u> clause begins on a new line directly below the <u>IF</u> clause. The cross-reference is signaled typographically with capitalization and verbally with the phrase *REFER TO*.

19.4 Pay special attention to cross-references and cross-referenced material whenever documents are revised or updated.

Summary

A system should be in place to track how all documents in a set are linked through cross-references. Whenever a document is revised, the accuracy of identification information in cross-references to that document (e.g., step numbers) must be checked.

This book advocates a user-centered approach to procedures—give the person performing the task the best procedure you can. You should be aware, however, that many of the cross-referencing techniques discussed in this chapter will make your job, as a procedure writer, more difficult, but the procedure user's job easier. This section discusses some of the things that you should do to ensure that cross-referencing does not introduce errors into procedures.

This problem is somewhat ironic, as cross-references are often used in an attempt to prevent errors from being made when procedures are revised. The use of cross-references can reduce the risk of errors in procedure revisions because the cross-references eliminate redundant passages in procedures, and thus help ensure that passages in need of revision are not overlooked. However, revisions in a procedure that affect aspects of the procedure, such as its name, number, or its step numbering sequence, are problematic if that procedure can be entered from other procedures via cross-references. These types of changes affect the features of a cross-referenced step that identify it in cross-references in other procedures. Thus, whenever a procedure is revised in a manner that changes such features, it is necessary to verify every cross-referencing step to that procedure throughout the procedure set.

Further, in a procedure where all steps are performed sequentially and no cross-references are used, it is only necessary to verify one path through the procedure. In a highly branched procedure there are many paths through the procedure and it becomes necessary to confirm that all paths are complete and that no path violates any pre-conditional information as it snakes through the procedure set. Each additional conditional cross-reference in a procedure creates a new path that a user can follow through the procedure. In addition to potentially bypassing important information, the complex structures created by conditional cross-references can lead to errors by introducing steps that change the dynamics of the system in ways that were not anticipated when other "downstream" steps were written (without the knowledge of what steps would be introduced up stream through some unusual combination of conditional cross-references). Thus, to be absolutely sure that no revision creates a problem in a procedure, writers must not only test a procedure subsequent to a major revision, but test every procedure that cross-references the modified procedure as well.

Complex structures created by nested cross-references create problems for procedure writers as well as users. It can be very difficult to ensure that a procedure is technically correct under all conditions when it contains complex layers of cross-references. Procedure writers often overlook problems along one or more paths through a procedure even when the structure contains only small amounts of branching (Weiss, 1990). The more complex the web of cross-referencing that ties a set of procedures together, the more likely it is that something will be missed when procedures are revised and verified.

In this chapter...

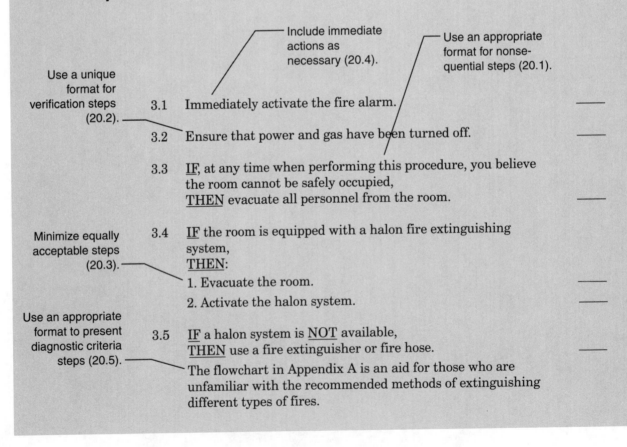

Include immediate actions as necessary (20.4).

Use an appropriate format for nonse-quential steps (20.1).

Use a unique format for verification steps (20.2).

3.1   Immediately activate the fire alarm.   ——

3.2   Ensure that power and gas have been turned off.   ——

3.3   <u>IF</u>, at any time when performing this procedure, you believe the room cannot be safely occupied,
<u>THEN</u> evacuate all personnel from the room.   ——

Minimize equally acceptable steps (20.3).

3.4   <u>IF</u> the room is equipped with a halon fire extinguishing system,
<u>THEN</u>:

     1. Evacuate the room.   ——

     2. Activate the halon system.   ——

Use an appropriate format to present diagnostic criteria steps (20.5).

3.5   <u>IF</u> a halon system is <u>NOT</u> available,
<u>THEN</u> use a fire extinguisher or fire hose.   ——

     The flowchart in Appendix A is an aid for those who are unfamiliar with the recommended methods of extinguishing different types of fires.

CHAPTER

TWENTY

Special Types of Steps

Steps should be tailored to the information that they present. A simple step consists of a verb and a direct object (e.g., *Open the relief valve*). In other types of steps, it is necessary to present additional information. For example, conditional steps (e.g., <u>*IF*</u> *header pressure is above 100 psia,* <u>*THEN*</u> *open the relief valve*) must present a condition as well as a verb and an object, and must use conditional terms according to the rules of formal logic.

Other, more complex types of steps, such as the following, have different requirements:

- *Nonsequential steps* are performed out of sequence with other steps. In these steps, in addition to specifying the action that must be performed, it is necessary to specify the criteria that define when the step must be performed. These criteria are typically related to time (e.g., a valve should be closed 10 minutes after it is opened) or to some parameter (e.g., a valve should be closed once a tank is full). In addition to a step specifying these criteria, the procedure should include some means of reminding operators to perform the step.

- *Verification steps* require users to determine whether a certain criterion is met and, if it is not, to take action to ensure that the criterion is met. Because steps of this sort are common in procedures, a concise, consistent format should be adopted for presenting them.

- *Equally acceptable steps* allow users to choose among alternative actions.

- *Diagnostic steps* present decision criteria that help users diagnose a fault or condition.

- *Immediate actions* must be performed without delay in an emergency.

20.1 Use an appropriate format for nonsequential steps (i.e., continuous steps, time-dependent steps, and concurrent steps).

Summary

Nonsequential steps should be presented so they clearly specify the criteria that govern when they should be performed. The nonsequential step should first appear in the procedure at the earliest point where it may apply and should be followed by reminders (e.g., on the facing page) for as long as necessary.

A central characteristic of procedures is that they present steps in the order. This aspect of procedures greatly simplifies their execution. The procedure user performs Step 1, Step 2, Step 3, and so on, through the last step in the procedure, at which time he or she has completed the task described in the procedure.

But it is not always possible to present steps in the order in which they will be performed. Four basic reasons can either act alone or conspire to obscure the correct order for the steps in a procedure to be performed: (1) there is technical rationale for allowing users to determine the correct order of step performance, (2) the step should be performed at a time that depends on some factor that varies or is not known as the procedure is written, (3) the step should be performed after a certain period of time has passed, or (4) two or more steps should be performed concurrently.

When presenting a nonsequential step in a procedure, it is important to provide users with the criteria that govern when (or if) the step should be performed. This should be done in the manner that is most appropriate for the type of step, although it is important that similar types of nonsequential steps be presented in a similar manner. It is also important to provide users with reminders to perform the steps; this section also discusses reminders.

Basic nonsequential steps

Occasionally, there simply is no rigid order in which the steps must be performed. In these instances, it is simply necessary to indicate to the user that the steps may be performed in any sequence, perhaps by using a note.

The use of these types of nonsequential steps should be limited, however, as they may introduce confusion—users may overlook or omit steps if they are skipping back and forth through the procedure. Unless there is a strong technical reason for allowing steps to be performed in alternative orders, it is generally best to decide on an order and present the steps in that order. If possible, the nonsequential steps should include any criteria that will be useful to users when deciding upon an order for performing the steps.

Continuous steps

It is possible that the time at which a step must be performed may be dependent not on the completion of the prior step, but on some system parameter; for example, a valve must be closed when a tank is full. These steps are known as *continuous steps*, because users must continuously keep them in mind until they are performed.

When dealing with continuous steps, the procedure writer cannot predict exactly how the system will respond as the procedure is executed, and thus does not know where in the sequence of steps to insert the continuous step. In the example cited, the flow into the tank may be affected by factors that have nothing to do with the particular procedure being executed. Thus, the procedure writer cannot include the step specifying that the valve be closed at the point in the procedure where the valve must be closed.

A continuous step should be presented in the procedure at the point where users may first be required to perform the action. Continuous steps are best presented in conditional statements, as shown in Example 58. The condition in the conditional statement indicates when the action should be performed. The continuous step should be followed by reminders, which are discussed at the end of this section.

Continuous steps can also be recurrent; for example, users may be required to repeatedly fill and drain a tank. In these instances, the step should clearly indicate that the step is to be performed repeatedly.

5.6   <u>IF</u>, at any time while performing this procedure, an SIAS actuates,
       <u>THEN</u> ensure full HPSI and charging flow.   ____

                          ✧ ✧ ✧

12.2   <u>WHEN</u> the overflow tank is full,
       <u>THEN</u> stop the charging pump.
       Continue in this procedure.   ____

Example 58. Use of conditional terms to present continuous steps. These nonsequential steps, which are dependent on system parameters, are best presented using conditional statements. Note the use of the phrase *Continue in this procedure* to indicate that Step 12.2 is not a hold point.

Time-dependent steps

Other steps are performed after a set period of time has passed. These steps are called *time-dependent steps*. For instance, a maintainer may be required to notify the shift supervisor within 30 minutes after taking a pump off line. Unless the procedure writer knows exactly how many subsequent steps in the procedure the maintainer will perform in 30 minutes, he cannot accurately insert a step into the procedure directing the maintainer to notify his supervisor *at the time the step is read.*

So, when writing a time-dependent step, you must assist the procedure user in tracking the time. It is important to provide space for users to note the time that "starts the clock" and to present a calculation aid that will enable them to calculate the time at which the action should be taken. Example 59 demonstrates one method of presenting this information.

Common sense should be used when deciding whether to incorporate a calculation aid in a time-dependent step. Obviously, if an action must be completed within a brief period of time (e.g., 10 seconds), the calculation is trivial and a calculation aid is unnecessary, although it *is* necessary to clearly state that the action must be performed within 10 seconds.

Time-dependent steps can also be recurrent; for example, users may be required to perform an action *every* 15 minutes. A calculation aid or checklist may also be appropriate in such a situation. Users could check off the action each time it is performed.

Note: *The following step initiates a time-limited sequence. Steps 3.2 through 3.6 are to be performed within 20 minutes.*

3.1   Determine the time by which Step 3.6 is to be completed.
1. Record the time that Step 3.2 is to be started.   _____
2. Add 20 minutes.   +   :20
3. Record the time that Step 3.6 is to be completed.   _____

3.2   Place the INCIDENT ACTION switch to TEST.   ____

3.3   Verify the amber ALARM TEST light on the AIA graphic
      panel is lit.   ____

3.4   REFER TO Steps 5.1–5.17 in this procedure.
      RETURN TO Step 3.5.   ____

3.5   Place INCIDENT ACTION switch to OFF.   ____

3.6   Push RESET pushbutton on AIA logic tester and record
      the correct time.   ____

Example 59. Time-dependent steps. This example demonstrates how a calculation aid can be used to assist users in performing a time-dependent step. This step would be followed on subsequent pages by reminders that the step still applied.

When there are many calculated times in a procedure, consider the use of an appendix to log all of the times. If such an appendix is used, procedure users can look up all the relevant times in one place rather than having to flip through the procedures.

Concurrent steps

Finally, a procedure may require users to perform tasks concurrently. Example 60 depicts the presentation of concurrent steps.

5.1 CONCURRENTLY PERFORM Steps 5.2 and 5.3.   _____

5.2 Prepare the reactant solution by performing the following:
    1. Add 10 grams of concentrate to 1000 ml water.
    2. Boil the solution for 30 seconds.   _____
    3. Naturally cool the solution to 100°F.   _____
                                                               _____

5.3 Prepare the test solution by performing the following:
    1. Strain the sample solution to remove the sediment.
    2. Let the sediment air dry to remove any moisture.   _____
    3. Crush the sediment with a mortar and pestle.
    4. Mix 50 grams of the sediment with 1000 ml water.   _____

5.4 <u>WHEN</u> the reactant solution has cooled to 100°F,
    <u>THEN</u> immediately combine the reactant solution
    with the test solution.   _____

Example 60. Concurrent steps. In this example, users are instructed to perform Steps 5.2 and 5.3 concurrently. Compare with Example 61.

The concurrent performance of tasks may lead to problems, as users who are required to do too much simultaneously may forget to perform actions. One method of avoiding concurrent steps is to break the concurrent steps into actions that can be presented sequentially, as shown in Example 61.

There are advantages and disadvantages to the approaches used in Example 60 and Example 61. The best way to present this type of information depends on the nature of the tasks being described. As a general rule, concurrent steps should be avoided, because of the potential for error. This potential can be exacerbated if users are performing more than one procedure at once. Yet, it may be difficult to integrate the individual steps that comprise each task into a single sequence of steps, either for technical reasons or simply because the resulting sequence of steps is unclear.

In Example 61, the steps may appear fragmented and out of context. Although, users performing the steps by rote may do better with Example 61, experienced users may desire the contextual grouping provided in Example 60.

5.1	Add 10 grams of concentrate to 1000 ml water to make the reactant solution. ____
5.2	Heat the reactant solution to 200°F. ____
5.3	While the reactant solution is heating, strain the sample solution to remove the sediment. ____
5.4	Naturally cool the reactant solution to 100°F. ____
5.5	While the reactant solution is cooling, let the sediment from the sample solution air dry to remove any moisture. ____
5.6	Crush the sediment from the sample solution with a mortar and pestle. ____
5.7	Mix 50 grams of the sediment from the test solution with 1000 ml water to make the test solution. ____
5.8	WHEN the reactant solution has cooled to 100°F, THEN immediately combine the reactant solution with the test solution. ____

Example 61. Concurrent steps broken up. Here, Steps 5.2 and 5.3 from Example 60 are broken up and combined into a single sequence of steps. Although this procedure no longer includes concurrent steps, it may be more difficult to understand because the steps are wordier and do not appear in context.

The procedure writer must decide on the best way to present concurrent steps. Consider the experience level and desire of users when making such decisions, and verify them during testing. The writers' guide should provide the necessary guidance to support these decisions.

The importance of reminders

Thus far, this section has discussed the initial presentation of nonsequential steps (i.e., the step itself). It is important that the step be followed by reminders to operators to perform the nonsequential action. Example 62 presents examples of the types of reminders that may be used.

The placement and emphasis of these reminders is important. They should appear in a consistent location on every page. Potential locations include the top of each page or the facing page. They should also be emphasized so that they stand out, but they should not be unduly emphasized so that they detract from the emphasis of other, more important information on the page, such as cautions. Figure 11 demonstrates placement on the facing page.

Note: *Continue to cycle pressurizer heaters every 15 minutes.*

✧   ✧   ✧

Notify the shift supervisor that the recirculation pump has been taken off line by the time noted in Step 5.1 in this procedure.

✧   ✧   ✧

IF, at <u>any</u> time while performing this procedure, an SIAS actuates, <u>THEN</u> ensure full HPSI and charging flow.

Example 62. Examples of reminders to perform nonsequential steps.
Reminders such as these should follow nonsequential steps when necessary. They should appear in a consistent location on each page (e.g., on the top of the page or on the facing page) and should be emphasized in an appropriate manner.

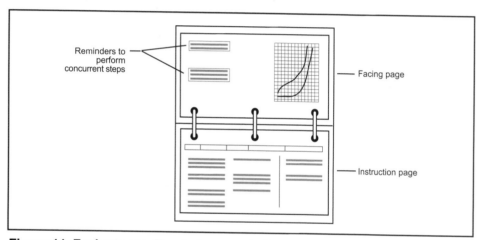

Figure 11. Facing page. The facing page is the page opposite the procedure page. It can be used to present supplementary information, such as reminders to perform concurrent steps.

20.2 Use a unique format for verification steps.

Summary

Verification steps should be presented in a consistent manner that clearly conveys the difference between verification steps (1) where users take action to ensure that the condition to be verified is met and (2) where users stop executing the procedure if the condition is not met.

Verification steps require operators to verify that a certain condition is met. Because verification steps can be common in procedures and can be especially problematic, they deserve special attention. There are two types of verification steps:

- In the first type, users (1) check if something is so; (2) if it is so, then go on; and (3) if it is not so, then make it so and go on.

- In the second type, users (1) check if something is so; (2) if it is so, then continue in the procedure; and (3) if it is not so, then stop executing the procedure and inform their supervisor.

Verification steps can be presented in a variety of ways, as shown in Example 63.

3.2	Verify open/open No. 1 Vent Valve.	____
	✧ ✧ ✧	
3.2	<u>IF</u> No. 1 Vent Valve is closed, <u>THEN</u> open No. 1 Vent Valve.	____
	✧ ✧ ✧	
3.2	Ensure that No. 1 Vent Valve is open.	____
	✧ ✧ ✧	
3.2	Insure that No. 1 Vent Valve is open.	____
	✧ ✧ ✧	
3.2	Assure that No. 1 Vent Valve is open.	____
	✧ ✧ ✧	
3.2	Check that No. 1 Vent Valve is open.	____

Example 63. A variety of ways of presenting verification steps. Although verification steps can be presented in a variety of ways, it is best to decide on a consistent means of presenting them. The first and second examples, while unambiguous, are wordy. The remaining four examples present the information concisely, but users must understand the meaning of the verb.

A consistent and concise format should be established for each type of verification step. Users encountering such a varied presentation of similar information in a procedure may attribute differences in meaning to spurious differences in presentation, may be unable to distinguish the one or two true differences in meaning lying behind the many differences in presentation, or both. It is best to choose and stick to one means of presenting each type of verification step. One approach is to use *ensure* when the user makes something so (the first instance above) and *verify* when the user stops executing the procedure is something is not so (the second instance above).

20.3 Minimize equally acceptable steps; when presenting these steps, do so using a unique format.

Summary

Equally acceptable steps should be minimized, as the presentation of unnecessary alternatives clutters the procedure and makes it more difficult to use. Present alternatives only when necessary. Provide criteria for distinguishing among alternatives when possible.

Equally acceptable steps are steps where "any one of several alternative steps or sequences of steps may be equally correct" (NRC, 1982, p. 23). When encountering these steps, users may choose among these alternatives.

Equally acceptable steps should be minimized. There will typically be more than one way of accomplishing a task, as many of the systems documented by procedure writers include redundancies and backups. Hence, in some procedures, it would be possible to present different, equally acceptable methods of accomplishing the same objectives for many of the tasks presented in the procedure. The result, however, would be a cluttered, confusing procedure that would continuously be presenting alternatives and requiring the users to make choices among them when such choices are unnecessary.

Procedure writers should limit the use of equally acceptable steps by presenting alternatives only in certain cases. One instance where it may be useful to present alternatives is when the procedure writer has reason to believe that the preferred alternative may not be available. Or, the presentation of equally acceptable steps may be considered a level-of-detail issue; if the procedure writer has reason to believe that an alternative may be useful to users and that they may not be aware of that alternative, then equally acceptable steps may be appropriate.

When alternatives are presented, it is often useful to present criteria that users may use when deciding among these alternatives. In such an instance, equally acceptable steps are best presented as conditional steps, as shown in Example 64.

4.18 <u>IF</u> Pump A is operational,
<u>THEN</u> use Pump A to fill the holding tank.
<u>IF NOT, THEN</u> use Pump B to fill the holding tank.   ___
    ___

Example 64. Use of a conditional statement to present alternatives. The use of a conditional statement clearly indicates that Pump A is the preferable alternative.

If neither of the alternatives is better than the other but it is still beneficial to provide users with alternatives, then an approach should be used that clearly indicates that only one alternative should be followed. Example 65 shows such an approach.

4.18   Use <u>one</u> of the following to fill the holding tank:

    • Pump A   ——

    • Pump B   ——

Example 65. Equally acceptable alternatives. In this case, there is no clear preference between Pump A or Pump B.

20.4 Include immediate actions in procedures when necessary.

Summary

Immediate actions, which are the initial steps that users take to control an emergency and are performed from memory, should be included in procedures when necessary.

Procedures for dealing with emergencies often include actions that procedure users must take immediately; for example, upon discovering a fire, a worker should immediately sound the fire alarm. Procedure users should be trained to perform these actions. The actions should also be included in procedures, but only as reminders.

Emergency procedures at nuclear power plants and similar facilities typically include immediate operator actions. NUREG-0899, *Guidelines for the Preparation of Emergency Operating Procedures* (NRC, 1982), states that immediate operator actions are those actions that operators should take immediately when there are indications of an emergency. These actions are taken to stop further degradation of existing conditions, to mitigate their consequences, and to allow operators to evaluate the situation. Operators normally memorize these actions and perform them without having to refer to an EOP (emergency operating procedure).

The American National Standards Institute provides the following examples of immediate operator actions for reactor operations (American Nuclear Society, 1989, p. 28):

- the verification of automatic actions

- assurance that the reactor is in a safe condition (e.g., shutdown of the reactor with sufficient reactivity margin and establishment of required core cooling)

- notification to plant personnel of the nature of the emergency

- determination that the reactor coolant system pressure boundary is intact

- confirmation of the availability of adequate power sources

- confirmation that containment and exhaust systems are operating properly in order to prevent uncontrolled release of radioactivity.

The list provides an idea of the types of actions that belong in an immediate actions section. If you are writing emergency operating procedures in a reactor facility, you can use this list (or other relevant sources) directly. If you are writing procedures (especially emergency procedures) in other types of facilities, determine the actions that must be performed without delay and consider incorporating them in an immediate actions section.

The NRC recommends that immediate operator actions should be included in a procedure as a back-up to user training. This sound guidance should be followed in any procedure that addresses an emergency situation. Immediate actions should also be identified as such. Typically, it is sufficient to include them in a section titled, *Immediate Actions*, or in some similar manner.

It should be stressed, however, that inclusion of immediate actions in a procedure is not a substitute for training. Because of their critical nature, operators should be able to perform immediate actions without referring to a procedure; the procedure is simply a back-up for operator training in this case.

In this chapter...

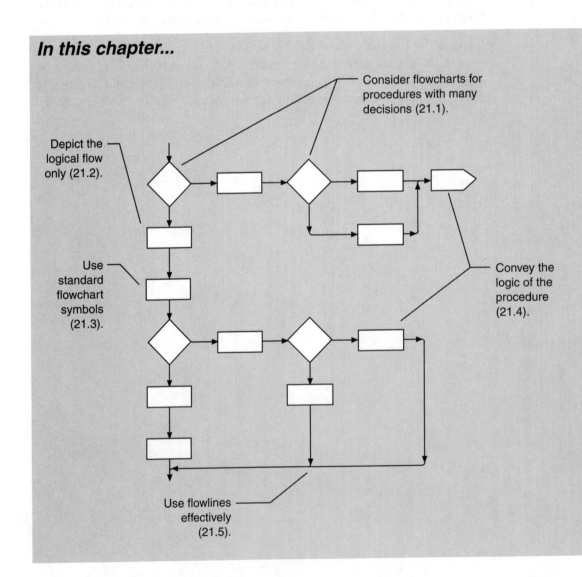

Consider flowcharts for procedures with many decisions (21.1).

Depict the logical flow only (21.2).

Use standard flowchart symbols (21.3).

Convey the logic of the procedure (21.4).

Use flowlines effectively (21.5).

CHAPTER

TWENTY-ONE

Flowcharts

Flowcharts are a graphical alternative to the text-based procedures that we have been discussing in this book.

21.1 Consider flowcharts for procedures that contain many decision points.

Summary

Consider flowcharts for procedures that contain many decisions, particularly diagnostic procedures. The linear-branching structure of the flowchart guides users to the next action and can reduce errors in these types of procedures. Flowcharts are unnecessary for presenting procedures that contain few decisions.

One of the fundamental characteristics of a procedure is that it is a linear document that presents steps in order. This is a strength so long as those steps are performed in the order they are written. However, in some procedures, users will skip steps or sequences of steps, depending on the conditions that hold as the procedure is executed. For example, a repair procedure might contain a series of steps that should be taken only if a particular part is worn, or a business procedure might contain a sequence of steps that applies to only one type of client.

190

Problems can arise as these types of procedures are performed, because procedure writers must use conditional statements and cross-references to guide users to steps that need to be performed. Users must skip steps and jump around in the procedure. All of this increases the chance of an error.

As we have mentioned several times in this book, flowcharts are often a superior means of presenting these types of procedures. The flowchart designer is not restricted to the linear flow of steps in the procedure. He can use flowlines to guide users to the steps that they must perform. This has been referred to as a linear-branching structure (Twyman, 1979). Flowpaths branch at decision points (diamond-shaped symbols), where users take a path that depends on the answer to the question in the decision symbol. Example 66 demonstrates the linear-branching structure by showing how a flowchart routes the user to an action that should only be taken if the reactor has tripped.

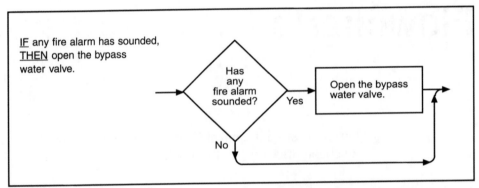

Example 66. An IF...THEN statement and a corresponding portion of a flowchart. When executing the written step procedure, users must mentally skip over the action if the condition is not true. When executing the flowchart, users remain on a flowline whether the condition is true or false; they do not skip anything (adapted from Barnes et al., 1989).

Diagnostic procedures

Diagnostic procedures demonstrate the strength of the flowchart format. As their name implies, a diagnostic procedure walks users through a series of decisions and actions, the goal being to diagnose and possibly remedy some unknown problem.

Users of these procedures often need all the help they can get. Humans are poor diagnosticians. The difficulties humans have when performing diagnoses stem from the difficulty we tend to have with decision making in general. Many researchers have investigated human decision making (e.g., Tversky & Kahneman, 1982), and have identified several factors that tend to make decision making difficult for us.

- We have difficulty accurately assessing probability or risk in uncertain situations; for example, people are unfamiliar with the statistical concept of regression to the mean, which predicts that things tend towards their average, so a football team having an exceptionally good season is more likely to have a worse season the following year.[36] This does not mean the team has gotten worse; random chance has simply brought its performance closer to where it belongs. Regression to the mean also means that if you do particularly poorly on a test, you are likely to do better on the next test (as a statistics professor once explained to one of the authors of this book, who had just done particularly poorly on a test, due to what seemed like unfair grading).

- We place undue emphasis on information we are familiar with; for example, because airplane crashes are covered so extensively by the mass media, we may overestimate our chance of being involved in such a crash.

- We tend to make decisions early in a process and then seek out information that reinforces those decisions, paying little heed to contradictory information. For instance, at Three Mile Island, operators misdiagnosed the situation and clung to that misdiagnosis in the face of contradictory information.

Thus, one of the important roles for procedures is that of a diagnostic aid that reduces these types of errors. By methodically walking the user through the diagnostic process, a well-written procedure can eliminate much human fallibility from the decision making that is so central to a diagnostic procedure. Compare Example 68 with Example 67, which present a series of decisions users must make when diagnosing a malfunction in a nuclear reactor, to see the superiority of the flowchart format.

Many researchers have compared flowchart procedures with step-by-step procedures and found flowcharts superior for presenting procedures that consist of many decisions (e.g., Horton, 1991; Kammann, 1975; Wright & Reid, 1973; Wright, 1971; Wason, 1968). However, studies of this type have a tendency to compare poor step-by-step procedures with good flowcharts, so the actual difference is not as great as that suggested by their results. If you use conditional terms and cross-references as described in Chapters 17 and 19, it is possible to write step-by-step procedures that effectively present decision criteria. Yet, when presenting complex decision criteria, a good flowchart probably remains superior to a good step-by-step procedure.

In addition to helping users, flowcharts help procedure writers by forcing them to systematically consider all possibilities. One of the authors of this book was asked to help prepare some overhead transparencies for a presentation on some fairly complex rules involving drug and alcohol testing. Flowcharts seemed the way to go. As the flowcharts were drawn, inconsis-

---

[36]For any statisticians out there, a better explanation of *regression to the mean* is as follows: "When some variable X is being used to predict some other variable Y, the predicted Y is closer to the mean of the Ys than X is to the mean of the Xs" (Loftus & Loftus, 1988, p. 467).

3.1   IF reactor power can __NOT__ be determined,
       __THEN__ GO TO Step 3.3 in this procedure.   ____

3.2   IF reactor power is less than or equal to 6%,
       __THEN__ GO TO Step 3.10 in this procedure.   ____

3.3   IF torus temperature is less than or equal to 110° F,
       __THEN__ GO TO Step 3.10 in this procedure.   ____

3.4   IF any ERVs are open,
       __THEN__ GO TO Step 3.6 in this procedure.   ____

3.5   IF drywell pressure is less than or equal to 3.5 psig,
       __THEN__ GO TO Step 3.10 in this procedure.   ____

3.6   IF any MSIVs are open
       __THEN__ bypass the low-low water level MSIV
       isolation interlocks.   ____

Example 67. Complex series of conditional statements. This series of conditional statements, which direct operators in diagnosing a problem in a nuclear power plant, can be difficult to follow. Compare this example with the flowchart in Example 68 (adapted from Moore et al., 1990).

tencies and omissions in the rules became obvious. They had not been evident when the rules had been described in print.

Disadvantages of flowcharts

Flowcharts draw their strength from their linear-branching structure. However, if the structure does not branch—if the flowchart simply depicts a sequence of action steps with no decisions—then there is really no advantage to using the graphically complex flowchart format. A simple list of steps will do.

Also, flowcharts do not convey hierarchical information very well (Horton, 1991). You may recall that, in text procedures, headings can be used to group steps and steps can be used to group substeps. Flowcharts, on the other hand, do not show these types of groupings well. All information is on one level. Also, flowcharts do not support learning or memorization well.[37]

Finally, flowcharts take up a lot of space, as we will discuss in Section 21.3. Be forewarned: effective flowcharts can require large sheets of paper.

---

[37]The same thing could be said of many of the principles discussed in this book, however. Procedures are optimized to support task performance, not learning.

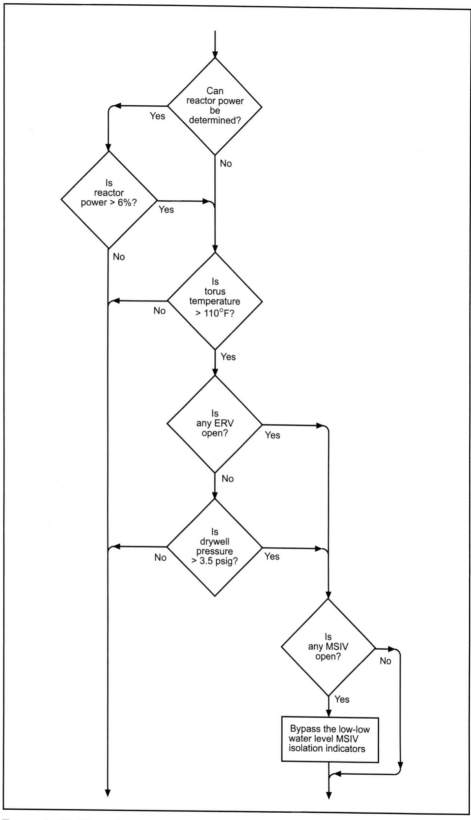

Example 68. Flowchart version of Example 67. The flowchart in this example is easier to follow than the series of steps in Example 67, as the logic can be visually traced (adapted from Moore et al., 1990).

21.2 Depict the logical flow only.

Summary

When designing a flowchart, depict only the flow of actions and decisions in the procedure—essentialize the flowchart.

Many things call themselves flowcharts. Computer programmers have used them for years to depict the logic flow of a piece of computer code. Many nuclear power plants use flowcharts for procedures; when we studied them for the Nuclear Regulatory Commission (Barnes et al., 1989) we recognized that some differed from the flowcharts used by computer programmers and dubbed them "big-picture flowcharts." They are a hybrid of flowchart and text procedures that present concurrent actions in parallel flowpaths. They are used in emergency operating procedures where users must perform several procedures concurrently. Nassi-Schneiderman flowcharts and nested-boxes flowcharts look nothing like the flowcharts described in this section; they use a series of nested boxes to present actions and decisions

So, an important order of business is to define what a flowchart is. We will do that here by limiting the information that is presented in a flowchart: flowcharts should convey only the actions and decisions in a procedure. They should not convey other information, such as inputs, outputs, responsibilities, cash flows, or whatever. Including this information, which is secondary to the task being performed, obscures that task, and makes the flowchart difficult to follow. This chapter will describe how to draw these flowcharts. These are not the only type of flowcharts that can be drawn, but they are generally the best for presenting procedures.

Limiting the information presented in a flowchart, or any graphic, can be a good idea. Graphics drawn by inexperienced designers often go awry because they try to present too much information.[38] Consider Example 69, which depicts a publication process. Compare this with Example 70, which presents the procedure that is embedded somewhere in Example 69.

Example 69 is very cluttered, and users really don't have a framework for deciphering the clutter. This problem is worth focusing on.

---

[38]Experienced designers, on the other hand, can effectively include a great deal of information in a graphic. Tufte devotes much of his excellent book *The Visual Display of Quantitative Information* (1983) to such complex, data-rich graphics. The effective design of such graphics is beyond the scope of this chapter.

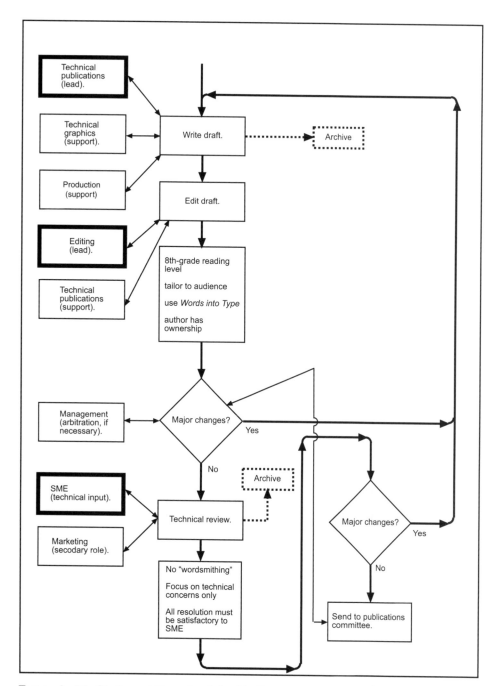

Example 69. Cluttered flowchart. In this flowchart, the underlying procedure is cluttered with information on responsibilities, detailed information on steps, and archiving points. As a result, the procedure is graphically busy and difficult to interpret.

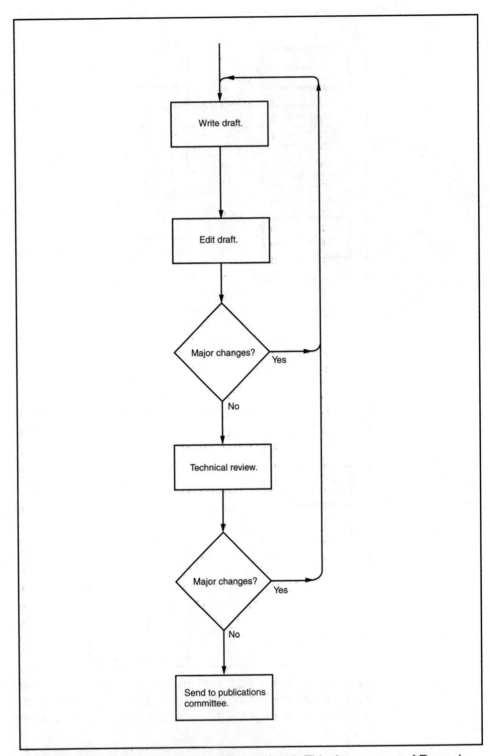

Example 70. Simplified version of Example 69. This the essence of Example 69—while the omitted information may be important, it does not belong in a flowchart procedure.

When we write, we (should) conform to a variety of rules. We use words with standardized meanings. We spell them correctly. We string them together in grammatical sentences. These rules have evolved alongside language, and we can communicate effectively because both writer and reader know them.

Corresponding rules do not exist for graphics, so the reader has to figure out what the writer had in mind. Anarchy can reign. Look at Example 71. A variety of questions are liable to come to mind as you do. Love, purpose, spirituality, and self esteem are apparently built on a footing of hard work and a foundation of physical fitness and honesty—that much is apparent. But why is the purpose pillar taller than the love and spirituality pillars, and why is the self esteem pillar taller still? For that matter, why are they pillars? What do they support? What do the dotted lines signify? *Happiness*, *Competence*, and *Burnout* appear to be a continuum, but how does *Varying aspects* fit in, and how does it relate to the foundation and footing? One senses that the designer of this graphic knows the answer to these questions, but has not been able to find a language to communicate them.

So, this chapter is an attempt to lay down some rules for one specific type of graphic—a procedural flowchart. Example 69 does not follow these rules, and it prompts questions.

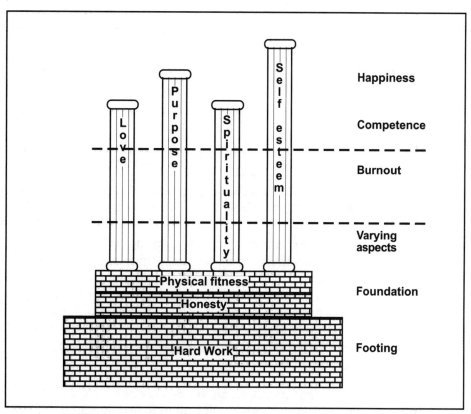

Example 71. Graphical anarchy. Interpretation of this graphic raises a variety of questions.

21.3 Use standard flowchart symbols.

Summary

Use an oval for entry and termination points, a rectangle for an action step, a diamond for a decision step, a rectangle with a pointed end for a cross-reference, and a shaded arrow for an cross-reference entry point.

Example 72 shows standard flowchart symbols. These symbols are generally similar to some of those recommended by the American National Standards Institute (1970). We do not recommend a complete adoption of the ANSI symbol set for procedural flowcharts, because many of the symbols are relevant only to data processing.

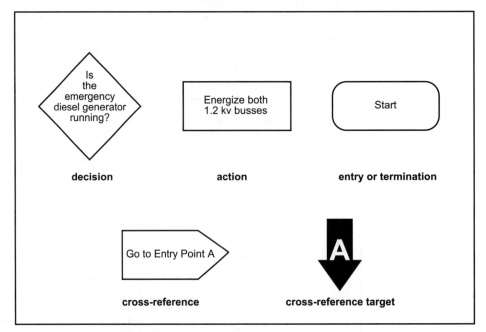

Example 72. Flowcharting symbols. These symbols are generally accepted and are thus the most likely to be understood by users.

The shaded arrow, a cross-referencing symbol, is not in the ANSI set. When users encounter a cross-reference, they are directed to a point identified with a shaded arrow (see Example 82). The arrow is shaded so that it stands out, because users will have to scan the flowchart to locate it. It is labeled so that users can associate it with the cross-reference. Basically, if users are told to go to Entry Point D, they should be able to easily find it. The design of the arrow supports this. Cross-references will be discussed in greater detail in Section 21.5.

One useful modification to this symbol set is shown in Example 73 (Barnes et al., 1989). It can be difficult to fit text into the decision symbol. The modification shown in Example 73 allows the symbol to hold more text. Note that it still looks like a diamond because the corners of the rectangle have been rounded. This symbol can be difficult to draw, however.

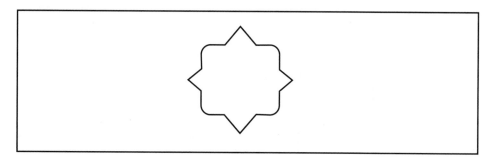

Example 73. Modified decision symbol. It is easier to fit text into this symbol than into a traditional diamond-shaped decision symbol.

21.4 Design the flowchart so that its organization conveys the logic of the procedure.

Summary

Design flowcharts so users can quickly overview the logic of the procedure.

A well-designed flowchart can convey information at two different levels. At one level, the user sees the individual steps that make up the procedure. At the other level, the flowchart provides macro-level information about the procedure—the flowchart can show the user where he is in the procedure and where he is going. This section discusses how to design flowcharts so that they provide this information.

Use of rows and columns

Compare Example 74 and Example 75. Both depict the same flowchart, but Example 75 arranges the symbols in a better way. It exhibits some structure. We can see that there is one main horizontal flowpath with two branches. One branch goes to another procedure and the other rejoins the main flowpath after the user takes a series of actions.

If the flowchart has been designed to fall into rows, the primary direction of movement should be from left to right; if it falls into columns, the primary direction of movement should be from top to bottom. From childhood, we have learned to read text from left to right, and research indicates that people read diagrams in the same manner (Winn & Holiday, 1982). The flowchart designer should respect these habits.

It is not enough that the flowchart simply fall into a nice grid, however. The movement through the rows and columns should be meaningful, such that a departure from the normal direction of movement indicates an abnormal situation. Example 76 duplicates Example 75 and shows the wording of the first decision symbol. The primary direction of movement in this flowchart is from top to bottom. At the decision symbol shown, users check temperature

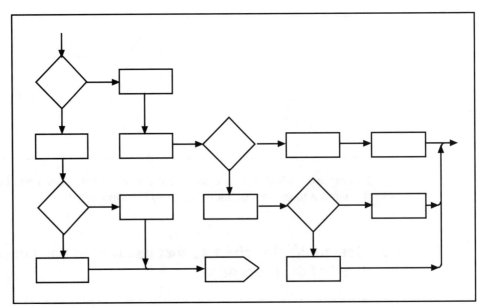

Example 74. Poorly designed flowchart. The designer of this flowchart has arranged the symbols to save space.

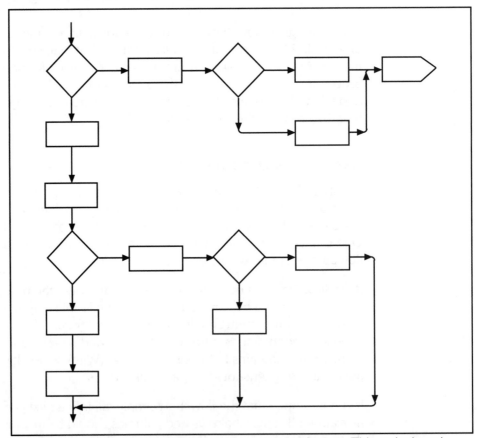

Example 75. Flowchart that falls into rows and columns. This redesigned version of Example 74 arranges the symbols in a more meaningful manner. The primary direction of movement is down, with branches to the right signifying contingencies.

alarm status. If no sensors have alarmed, then status is normal and they continue down. If a sensor has alarmed, they move to the right. This is a change in direction, and it signifies that status is no longer normal.

This is what we mean when we say that a flowchart can convey macro-level information. The flowchart is in a sense a map of the logic of the procedure, and changes in direction convey changes in meaning. Users who understand this convention can overview the flowchart and see the general logic of the procedure.

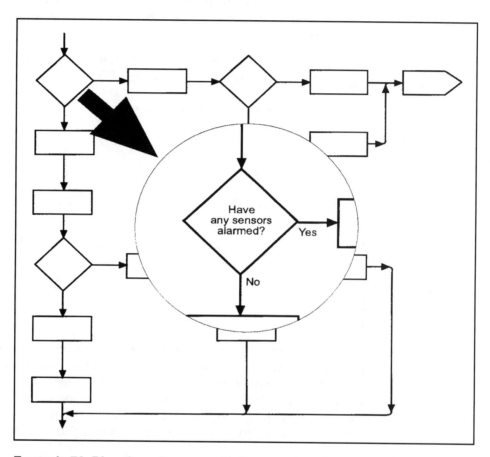

Example 76. Direction of movement. One step from Example 75 is shown. If expected conditions hold, sensors will not have alarmed and users will continue moving downward in the flowchart. If expected conditions do not hold, sensors will have alarmed and users will move to the right.

Exits from decision symbols

This brings up the issue of how to word questions in decision symbols, and how to label the exits, because this is what controls the direction that flow-chart users move from a decision symbol. Ideally, the flowchart will meet two criteria:

- As discussed above, an expected response will cause users to continue along the primary direction of movement in the flowchart.

- The *Yes* and *No* labels will be placed consistently at each decision symbol; for example, all *Yes* labels will be at the bottom of the decision symbol.

For these two criteria to be met, the flowchart designer must vary the word-ing of the question, as shown in Example 77.

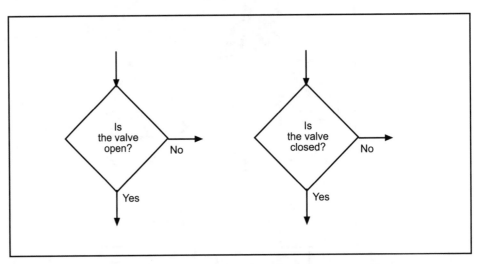

Example 77. Varying the wording of the question. Assume that two conventions have been established: the expected direction of movement is down and the *Yes* label is always at the bottom of a decision symbol. If the valve is expected to be open, the question should be worded as on the left; if it is expected to be closed, the question should be worded as on the right.

The advantage of consistently placing exits is that users will know where to find them—if the answer is yes, they consistently move to the right, for example. But designing the flowchart in this manner requires that the steps be worded in a specific way, and they won't always cooperate. Example 78 shows a flowchart step that has been forced into an unwieldy negative phrasing to control the placement of the exit labels. In such cases it is better to write the steps clearly than to have exits always be consistent.[39]

---

[39]Another school of thought holds that exits labels from decision symbols should always be consistently placed and the flowchart should go where it goes. This is certainly a viable ap-proach; however we believe there is greater advantage to showing the macro-level organiza-tion of the flowchart by having a primary flowpath.

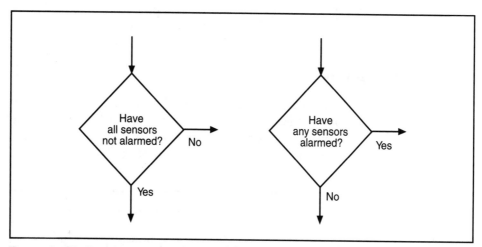

Example 78. Poorly worded decision step. The wording in the symbol on the left is necessary to force the *Yes* exit to the bottom of the symbol, but is likely to be misunderstood. The wording in the symbol on the right is preferable.

Note that a worst case would be to have *one* inconsistent decision symbol. If the *Yes* label is always on the bottom except for one decision symbol, then users' expectations will be reinforced as they continually encounter the *Yes* on the bottom. When they reach the one decision where it is on the side, an error becomes more likely. If you are forced to inconsistently label exits, then let users know by being consistently inconsistent.

Flowchart size

In order for users to see the macro-level organization of a flowchart, they must see all or most of the flowchart at once. If you go back and look at Example 74 and Example 75, you can see that the well-designed flowchart (Example 75) requires more space than the poorly designed flowchart. So, if users must see all of the flowchart at once and the flowchart will be big, than it must be printed on a big sheet of paper. If you are going to design effective flowcharts for complex procedures, you should accept this fact.

Page breaks can be placed in flowcharts, by using the cross-referencing symbol. These breaks should be placed so that they affect a minimum number of flowlines.

21.5 Use flowlines effectively.

Summary

Include an arrow on each flowline segment. Join flowlines that go to the same location. Curve flowlines at corners and when they join other flowlines. Avoid flowlines that cross. Use a bubble if flowlines must cross.

Flowlines convey movement, and their proper use is key to a well-designed flowchart.

Arrows

Arrows are a powerful aspect of flowchart design, as they direct movement through the flowchart. Use an arrow on each segment of a flowline, as show in Example 79. Repeat arrows on long flowline segments, particularly if they move in a non-standard direction (right to left or bottom to top).

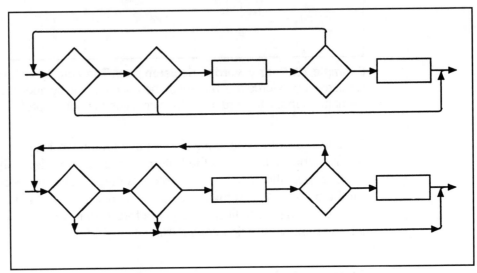

Example 79. Use of arrows. The flowchart on the top uses too few arrows on the upper and lower flowpaths. The flowchart on the bottom correctly uses an arrow on each line segment and repeats the arrows on the right-to-left loop.

Joining flowlines

Multiple flowlines will often go to the same point. In such cases they should be joined, as shown in Example 80. Further, they should join with rounded corners, like train tracks, to send users in the correct direction at each intersection.[40] Example 68, which is larger, shows this more clearly.

Crossing flowlines

Ideally, flowlines should not cross. Users could make a "wrong turn" at the intersection of the flowlines. Crossing flowlines can also obscure the organization of the flowchart. Example 81 illustrates this.

---

[40]Many software packages offer tools to draw flowcharts, and some are specifically designed to do so; however, we have never seen one that supports this simple but critical aspect of flowchart design. It would be a worthy addition to any flowcharting program.

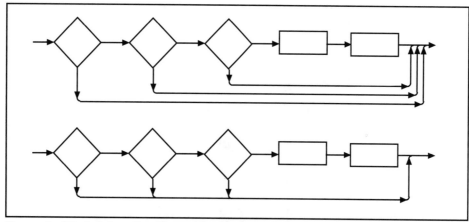

Example 80. Joining flowlines. Flowlines that go to the same place should join, as shown on the bottom. They should also join like train tracks, to further guide movement in the correct direction.

Flowcharts should be designed to minimize crossing of flowlines. Example 81 cannot be satisfactorily redesigned by moving the symbols to eliminate the crossed flowlines.[41] The designer must turn to other means. Example 82 shows the three ways that this problem can be addressed. Each has advantages and disadvantages.

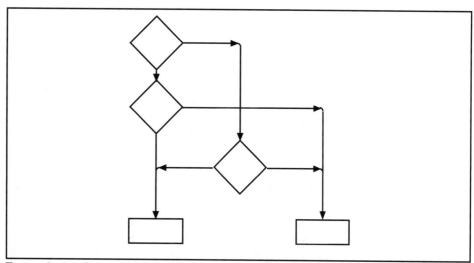

Example 81. Crossing flowlines. Users could make a wrong turn at the point where the flowlines cross (reproduced from Barnes et al., 1989, p. 12-18).

---

[41]As shown below, the price for eliminating the crossing flowlines is too high—a long flowline with several changes in direction that appears to frame the other steps.

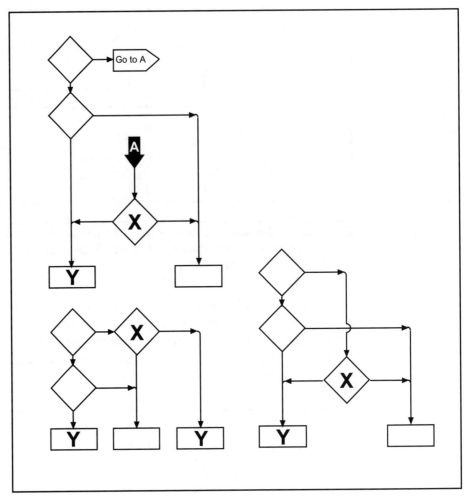

Example 82. Handling flowlines that cross. Crossing of flowlines can be eliminated in one of three ways: (1) by using a cross-reference, (2) by repeating steps, and (3) by using a bubble in the flowline at the point where they cross.

- One approach is to use a cross-reference, as shown in flowchart at the top of Example 82. As cross-references can also introduce errors if not followed correctly, this is not always the optimal answer. However, if the cross-reference is to a large group of steps that belong together (i.e., they would all be in the same section in a text procedure), then a cross-reference would be suitable.

- Steps could also be repeated, as shown in the lower left of Example 82, where Step Y is repeated. This may be suitable if only a few steps are involved. A disadvantage is that the structure of the flowchart does not depict the logic of the procedure as effectively, because a user who is overviewing the flowchart cannot see that the steps are the same. The flowchart is also more difficult to maintain, because any change in the duplicated steps must be made twice.

- Finally, a "bubble" could be used to differentiate the lines as they cross, as shown in the lower right of Example 82. This convention is well established, so users should understand it. It also does not distort the structure of the flowchart by repeating identical steps. In this case, it is the simplest and best solution.

PART

FIVE

Conclusion

CHAPTER
TWENTY-TWO

Some Closing Themes

As a means of wrapping things up, this chapter will discuss some of the themes that have guided the preparation of this book. These themes represent the philosophical approach that lies behind much of the guidance and point out some of the complexities and subtleties of procedure writing.

22.1 The nature of writing: Cookbook versus craft

This book is not a procedure for writing procedures. Although we have made every effort to make this book useful to the procedure writer and believe that the material presented here will be very helpful to you as you attempt to write better procedures, it is important to understand this limitation—this book isn't a cookbook. You can use these principles as cookbook instructions to a certain extent, but problems will often arise when you try to apply a principle in a unique situation or where two principles conflict with each other. In these situations, you will have to rely on your skills as a writer to sort things out, just as a car mechanic sometimes relies on intuition when fixing an engine or a surgeon sometimes relies on instinct while operating. In this sense, you must sometimes treat procedure writing as a craft rather than a science.

In other words, the principles here are advisory, and you should not lose sight of your end goal—communicating clearly—as you apply them. Experienced writers treat guidelines with care. Dave Farkas (1995, p. 588) wonders, "Does instruction based on these kinds of guidelines hinder students from developing greater subtlety of expression?" In *Dynamics in Document Design*, Karen Schriver (1997, p. xxiv) writes,

> I am wary of books that emphasize guidelines for writing and design. It's not that guidelines are intrinsically inappropriate; they are often quite helpful. The problem is that books organized around guidelines tend to trivialize the complexity of decision-making in document design, reducing writing and design to a list of prescriptive and often arbitrary dos and don'ts. Moreover, they tend to underestimate the knowledge, sensibilities, and skills that writers and graphic designers need in order to develop their expertise.

Principles deal with absolutes of right and wrong; writers seldom do. Instead, the writer deals with shades of meaning and subtleties—almost always, there is more than one way to say something. Consider Example 83, which presents several different ways of making the same statement.

We're out of food. I'm going to the store.

We are out of food. I am going to the supermarket.

There's no food in the house, so I'd better go to the store.

I'm going shopping, because there isn't a thing to eat in the house.

Example 83. Different ways of saying the same thing. There are many different ways to convey the same idea. No one of these ways is necessarily correct.

Procedure writers do not have the freedom to choose among these many alternatives. Many principles in this book reduce the options you will face when writing a procedure; for example, steps must begin with an action verb, conditional term, or modifier; all action verbs must be taken from an approved list; decision criteria must be written according to the techniques of formal logic; and so on. As a result of these rules, procedures will be more precise, because information is presented in a manner that research or historical practice has shown to be superior and because information is presented consistently.

Despite these efforts to increase precision, procedure writers are still working with the English language and cannot be completely freed from its inherent qualities. This fact has important implications for this book and the way you will use it. There are very few absolute rights and wrongs in procedure writing. If there were, we would not have bothered writing this book; instead, we would have simply written a writers' guide for the ultimate procedure and recommended that it be followed. But there is no ultimate procedure. As a procedure writer, you will have to make judgment calls. The purpose of this document is to help you to make those decisions. But do not look to it for proclamations of right or wrong in all situations.

Three examples may clarify this point. One is concerned with type size. Section 10.1 provided a visual angle formula for determining type size. This formula yields a neat, precise numerical answer for the optimal size of type, but this formula alone was not adequate for specifying a type size; line length, font, and other factors that could not be incorporated in the formula had to be considered as well. As a result, typesetters and printers seldom use the visual angle formula; instead, they use their trained eye to determine what looks the best—they approach the issue as a craftsperson, not a scientist.

A second example involves readability formulas. Many researchers have investigated techniques for quantifying how difficult a passage is to read. These formulas are based on sentence length, word length, proportion of words that appear on a list of "simple" words, number of syllables per word, and so on. Like the visual angle formula, readability formulas attempt to quantify an aspect of writing.

And, like the visual angle formula, readability formulas ignore a host of factors that also affect readability but do not lend themselves to quantification. Readability formulas ignore grammar, use of figures and tables, a document's organization and design, and many other factors (Giles, 1990). As discussed throughout this book, these attributes of a document all have an immense effect on its understandability. Because readability formulas ignore so much, technical communicators discount their usefulness, sometimes in strong language:

> While some authorities recommend readability formulas—if the writer recognizes the formula as a tool limited by the variables manipulated—overwhelming argument from other experts suggests that the formulas should be ignored because they can mislead writers by lulling them into a false sense of security or into writing stilted prose to fit the formula. (Giles, 1990, p. 131)

Readability formulas are another example of a failure of the cookbook approach. Effective writing cannot be judged by whether the writer got the recipe right, perhaps by using words and sentences of the perfect average length, but must be judged by how well the writer applied his craft.

The third example is concerned with verb choice. It is important that all action verbs in procedures be taken from an approved list (see Section 6.1). When compiling this list, it is important to eliminate redundancy, so that there is a unique, one-to-one correspondence between verbs and actions. This makes perfect sense in the abstract, but in practice it can be difficult to decide when two verbs are redundant and when they are not. For example, do *inform* and *tell* mean the same thing? They do in one sense—both indicate that information is being provided, as in *Inform site management that the reactor has tripped* and *Tell site management that the reactor has tripped*. In this situation, one could be eliminated—probably *inform*, because it is the longer of the two.

However, *tell* can be used in another sense—when instructing someone to do something. Thus, *Tell Chemistry to sample for boron* is another acceptable use of *tell*. But what if a procedure instructs a subordinate to "tell" a superior to do something (e.g., *Tell the shift supervisor to declare a site emergency*)? Depending on the politics at a particular facility, *tell* may not be appropriate in these situations. So should the verb list include another verb, such as *ask*, for situations when subordinates are dealing with superiors? Is the issue worth the complexity of one more verb on the list, and the potential of confusion by users who are not familiar with the difference?

Other connotations of *tell* and *inform* may intrude on matters. *Inform* may be understood by some as implying that the person who informs must ensure that the listener understands (or becomes *informed*). *Tell*, on the other hand, may not carry this implication. Once you have told someone you have done your part; if he doesn't understand, that's his problem. This is a subtle difference, and it may not be apparent or important to everyone. But is it important enough to dictate that both verbs be included in the verb list?

There are no correct or incorrect answers to these questions; the correct answer will depend on the particular situation at a facility. This example demonstrates some of the subtle shades of meaning that affect word use in procedures. These shades of meaning cannot be quantified; instead, they hinge on the feelings that we associate with a word.

The importance of training

Our intention in presenting this discussion is not to be discouraging; we are merely being forthright about what this book has to offer. This book will be of much use to you, but you need more—you need some training in technical communication. This training will enable you to develop the skills as a writer—as a craftsperson—that are necessary for applying the guidance presented here in an optimal manner. If you have already had classes such as these, that's good. If you haven't, some training in technical communication could be quite useful to you.

To take the cookbook analogy literally, consider a novice cook and a trained chef who both prepare the same recipe. The trained chef will certainly prepare a tastier, more succulent dish. Why? Because, although both had access to the same recipe, the chef brought years of training and experience to the task and was able to do a better job. Similarly, with skills in technical communication, you can use this book to prepare procedures that are better than those prepared by someone who merely follows this book and does not have the additional training.

Technical communication (or writing) classes are relatively common. They are offered at two- and four-year colleges and may be offered at some vocational schools. If you work at a large facility, perhaps they are offered somewhere on site. You might be able to attend one of these classes or, for a large enough group of procedure writers, it may be possible to arrange a special class.

Don't be too concerned if you are taking a class in technical writing rather than procedure writing. Few classes specifically teach procedure writing. Further, the skills you learn in a technical communication class will be useful to you as a procedure writer—especially when combined with the information in this book. A technical communication class should teach an approach that can be applied to any technical document. This approach should work for procedures as well as any other documents that you prepare.

22.2 Correctness

Procedures must be correct. This point is obvious—an incorrect procedure will lead users to take incorrect actions. As a procedure writer, much of the work you do is intended to keep errors out of procedures—your research into background documents, your subject matter expertise, your interviews with users and subject matter experts, and the user testing process are all important in this regard.

A procedure that is correct but is misunderstood is as bad as an incorrect procedure. To take an obvious example, a technically correct procedure that was written in a foreign language would be useless. There are other, more subtle ways that a "correct" procedure may be misunderstood. One occurs when the procedure assumes knowledge that the procedure user does not possess. Say that a procedure writer instructs users to start a pump, but does not include instructions to check for abnormal vibration. Now assume that this procedure is executed by a novice user who fails to check for vibration and the pump is in fact faulty; as a result, an expensive pump is damaged. The user may argue that the procedure was not correct because it omitted instructions to check for vibration, while the procedure writer may argue that the user should have known to do that. Obviously, in situations such as these, arguments over whether the procedure was "correct" are moot; the procedure was not executed successfully, and that is what matters.

Dye (1988) argues that problems such as this render the distinction between correctness and usability meaningless. While this position may be viewed as extreme, correctness and usability must be evaluated as two facets of the same issue. Compromises in usability for the sake of correctness can never be justified.

But it can be dangerous to concentrate too much on correctness: it is possible to try to hold procedures to an arbitrary standard of correctness that is so stringent that we lose sight of the whole point of the procedure. Writing that tries too hard to be correct "haggles over trifles and refuses to know when errors and confusion no longer matter" (Follett, 1966, p. 9). For instance, you don't cross a bridge, you cross a river; you drink a cupful of coffee rather than a cup of coffee. Yet to correct errors at so fine a level is to split hairs with little regard for what really matters—will the reader understand what has been written? There is no ambiguity in either of these expressions, so the answer is yes.

Further, in some cases, an "incorrect" term is preferable to a correct term. For example, a spiral staircase is, technically speaking, a helical staircase, because a spiral exists in only two dimensions while a helix, like a staircase, exists in three dimensions. When a reporter gets a scoop on a story, he has actually gotten a beat if he obtained the information by honorable means (Follett, 1966). Similarly, a *workaholic* should be a *workic*, because the suffix *-ic* in *alcoholic* denotes the addiction; if *workaholic* is correct, then *alcoholaholic* must also be correct. These expressions are all "incorrect," but if we speak of helical staircases, reporters beating a story, or workics, we will not be communicating effectively. People won't know what we mean, and that is what is important.

An analogous situation from procedure writing would occur when someone complained that a step that says, *Open the valve*, is incorrect because the user isn't opening a valve, he's flipping a switch. The distinction is meaningless—assuming that users are trained to know which switch operates the valve.

Similar problems can occur with conditional steps. Consider the following: *IF, at any time while performing this procedure, an operating diesel generator's 4.16 kV bus is de-energized, THEN energize the 4.16 kV vital bus.* A complaint with this step might be that there are actually two conditions in the antecedent: a diesel generator must be operating and its 4.16 kV bus must be de-energized. Thus, a more "correct" way to write the step would be, *IF, at any time while performing this procedure, a diesel generator is operating AND its 4.16 kV bus in de-energized, THEN energize the vital 4.16 kV bus.* But this version may be more difficult to understand. Because this step is taken from a procedure that addresses a loss of off-site power, it is a reasonable assumption that a diesel generator will be running, so the first condition will always be met. The second condition is the critical condition, but, by appearing as the second of two conditions, it is not emphasized as heavily. An alternative might be to recast the step, maintaining the two conditions: *IF, at any time while performing this procedure, a 14.6 kV bus is de-energized AND that bus is linked to an operating diesel generator, THEN energize the 4.16 kV vital bus.* But this alternative is longer and worded more awkwardly. Both of these alternatives are solutions to a non-existent problem—the initial wording of the step was clear and concise.

True, this is a complex and subtle point, but, as a procedure writer, you will be dealing with issues such as these on a daily basis. If you do not deal with them effectively, your procedure writing efforts can grind to a halt. Obviously, the rules governing conditional terms are important and must be followed; 95 percent of the time they will lead to steps that are clear and easy to understand. But you have some leeway in how you apply these rules, and this is an instance where a rigid interpretation of rules governing conditional terms—in pursuit of a step that is more "correct"—in actuality makes the step more difficult to understand. This example also illustrates the point made in Section 21.1, that you cannot cookbook the procedure writing process. The rules on conditional terms have to be applied with an *eye* towards the writer's craft.

This discussion is not intended to dismiss the importance of correct procedures, of course. The intention is to convey the point that a procedure is correct if its users will understand it in the manner the writer intended. It is as simple as that. Debates over the "correctness" of a word or step are rendered moot if users will interpret the word or step in the manner intended. That's the final standard.

22.3 Consistency

A recurring theme in this book is consistency. We're returning to it once more because consistency is important—it's the hallmark of a good procedure. Similar thoughts should be expressed in a similar manner, or else the writer runs the risk that the reader will perceive his writing as undisciplined or, worse, will attribute differences in meaning to spurious differences in presentation. Take the time yourself to review procedures for consistency and then get someone else to look at them. It is that important.

22.4 Don't blame everything on the procedure

One of the authors of this book was witnessing an exercise in a nuclear power plant simulator where an operator misread a step. This step contained a list of actions that the operator misinterpreted as a list of conditions. As a result, he made an error. In the briefing following the exercise, the problem was discussed and one observer suggested that the action verb be underlined so that it would be clear that the step was, in fact, an action.

Other people involved in the briefing hesitated to agree with this change. The step was clearly written and did not include conditional terms, so there was no clue as to what had confused the user. They wondered why the operator had misread the verb. Would underlining help?

Their concerns were well founded. What had actually happened was that the operator simply wasn't paying attention to the procedure. That happens. And, if the user isn't paying *any* attention to the procedure, it can be the most usable procedure in the world and it will not improve task performance. So underlining the action verb would not have made any difference and would have made the procedure more difficult for a user who was paying attention to understand. He would wonder why that action verb and no other action verb was underlined. Was it somehow different? Thus, emphasizing the action in response to this situation would have been the wrong thing to do.

This example demonstrates several things. First, emphasis is not the answer to every problem. Second, changes to procedures should not be made based on one incident if that incident was a fluke. Finally, don't always blame the procedure when something goes wrong.

This last point is important. True, many errors can be attributed to procedures; if they could not be, there would be little reason for preparing this book. But too often, the response to *any* human performance problem is to revise the procedure or write a new one. Some problems are the result of inexperience, inattention, a lack of training, or even deliberate malice. These problems have nothing to do with procedures. If a procedure is changed to "address" these problems, the result is frequently that the true cause of the problem has not been addressed and the procedure is more difficult to use. Fixing individual bits of procedures due to individual errors can introduce tremendous inconsistencies into procedures. Over-proceduralization, where there is a procedure for everything, can also result. In this situation, users may be more likely to resent procedures because they are words and difficult to use; this resentment can lead to errors in those instances where a procedure is necessary, but the user fails to use the procedure or pays only cursory attention to it.

22.5 Writer knowledge versus user knowledge

It is usually appropriate for procedure writers to view their users as people who know less than the writers about the *specific information* covered in the procedures. This is not to say that the readers know less about the system, process, or equipment covered in the procedure than the writer, nor is it to say that the writer is necessarily smarter or wiser than the reader. However, the writer generally has access to many resources that are unavailable to the procedure user. For example, when attempting to determine the best way to perform some task, the writer may consult numerous basis documents; interview technical experts; interview users; draft different versions of the procedure and test them in simulations; and, perhaps most importantly, take time to think about, ponder, and mull over the options. Procedure users rarely have such luxuries. The user must decide upon a course of action and take it. This difference, in fact, is one of the basic reasons for writing procedures at all—in order to allow someone to take the time to find the best way of performing a task and documenting that method to help others perform the task.

This premise that the writer knows more (or at least had access to more resources) than the reader is reflected in numerous aspects of the form and use of procedures. Perhaps most importantly, this premise is reflected in the content of procedures. For example, as explained in the discussion of equally acceptable steps, the writer should not tell the reader about every method by which a task could be performed, the writer should (usually) choose the best method and present that method only in the procedure. However, the discussion of equally acceptable steps also stated that sometimes the writer should provide the reader with options. Why should the writer let the reader select from among options when, presumably, the writer has more resources than the reader for making such decisions? Quite simply, despite all of the advantages the writer has over the reader for acquiring and analyzing information, he or she does not always know more than the reader does about the specific information presented in the procedure, because the reader knows (or at least has the opportunity to know) things about the equipment, process, or system covered in the procedure that are *unique to the particular moment* that the procedure is being executed. The fact that the reader has access to such information, which the writer cannot possibly obtain, underlies the general principle presented here.

The general principle, then, is that the writer should provide the reader with options only when the reader has information that informs decisions (or judgments) that the writer cannot obtain. Generally this information is limited to the status of the system or equipment documented in the procedure that will vary from one occasion to another. When such variables affect the optimum way that the procedure should be performed, the writer should not only allow the user to make decisions or judgments but should either force the user to do so (e.g., through conditional statements that demand that the user assess the status of the system and make decisions based upon the outcome of those decisions) or encourage the user to do so (e.g., through equally acceptable steps or unconditional external cross-references). If possible, the writer should simplify the decision making for the user by giving the user objective decision criteria upon which to base decisions. Regardless of how variable the system is, the writer still has the luxury of time to assess alternatives. Thus, the writer can figure out exactly what options might be available and what factors favor each option. On some occasions, however, the variables become too numerous and too far-reaching for the writer to simplify the decision-making process by incorporating decision points for all of the variables into the procedure. It is at this point that the writer should turn the responsibility of choosing approaches over to the user and let the user make judgments. Once the writer has made this decision, his responsibilities expand to making sure that the reader is told what he or she needs to know to make informed judgments (e.g., global and contextual information about the procedure become more important than ever).

In summary, writers should attempt to find the best way of performing tasks and document those methods in procedures. When this is not possible, writers should attempt to provide users with objective criteria for making decisions (e.g., conditional statements). The least preferred presentation, but a correct choice on some occasions, is to simply provide users with options and the information needed to make informed judgments. The choice of presentation will depend upon the relative amounts of information available to the writer and the user. As the amount of relevant information that is available to the user but not the writer increases, so should the amount of choice handed over to the user.

As a final note, the principle discussed here might be broadened just a bit further to state the single principle that underlies all of the guidance presented here. This principle might also be considered the single fundamental core principle of effective procedure writing. This global principle, simply stated, is "honor thy user."

APPENDIX

Example Styles

This appendix provides the formatting specifications for the examples used in this book. This book was prepared with Microsoft Word and converted to PageMaker for printing. Style sheets were used to standardize formatting. Style sheets allow you to define a style by specifying formatting (font, line spacing, indentation, etc.), then to apply all that formatting simply by calling up the style name. They are a great tool for increasing consistency and for freeing writers from concern over the drudgery of formatting. We highly recommend their use.

This appendix shows the styles that we used. All are paragraph styles. Because we deliberately kept the examples as simple as we could, you may find that you need other styles besides these if your procedures are more complex than our examples.

Normal *Every style is based on the normal style (unless otherwise specified), so every style has this formatting unless conflicting formatting is specified for that style.*

Century Schoolbook, 10 point. *We chose Century Schoolbook primarily because it contrasted with the Southern font used for the text of this book. You don't have to use it.*

Line spacing at least 12 points. *The font is 10 point and the line spacing is 12 points, so there are 2 points of leading, or extra space between lines. Leading can make type easier to read.*

Space before 12 points. *This is the default spacing—one blank line between each paragraph.*

Indent: right 0.58 in *The text ends 0.58 inches from the right margin, leaving room for the placekeeping aid.*

Keep lines together. *So line breaks don't occur in the middle of paragraphs.*

Don't hyphenate. *Hyphenation is a bad idea in procedures.*

Blank Line *Used to insert a blank line where necessary. This style was seldom used, because the space before or after each style is normally used to insert blank lines.*

Based on Normal

Line spacing exactly 12 points.

Space before 0 points. *This overrides the default of 12 points before set in the Normal style.*

Bullet.Step *A bulleted item in a list following a step.*

Based on Normal

Indent: left 0.42 in, hanging .025 in

Space before 3 points *So a bulleted item is close to the paragraph or bulleted item that proceeds it..*

Bulleted *This puts in the bullet character.*

Tabs: 4.98, right flush Used for the placekeeping aid. *At the end of the item, press tab, then type three underlined spaces. They will align with the right margin.*

Bullet.Number *A numbered item following a bulleted item.*

Based on Number

Indent: left 0.69 in *So the bullet aligns with the text of the item above it.*

Caution

Based on Warning

Border: single solid line, 1½-point line width

Border spacing: 1 point

Heading 1 *A first-level heading.*

Based on Step

Font: 11 point, bold

Note

Based on Normal

Font: italic

Indent: left 0.42 in, right 0.6 in

Space before 18 points, space after 6 points

Number.Step *A numbered item in a list following a step.*
 Based on Bullet.Step
 Indent: right 0.62 in

Paragraph.Step *A paragraph that follows a step.*
 Based on Step.
 Indent: first line 0 in *No hanging indent.*
 Space before 3 points

Step

 Based on Normal
 Indent: hanging 0.44 in
 Tabs: 0.44 in, 4.98 right flush *The first tab is used to align the text after the step number; the second is used for the placekeeping aid.*

Warning

 Based on Normal
 Space before 18 points, after 6 points
 Border: 1½-point line width
 Border spacing 1 point

Glossary

acronyms: Acronyms are abbreviations for a group of words, formed from the first letter of each word. Periods do not separate letters in an acronym. Often, acronyms themselves are pronounced like words. For example, the acronym *NASA* (pronounced *nah-suh*) stands for the National Aeronautics and Space Administration.

action verb: An action verb is a verb that directs the user to perform a task in an action step. The action verb is typically the first word in the step.

action step: See step.

active voice: Active voice is a sentence construction that shows the subject of the sentence acting. For example, *John checked out the book* is an active voice sentence. In a passive voice sentence, the subject is being acted upon, as in *The book was checked out by John.*

appendix: Supplementary material at the end of the procedure. Appendices include information that covers a specific subject or function. They are required for procedure completion but are used separately. An example of an appendix is a checklist. Appendices are sometimes called attachments.

attachment: See appendix.

blocks of text: Blocks of text are groups of words.

bold type: Bold type is heavier and darker than regular type. Bold type contrasts more with its white background and captures the reader's attention more quickly, provided that it (or other emphasis techniques) are not over-used.

case: The case of a noun changes depending on whether the noun form is subjective (we), objective (us), or possessive (our). Case also refers to capital letters (upper case) and smaller letters (lower case). See type case.

cautions: Cautions alert users to potential hazards in conditions, practices, or procedures that may damage products and equipment or adversely affect site operations. See warnings.

check-off spaces: A box or line on which to place a check mark to indicate that a step has been successfully completed.

coding techniques: Coding techniques are emphasis techniques that identify information; for example, full capitalization and underlining identifies conditional terms.

concurrent steps: Concurrent steps are two or more steps that are performed at the same time.

conditional cross-reference: A cross-reference in a conditional statement:

IF the steam generator levels can maintain heat removal,
THEN GO TO Step 3.5 in this procedure.

conditional statements: Also called logic statements, conditional statements are instructions that indicate an action should be performed only if certain conditions are met. Conditional terms such as IF, WHEN, THEN, NOT, AND, and OR are used to present conditional statements.

conditional terms: IF, WHEN, THEN, NOT, IF NOT, AND, and OR. Conditional terms are used in conditional statements according to the rules of Boolean logic.

continuous steps: Continuous steps are those that apply for a period of time while the procedure is being executed.

cover page: The cover page is the first page of the procedure.

cross-references: A cross-reference is a reference from one section of a procedure to another part of the same procedure or to a different procedure.

diagnostic steps: Steps that assist users in determining the nature of a situation. A flowchart is often a useful format for diagnostic steps.

emphasis techniques: Emphasis techniques are the typographical, spatial, or graphic techniques that emphasize or code information in the procedure.

equally acceptable steps: These are steps that specify a number of equally acceptable alternative actions.

font: A font is all the characters and punctuation marks of one style of type.

format: The way the pages of a document look.

framing: Enclosing in a box.

grammar: The written official rules, and unwritten common-knowledge rules, governing how words are put together to form a language. Grammar pertains to spoken as well as written communication.

headings: Headings are short phrases that introduce the beginning of a section by describing that section.

hierarchy: A hierarchy is a group of ideas organized or classified according to rank or importance.

human factors: Human factors is the discipline that studies how human beings interact with technology as well as how technology affects human performance, primarily in industrial settings.

imperative mode: A sentence in the imperative mode (or mood) is considered a command. It is understood that the subject of the sentence is *you* although this word is not used. The sentence *Check the SI system in one hour* is written in the imperative mode.

justified text: Text with straight margins on the left and right, so that *every* line begins and ends the same distance from the left or right margin.

left-justified text: Text that is aligned along the left margin of a page.

level of detail: The amount of technical detail presented in a procedure. Steps that are written at a low level of detail include only general instructions and rely heavily on user training. Steps that are written at a high level of detail precisely specify all actions.

line spacing: Line spacing is the dimension measured perpendicularly from the baseline of one line of text to the baseline of the next line.

logic statements: See conditional statements.

logic terms: See conditional terms.

margins: A uniform amount of white space at the top, bottom, right side, and left side of a page.

model: A representation of a process. For example, a model of the reading process helps people understand how people gain information from printed text.

nonsequential steps: These are steps that appear where they are first required but that may need to be performed later in the sequence of actions. Nonsequential steps include continuous steps, time-dependent steps, and repeated steps.

notes: Notes provide important supplemental non-safety-related information to users. Information may be presented in a note if it would otherwise be difficult to incorporate into the procedure.

objective, statement of: A brief description of the purpose of a procedure that appears at the beginning of the procedure.

passive voice: Passive voice is a sentence construction in which the subject of the sentence is acted upon. Passive voice sentences always use some form of *to be* in front of the verb. They have the potential to become wordy or confusing; therefore, active voice is usually preferable to passive voice. *The pump was activated by the operator* is an example of a passive voice sentence. See active voice.

placekeeping aids: Placekeeping aids are used to help the user know what steps have been accomplished in a procedure. Check-off boxes are one type of placekeeping aid used to indicate that an action has been accomplished.

point: A typographical measure equal to approximately 1/72 inch.

positive statement: A sentence that does not contain a negative form of a verb is a positive statement. For example, *Do not leave the door open* is a negative statement. *Leave the door closed* is a positive statement that has the same meaning as the negative statement. Positive statements are generally easier to understand.

punctuation: The set of standard symbols used in writing to separate words into sentences, phrases, and clauses, and to help a reader understand the text.

ragged-right margins: When the white space along the right side of a page varies according to line lengths of text, the right margin is ragged (i.e., uneven).

range: An amount of acceptable variation in an instrument reading.

readability: The ease with which a person can read and understand text.

recurrent steps: Recurrent are steps that are performed repeatedly at various times.

repeated steps: See recurrent steps.

right-justified text: Text that is aligned along the right margin of a page.

sans serif: Literally, *without serifs*. Sans serif fonts do not have short lines at the end of the strokes in their letters.

schema: A schema is a mental structure that represents a person's knowledge of the world based on personal experience. People constantly build new schemata (the plural of *schema*) and add to old schemata as they encounter experiences each day. These schemata help people interpret and store information gained through these experiences. For example, while reading text a person might draw from a schema for punctuation marks that helps the person know that periods signify the end of a sentence.

serif: The short lines at the end of the strokes in letters in some typefaces are called serifs.

single-column format: A format where the text forms one column.

spacing, line: See line spacing.

spatial emphasis: Use of white space to highlight information.

step: A step provides instructions for performing a specific action.

symbols: Symbols are printed or written signs used to represent an operation, element, quantity, quality, or relation.

syntax: Syntax is the way in which words are combined to form phrases and sentences.

time-dependent steps: Steps that are performed after a set period of time has passed. When presenting a time-dependent step, it is important to provide space for users to note the time that "starts the clock" and to present a calculation aid that will enable them to calculate the time at which the action should be taken.

transitions: See cross-references.

true emphasis techniques: Emphasis techniques that identify important information. See coding techniques.

twelve-point type: This is a type font's specified size based on characters of the font formerly having been cast in lead blocks that measured 12 points high. Different fonts that are all twelve-point type fonts will look different in size because the widths and heights of individual characters in each font vary from one another.

two-column format: Procedures that are presented in two columns. The left-hand column can present actions while the right-hand column presents details. An alternative two-column format presents the actions in the left-hand column and contingencies in the right-hand column.

type case: Type case refers to whether letters are presented in all capitals, mixed case, or all lowercase. For blocks of text, mixed case is easier to read than all capitals.

type face: See font.

type size: This dimension pertains to the height of a block of lead in which a letter would have been cast. Type size is typically greater than the actual height of letters in a typeface.

typography: Typography is the arrangement and appearance of type on a page.

validation: A formal check of a procedure's accuracy and usability. Technically, there are two different processes, verification and validation, although they are often considered as one. Comprehensive verification and validation consists of simulator exercises, control room and plant walkthroughs, and desktop reviews. This book uses the simpler term *testing*.

verification: See validation.

visual angle: Visual angle is the angle subtended at the eye by a letter of type (or anything else on the page). When determining the optimal type size for a printed document, writers can use a formula to calculate the visual angle and to ensure that typed characters are sufficiently large for the viewer's eye to discern at a given distance.

walkdown: A walkdown consists of physically visiting and observing the location in which the activities are to be performed and the equipment that will be used. A walkdown is performed to ensure that the equipment and environment are actually as envisioned and the people involved can perform the required tasks.

walkthrough: A walkthrough is the cumulative, detailed check of a process and facility. Activities that may be used to complete walkthroughs include walkdowns, simulations, or modeling.

warnings: Warnings alert procedure users to potential hazards that may lead to death, injury, or radioactive release. See cautions.

white space: White space is blank space on a printed page. White space commonly defines the margins of a page and separates lines of text, words, and characters from one another on a printed page.

x-height: The height of the lower-case letter *x* (and *a*, *c*, *e*, and so on) in a font of type. If graphic designers use the visual angle formula to determine the optimal type size for a document, they should equate the results of that formula with the x-height of the letters in a font rather than with the font size itself.

References

Allen, P.R. (1995). Save money with a corporate style guide. *Technical Communication, 42*(2), 284–289.

Allen, P.R. (1996). User attitudes towards corporate style guides: A survey. *Technical Communication, 43*(3), 237–243.

American National Standards Institute. (1970). *Flowchart Symbols and Their Use in Information Processing* (ANSI X3.5–1970). New York: American National Standards Institute.

American Nuclear Society. (1989). *American National Standard Administrative Controls and Quality Assurance for the Operational Phase of Nuclear Power Plants* (ANSI/ANS-3.2-1988). La Grange Park, IL: American Nuclear Society.

Anderson, B. (1963). The short-term retention of active and passive sentences. Unpublished doctoral dissertation, Johns Hopkins University. Cited in Coleman, 1963.

Anderson, P.V. (1991). *Technical Writing: A Reader-Oriented Approach* (2nd Ed.). San Diego, CA: Harcourt Brace Jovanovich.

Anderson, R.C., Reynolds, R.E., Schallert, D.L., & Goetz, E.T. (1977). Frameworks for comprehending discourse. *American Educational Research Journal, 14*(4), 367–381.

Bailey, R.W. (1982). *Human Performance Engineering: A Guide for System Designers*. Engelwood Cliffs, NJ: Prentice-Hall, Inc.

Ballard, J.C., & Rode-Perkins, S.L. (1987). How to create mass media print warnings. *Technical Communication, 34*(2), 84–88.

Barfield, W. (1986). Expert-novice differences for software: Implications for problem-solving and knowledge acquisition. *Behavior and Information Technology, 5,* 15–29.

Barnes, V.E., & Radford, L.R. (1987). *Evaluation of Nuclear Power Plant Operating Procedures Classifications and Interfaces* (NUREG/CR-4613). Washington, DC: Nuclear Regulatory Commission.

Barnes, V.E., Bramwell, A.T., Olson, J., Wieringa, D.R., & Wilson, R.A. (in press). *The Extent, Nature, Causes, and Consequences of Procedure Violations in U.S. Nuclear Power Plants: A Follow-up to Chernobyl* (NUREG/CR-5786). Washington, DC: Nuclear Regulatory Commission.

Barnes, V.E., Moore, C.J., Wieringa, D.R., Isakson, C.S., Kono, B.K., & Gruel, R.L. (1989). *Techniques for Preparing Flowchart-Format Emergency Operating Procedures* (NUREG/CR-5228). Washington, DC: Nuclear Regulatory Commission.

Benson, P.J. (1985). Writing visually: Design considerations in technical publications. *Technical Communication, 32*(4), 35–39.

Berkin, M.M. (1964). Performance decrement under psychological stress. *Human Factors, 6,* 21–30.

Bernstein, T.M. (1965). *The Careful Writer: A Modern Guide to English Usage.* New York: Atheneum.

Berry, E. (1981). How to get users to follow procedures. *Journal of Systems Management, 1,* 22–25.

Boggan, S., Farkas, D., & Welinske. (1996). *Developing online help for Windows 95™.* London: International Thompson Computer Press.

Bovair, S., & Kieras, D.E. (1989). *Toward a Model of Acquiring Procedures from Text* (Report No. 30). Ann Arbor, MI: University of Michigan.

Brooke, J., & Duncan, K. (1981). Effects of system display format on performance in a fault location task. *Ergonomics, 24,* 175–189.

Brown, A. (1989). *In Print: Text and Type in the Age of Desktop Publishing.* New York: Watson-Guptill Publications.

Bruce-Briggs, B. (1988). *The Shield of Faith: Strategic Defense from Zeppelins to Star Wars.* New York: Touchstone.

Brusaw, C.T., Alred, G.J., & Oliu, W.E. (1987). *Handbook of Technical Writing.* New York: St. Martin's Press.

Burnett, R.E. (1990). *Technical Communication* (Second Edition). Belmont, CA: Wadsworth.

Chall, J.S. (1984). Readability and prose comprehension: Continuities and discontinuities. *Understanding Reading Comprehension: Cognition, Language, and the Structure of Prose* (pp. 233–247). Newark, DE: International Reading Association.

Coleman, E.B. (1963). Learning of prose written in four grammatical transformations. *Journal of Applied Psychology, 47*(5), 332–341.

Dixon, P. (1987). Actions and procedural directions. *Coherence and Grounding in Discourse* (pp. 70–89). Philadelphia, PA: John Benjamins Publishing Co.

Duchastel, P.C. (1982). Textural display techniques. In D.H. Jonassen (Ed.), *The Technology of Text* (pp. 167–192). Englewood Cliffs, NJ: Educational Technology Publications.

Duffy, T.M. (1985). Preparing technical manuals: Specifications and guidelines. In D.H. Jonassen (Ed.), *The Technology of Text: Volume Two* (pp. 370–392). Englewood Cliffs, NJ: Educational Technology Publications.

Dye, K.L. (1988). When is a document accurate and complete? *IPCC 1988 Conference Record: On the Edge: A Pacific Rim Conference on Technical Communication*, Seattle, Washington, October 5–7, 1988 (pp. 269–272). New York: Institute of Electrical and Electronic Engineers.

Echeverria, D., Barnes, V., Bittner, A., Fawcett-Long, J., Moore, C., Terrill, B., Westra, C., Wieringa, D., & Wilson, R. (1994). *The Impact of Environmental Exposures on Human Performance: Volumes I and II* (NUREG/CR-5680 and NUREG/CR-7675). Washington, DC: Nuclear Regulatory Commission.

Farkas, D. (1995). Four research ideas. *Technical Communication, 42*(4), 587–589.

Farkas, D., & Farkas, N. (1981). Manuscript surprises: A problem in copy editing. *Technical Communication, 28*(2), 12–22.

Felker, D.B., Pickering, F., Charrow, V.R., Holland, V. M., & Redish, J.C. (1981). *Guidelines for Document Designers*. Washington, DC: American Institutes for Research.

Follett, W. (1966). *Modern American Usage: A Guide*. New York: Hill and Wang.

Fuchs, F., Engelschall, J., & Imlay, G. (1981). *Human Engineering Guidelines for Use in Preparing Emergency Operating Procedures for Nuclear Power Plants* (NUREG/CR-1999). Washington, DC: Nuclear Regulatory Commission.

Giles, T.D. (1990). The readability controversy: A technical writing review. *Journal of Technical Writing and Communication, 20*(2), 131–138.

Glynn, S.M., Britton, B.K., & Tillman, M.H. (1985). Typographical cues in text: Management of the reader's attention. In D.H. Jonassen (Ed.), *The Technology of Text: Volume Two* (pp. 192–209). Englewood Cliffs, NJ: Educational Technology Publications.

Gould, J.D., Alfaro, L., Finn, R., Haupt, N., & Minuto, A. (1987). Reading from CRT displays can be as fast as reading from paper. *Human Factors, 25*(9), 497–517.

Green, T.R. (1977). Conditional program statements and comprehensibility to professional programmers. *Journal of Occupational Psychology, 50,* 93–109.

Gringas, B. (1987). Simplified English in maintenance manuals. *Technical Communication, 34*(1), 24–28.

Harbaugh, F.W. (1991). Accentuate the positive. *Technical Communication, 38*(1), 73–74.

Harris, J.E., & Wiklund, M.E. (1989). Consumer acceptance of threatening warnings in the residential environment. *Proceedings of the Human Factors Society 33rd Annual Meeting* (pp. 989–993). Santa Monica, CA: Human Factors Society.

Hartley, J. (1982). Designing instructional text. In D.H. Jonassen (Ed.), *The Technology of Text* (pp. 193–214). Englewood Cliffs, NJ: Educational Technology Publications.

Hart, M.H. (1998). *The 100: A ranking of the most influential persons in history.* Secaucus, NJ: Carol Publishing Group.

Hartley, J. (1985). *Designing Instructional Text* (2nd Ed.). New York: Nichols.

Hartley, J., & Burnhill, P. (1977). Fifty guidelines for improving instructional text. *Programmed Learning and Educational Technology, 14*(1), 65–75.

Hartley, J., & Jonassen, D.H. (1985). The role of headings in printed and electronic text. In D.H. Jonassen (Ed.), *The Technology of Text: Volume Two* (pp. 237–263). Englewood Cliffs, NJ: Educational Technology Publications.

Hartley, J., & Rooum, D. (1983). Sir Cyril Burt and typography. *British Journal of Psychology, 74*(2), 203–212.

Hartley, J., & Trueman, M. (1983). The effects of headings in text on recall, search and retrieval. *British Journal of Educational Psychology, 53,* 205–214.

Herriot, P. (1969). Comprehension of active and passive sentences as a function of pragmatic expectations. *Journal of Verbal Learning and Verbal Behavior, 8,* 166–169.

Holland, V., Charrow, V., & Wright, W. (1988). How can technical writers write effectively for several audiences at once? In L. Beene & P. White (Eds.), *Solving Problems in Technical Writing* (pp. 27–54). New York: Oxford University Press.

Horn, R.E., & Kelly, J.N. (1981). *Structured Writing: An Approach to the Documentation of Computer Software.* Waltham, MA: Information Mapping, Inc.

Horton, W. (1991). *Illustrating Computer Documentation: The Art of Presenting Graphically on Paper and Online.* New York: John Wiley & Sons, Inc.

Houp, K.W., & Pearsall, T.E. (1988). *Reporting Technical Information* (6th Ed.). New York: Collier Macmillan.

Huckin, T.N. (1983). A cognitive approach to readability. In P.V. Anderson, R.J. Brockmann, & C.R. Miller (Eds.), *New Essays in Technical and Scientific Communication: Research, Theory, Practice* (pp. 90–110). New York: Baywood Publishing Company.

Internal Revenue Service. (1990). *Form 1040.* Washington, DC.

James, G. (1985). *Document Databases.* New York: Van Nostrand Reinhold.

Jeffrey, R.C. (1967). *Formal Logic: Its Scope and Limits.* New York: McGraw-Hill.

Jonassen, D.H. (1982). Introduction to section one: Implicit structures in text. In D.H. Jonassen (Ed.), *The Technology of Text* (pp. 5–14). Englewood Cliffs, NJ: Educational Technology Publications.

Kammann, R. (1975). The comprehensibility of printed instructions and the flowchart alternative. *Human Factors, 17*(2), 183–191.

Kantowitz, B.H., & Sorkin, R.D. (1983). *Human Factors: Understanding People-System Relationships.* New York: John Wiley and Sons.

Kieras, D.E. (1978). Good and bad structure in simple paragraphs: Effects on apparent theme, reading time, and recall. *Journal of Verbal Learning and Verbal Behavior, 17,* 13–28.

Lannon, J.M. (1991). *Technical Writing* (5th Ed.). New York: Harper Collins.

Lanyi, G. (1994). *Managing Documentation Projects in an Imperfect World.* Columbus, OH: Battelle Press.

Larkin, J.H., & Simon, H.A. (1987). Why a diagram is (sometimes) worth ten thousand words. *Cognitive Science, 11,* 65–99.

Loftus, G.R., & Loftus, E.F. (1988). *Essence of Statistics,* 2nd ed. New York: Alfred A. Knopf.

Lorch, R.F. Jr., & Lorch, E.P. (1985). Topic structure representation and text recall. *Journal of Educational Psychology, 77*(2), 137–148.

Mackh, G.E., & Rew, L.J. (1991). Using access aids to boost information retrieval. *Technical Communication, 38*(2), 210–219.

Marshall, S.L. (1978). *Men Against Fire: The Problem of Battle Command in Future War.* Glouchester, MA: Peter Smith.

McCallum, M., Morgan, J., Wieringa, D.R., Kinghorn, R.A., & Kantowitz, B.H. (1994). *Procedures Software Tool (PST) Requirements Analysis and Functional Description* (TR-103247). Palo Alto, CA: Electric Power Research Institute.

McCarthy, R.L., Finnegan, J.P., Krumm-Scott, S., & McCarthy, G.E. (1984). Product information presentation, user behavior, and safety. *Proceedings of the Human Factors Society 28th Annual Meeting.* Palo Alto, CA: Human Factors Society.

Meyer, B.J. (1985). Signaling the structure of text. In D.H. Jonassen (Ed.), *The Technology of Text: Volume Two* (pp. 64–89). Englewood Cliffs, NJ: Educational Technology Publications.

Miller, D.F. (1996). Communicating in spite of three-letter acronyms, Part II: Being a force for salvation (of meaning). *Intercom: The Society for Technical Communication Magazine, 43*(2), 10–12.

Moore, C.J., Kono, B.K., Wieringa, D.R., Barnes, V.E., Isakson, C.S., & Gruel, R.L. (1990). Graphic design tools for promoting the usability of flowchart-format procedures and other functional graphic images. *Proceedings of the Society for Technical Communication* (3rd Region 7 Conference, Portland, OR, October 12–13, 1990) (pp. 94–107). Arlington, VA: Society for Technical Communication.

Morgenstern, M.H., Barnes, V.E., Radford, L.R., Wheeler, W.A., & Badalamente, R.V. (1985). *Development, Use and Control of Maintenance Procedures in Nuclear Power Plants: Problems and Recommendations* (NUREG/CR-3817). Washington, DC: Nuclear Regulatory Commission.

Nuclear Regulatory Commission (NRC). (1982). *Guidelines for the Preparation of Emergency Operating Procedures* (NUREG-0899). Washington, DC: Nuclear Regulatory Commission.

Nuclear Regulatory Commission (NRC). (1989). *Lessons Learned from the Special Inspection Program for Emergency Operating Procedures* (NUREG-1358). Washington, DC: Nuclear Regulatory Commission.

Parker, R.C. (1988). *Looking Good in Print: A Guide to Basic Design for Desktop Publishing.* Chapel Hill, NC: Ventana Press.

Payne, J.W. (1976). Task complexity and contingent processing in decision making: An information search and protocol analysis. *Organizational Behavior and Human Performance, 16*(2), 366–387.

Pinker, S. (1994). *The Language Instinct: How the Mind Creates Language.* New York: William Morrow and Company.

Porter, K. (1991). Usage of the passive voice. *Technical Communication, 38*(1), 87–88.

Poulton, B., & Brown, C.H. (1968). Rate of comprehension of an existing teleprinter output and of possible alternatives. *Journal of Applied Psychology, 52,* 16–21.

Poulton, E.C. (1972). Size, style, and vertical spacing in the legibility of small typefaces. *Journal of Applied Psychology, 56,* 156–161.

Rogers, W.H., & Moeller, G. (1984). Comparison of abbreviation methods: Measures of preference and decoding performance. *Human Factors, 26*(1), 49–59.

Schriver, K.A. (1997). *Dynamics in Document Design.* New York: John Wiley & Sons.

Sherman, M.A. (1973). Bound to be easier? The negative prefix and sentence comprehension. *Journal of Verbal Learning and Verbal Behavior, 12,* 76–84.

Simon, J. (1980). *Paradigms Lost: Reflections on Literacy and Its Decline.* New York: Clarkson N. Potter.

Slobin, D.I. (1966). Grammatical transformation and sentence comprehension in childhood and adulthood. *Journal of Verbal Learning and Verbal Behavior, 5,* 219–227.

Slovic, P., Fischhoff, B. & Lichtenstein, S. (1982). Facts versus fears: Understanding perceived risk. In D. Kahneman, P. Slovic, & A. Tversky (Eds.), *Judgment Under Uncertainty: Heuristics and Biases.* Cambridge, MA: Cambridge University Press.

Smith, S.L. (1979). Letter size and legibility. *Human Factors, 21*(6), 661–670.

Souther, J.W., & White, M.L. (1984). *Technical Report Writing.* Malabar, FL: Robert E. Kriegger Publishing Company.

Spyridakis, J.H. (1989a). Signaling effects: A review of the research—Part I. *Journal of Technical Writing and Communication, 19*(3), 227–240.

Spyridakis, J.H. (1989b). Signaling effects: Increased content retention and new answers—Part II. *Journal of Technical Writing and Communication, 19*(4), 395–421.

Spyridakis, J.H., & Standal, T.C. (1987). Signals in expository prose: Effects on reading comprehension. *Reading Research Quarterly, 22*(3), 285–298.

Spyridakis, J.H., & Wenger, M.J. (1990). Cognitive dimensions of reading comprehension. *Proceedings of the Society for Technical Communication* (3rd Region 7 Conference, Portland, OR, October 12–13 1990) (pp. 124–128). Arlington, VA: Society for Technical Communication.

Stevens, K.C. (1981). Chunking material as an aid to reading comprehension. *Journal of Reading, 25*(2), 126–129.

Sticht, T. (1985). Understanding readers and their uses of texts. In T.M. Duffy & R. Waller (Eds.), *Designing Usable Texts* (pp. 315–340). New York: Academic Press.

Stratton, C.R. (1984). *Technical Writing: Process and Product*. New York: Holt, Rinehart and Winston.

Strunk, W. & White, E.B. (1979). *The Elements of Style* (3rd Ed.). New York: Macmillan.

The Chicago Manual of Style (14th Ed.). (1993). Chicago, IL: University of Chicago Press.

The Random House Dictionary of the English Language. (1967). New York: Random House.

Tinker, M.A. (1955). Prolonged reading tasks in visual research. *Journal of Applied Psychology, 39*, 444–446.

Tinker, M.A. (1963). *Legibility of Print.* Ames, IA: Iowa State University Press.

Tinker, M.A., & Paterson, D.G. (1928). Influence of type form on speed reading. *Journal of Applied Psychology, 12*, 359–368.

Towell, J. (Ed.) (1989). *Acronyms, Initialisms, and Abbreviations Dictionary* (13th Ed., Vol. 1). Detroit, MI: Gale Research Inc.

Trollip, S.R., & Sales, G. (1986). Readability of computer-generated fill-justified text. *Human Factors, 28*(2), 159–163.

Tufte, E.R. (1983). *The visual display of quantitative information.* Cheshire, CT: Graphics Press.

Turnbull, A.T., & Baird, R.N. (1980). *The Graphics of Communication* (4th Ed.). New York: Holt, Rinehart, and Winston.

Tversky, A. & Kahneman, D. (1982). Judgment under uncertainty: Heuristics and biases. In D. Kahneman, P. Slovic, & A. Tversky (Eds.), *Judgment Under Uncertainty: Heuristics and Biases* (pp. 2–20). Cambridge, MA: Cambridge University Press.

Twyman, M. (1979). Schema of graphic language. In E. Wrols & H. Bouma (Eds.), *Processing of Visible Language*. New York: Plenum Press.

van der Meij, H., & Carroll, J.M. (1995). Principles and heuristics for designing minimalist instruction. *Technical Communication, 42*(2), 243–261.

Vartabedian, A.G. (1971). The effects of letter size, case, and generation method on CRT display search time. *Human Factors, 13,* 363–368.

Waller, R. (1982). Text as diagram: Using typography to improve access and understanding. In D.H. Jonassen (Ed.), *The Technology of Text* (pp. 137–166). Englewood Cliffs, NJ: Educational Technology Publications.

Washington State Office of Financial Management. (1990). *Investment in Human Capital Study: Executive Summary and Synthesis*. Olympia, WA: Office of Financial Management.

Wason, P.C. (1959). The processing of positive and negative information. *Quarterly Journal of Experimental Psychology, 11,* 92–107.

Wason, P.C. (1961). Responses to affirmative and negative binary statements. *British Journal of Psychology, 52,* 133–142.

Wason, P.C. (1968). The drafting of rules. *The New Law Journal, 118*(5341), 548–549.

Weiss, E.H. (1990). Visualizing a procedure with Nassi-Schneiderman charts. *Journal of Technical Writing and Communication, 20*(3), 237–254.

White, J.V. (1982). *Editing by Design: A Guide to Effective Word-and-Picture Communication for Editors and Designers*. R.R. Bowker Company: New York.

Wieringa, D.R., McCallum, M.C., Morgan, J., Yasutake, J.Y., Isoda, H., & Schumacher, R.M., Jr. (1996). Automating the writing process: Two case studies. In P. Sullivan & J. Dautermann (Eds.), *Electronic Literacies in the Workplace: Technologies of Writing*. Urbana, IL: National Council of Teachers of English.

Winn, W., & Holliday, W. (1982). Design principles for diagrams and charts. In D. H. Jonassen (Ed.), *The Technology of Text* (pp. 277-299). Englewood Cliffs, NJ: Educational Technology Publications.

Wogalter, M.S., Godfrey, S.A., & Fontenelle, G.A. (1987). Effectiveness of warnings. *Human Factors, 29*(5), 599–612.

Words Into Type. (1974). Englewood Cliffs, NJ: Prentice-Hall, Inc.

Wright, P. (1971). Writing to be understood: Why use sentences? *Applied Ergonomics, 2*(4), 207–209.

Wright, P. (1985). Is evaluation a myth? Assessing text assessment procedures. In D.H. Jonassen (Ed.), *The Technology of Text: Volume Two* (pp. 418–436). Englewood Cliffs, NJ: Educational Technology Publications.

Wright, P., & Reid, F. (1973). Written information: Some alternatives to prose for expressing the outcomes of complex contingencies. *Journal of Applied Psychology, 57*(2), 160–166.

Zach, S.E. (1980). Control room operating procedures: Content and format. *Proceedings of the Human Factors Society, 24th Annual Meeting* (pp. 125–127). Santa Monica, CA: Human Factors Society.

Zimmerman, C.M., & Campbell, J.J. (1988). *Fundamentals of Procedure Writing* (2nd Ed.). Columbia, MD: GP Publishing, Inc.

Index